# THE

# FORTY

# CHAPTERS

## OF AL-KINDĪ

*Traditional Horary*
*& Electional Astrology*

TRANSLATED AND EDITED BY
**BENJAMIN N. DYKES, PHD**

---

The Cazimi Press
Minneapolis, Minnesota
2011

Published and printed in the United States of America
by the Cazimi Press
621 5<sup>th</sup> Avenue SE #25, Minneapolis, MN 55414

Library of Congress Control Number: 2011925120

**ISBN-13: 978-1-934586-19-8**

# ACKNOWLEDGEMENTS

I would like to thank the following friends and colleagues, in alphabetical order: Chris Brennan, Charles Burnett, Martin Gansten, and Richard Schacht. Special thanks go to Dorian Greenbaum and Deb Houlding for inspiring and facilitating this project.

# TABLE OF CONTENTS

# BOOK ABBREVIATIONS

| | | |
|---|---|---|
| *BOA* | Bonatti, Guido | *The Book of Astronomy* |
| *CA* | Lilly, William | *Christian Astrology* |
| *Introduct.* | Sahl bin Bishr: | *The Introduction* (in *WSM*) |
| *Judges* | Various | *The Book of the Nine Judges* |
| *On Quest.* | Sahl bin Bishr: | *On Questions* (in *WSM*) |
| *PN* | Various | *Persian Nativities* (vols. I-III) |
| *Search* | Hermann of Carinthia | *The Search of the Heart* |
| *WSM* | Sahl bin Bishr & Māshā'allāh: | *Works of Sahl & Māshā'allāh* |

# TABLE OF FIGURES

Note: All figures are by Benjamin Dykes, based on the texts;
Figure 62 is based on an Arabic *Letter* by al-Kindī.

# INTRODUCTION

## §1: *The Forty Chapters* & the *EMA* series

I am happy to present the first complete translation in 850 years of a famous volume of traditional horary and electional astrology, al-Kindī's *The Book of the Judgments of the Stars*, popularly known as *The Forty Chapters* (hereafter, *Forty Chapters*). It is the second horary volume in my *Essential Medieval Astrology* (*EMA*) translation cycle,[1] and is a companion to both *The Search of the Heart* (2011) and *The Book of the Nine Judges* (2011). Hermann of Carinthia's *Search* is a valuable guide to a little-known and distinct branch of horary practice, called the "understanding of thoughts," as well as the finding of hidden or lost objects, timing procedures, and the use of numerical procedures to identify special significators or "victors" (also known as a *mubtazz* or *almuten*). Hugo of Santalla's *Judges* is a collection of several important horary works (including material on thoughts and victors). Together, these three volumes present a well-rounded picture of all areas of traditional horary practice.[2]

Unlike most other books in the *EMA* cycle, al-Kindī begins his work with an introduction to some basic principles in traditional astrology. Still, it is not quite a beginner's book, and students would do well to accompany it with my *Introductions to Traditional Astrology* (hereafter, *ITA*), which has much commentary and information on all basic topics, not to mention a longer glossary than is contained here. Throughout *Forty Chapters* I make reference to it.

So, while not a beginner's course, *Forty Chapters* is a good introduction to questions and elections, and was used by such famous astrologers as al-Rijāl[3] and William Lilly. It contains a number of sections with valuable advice on general approaches to interpretation, and will repay much study.

---

[1] See Appendix A.
[2] In fact, there are important overlaps between these three volumes, since Hermann relied on one of the two Latin translations of *Forty Chapters* for some of his material, and most of *Forty Chapters* was used by Hugo for *Judges*.
[3] Often known in the Latin West as "Haly Abenragel." See below.

## §2: Al-Kindī's life, work, & influence on later astrology

The famous philosopher and scientific author, Abū Yūsuf Ya'qūb bin Ishāq al-Kindī, known as the "first philosopher of the Arabs," was born in about 801 AD, at a time of increasing sophistication, luxury, and learning in the Muslim world. Charlemagne and the Carolingian Renaissance held sway in the West, and the court of the *1,001 Arabian Nights*, scientists, and astrologers were creating legendary figures in the East. Al-Kindī belonged to a noble branch of the Kinda tribe in the Yemen. His family, which claimed one of the Companions of the Prophet Muhammad as an ancestor, would have been proud of his accomplishments as his fame and connections grew. After some education in Kūfa or Basra, he completed his training in Baghdad, where he coordinated an early circle of translators and writers, rendering texts from Greek and other languages into Arabic (sometimes as exact translations, sometimes as interpretive paraphrases). It was the perfect time for such activities, since the 'Abbasid Caliphate was well known for its support of Greek and Persian learning. Since the 760s, leading elites had hired professional Persian astrologers (such as Māshā'allāh, 'Umar al-Tabarī, and Sahl bin Bishr) and administrators, and particularly under Caliphs Hārūn al-Rashīd (r. 786-809) and al-Ma'mūn (r. 813-833) they sponsored the famous "House of Wisdom"—which was not a building, but a broad movement of translation, study, archiving, and scientific work.

Some time after arriving in Baghdad, the Arab al-Kindī came to be connected with the court of al-Ma'mūn, putting his professional dates at the court right after the deaths of the astrologers Māshā'allāh and 'Umar al-Tabarī (ca. 815 AD), and during the career of the astrologer Sahl bin Bishr (who is said to have worked for al-Hasan, a vizier under al- al-Ma'mūn).[4] Al-Ma'mūn's brother and successor, al-Mu'tasim (r. 833-842) made al-Kindī the tutor to his own son.

Al-Kindī himself seems not to have been a translator, but as part of overseeing a circle of translators he wrote many works explaining Greek and Persian thought to an Arabic-speaking world. Philosophically, he claimed to be an Aristotelian; but the Aristotle of that time was heavily filtered through numerous layers of Neoplatonic thought. At any rate, al-Kindī was not

---

[4] For modern translations of works by Māshā'allāh and Sahl, see my *Works of Sahl & Māshā'allāh* (2008) and *Persian Nativities I* (2009). For a short natal work by 'Umar, see *Persian Nativities II* (2010). *The Book of the Nine Judges* (2011) contains much or all of a horary work by 'Umar.

narrowly ideological, and moreover wrote in virtually every possible discipline: from comparing Euclid and Aristotle on optics, to writing numerous shortish works on astrology (in addition to *Forty Chapters*), to influential pieces on the proper proportions to be used in mixing medicines,[5] and much more. Most of these hundreds of short works and letters are lost in Arabic, but many of the more important ones survive, some in Latin translation.

Astrologically, he is well known for five things. First, *Forty Chapters* presented him as an accomplished astrological authority: it was not only used rather extensively by al-Rijāl (known in the West as Haly Abenragel) and al-Qasrānī,[6] but was one of the three major works incorporated into the 12th-Century *Judges*. Al-Bīrūnī borrows from §§44-55 of al-Kindī, in his own §§486-88, and much later, William Lilly's *Christian Astrology* contained long, uncredited passages from *Forty Chapters* (see below).

Second, al-Kindī used Persian mundane astrology to predict the end of Arab dominion in about 1293 AD.[7] There were various Islamic dynasties and sultanates in addition to the Caliphate at that time, but the Mongols had overthrown the 'Abbasids about 35 years earlier, in 1258 AD. Al-Kindī first uses gematric methods to establish 693 years, then compares this with cycles of Saturn-Mars conjunctions in Cancer. At any rate, his dates are tantalizingly close.

Third, al-Kindī wrote two letters (combined into one in Latin) on astrological weather prediction, which were foundational for later work on this topic in the Latin West.[8]

Fourth, al-Kindī has the dubious distinction of impelling the famous Abū Ma'shar towards astrology.[9] According to the standard story, Abū Ma'shar

[5] The Arabic heading of the letter claims that al-Kindī had "actually used" these formulas in practice (Burnett 1993, p. 100).
[6] For a late 9th-Century compilation made from seven astrologers' works, called the *Book of Questions on the Science of the Judgment of the Stars*: see Sezgin pp. 134 and 138. Burnett (1993, p. 86) says that some of al-Qasrānī's excerpts do not match the Arabic manuscript of *The Forty Chapters* itself.
[7] See Burnett and Yamamoto (2000), pp. 525-43 for a translation and discussion of this letter.
[8] I will translate this material for my forthcoming mundane installment of the *EMA* cycle, *The Astrology of the World*.
[9] Al-Kindī was also claimed to be among the best astrologers in judicial astrology (see below), but to me that sounds unlikely. Al-Kindī was already known more as a compiler and philosophical writer than as a practicing astrologer, and the few charts from his lifetime (Ch. 7.3 below) were cast just before his death, at unlikely morning hours for an elderly astrologer to take questions about missing objects—especially so many of them in

was an astrology skeptic who made his views known to al-Kindī. Al-Kindī responded wisely that one should study a subject before criticizing it. Abū Ma'shar took his advice and the rest, as they say, is history: Abū Ma'shar was certainly known in the Latin West as one of the best and most authoritative astrologers of all time. Nevertheless I say that this distinction of al-Kindī's is "dubious," because some other Arabic-speaking astrologers of the Middle Ages rather wished that Abū Ma'shar had stayed away from astrology. The scholar al-Bīrūnī criticized Abū Ma'shar's scholarly honesty,[10] and al-Rijāl moans that Abū Ma'shar is frequently inaccurate, and is like a man trying to collect firewood at night![11]

Fifth, through his *On the Stellar Rays*,[12] al-Kindī was also known as a scientific theorizer on how astrology and magic work. The basic idea of the book is that the stars become influential, and have causal interactions with the world, due to rays which they emit and which may be studied geometrically.

As for his views on astrology in general, al-Kindī may think (in his *Discourse on the Soul*) that the soul comes to be associated with the planetary spheres after death; but at any rate he views the heavens as instruments of Divine Providence. In fact, the stars have rational souls and move in obedience to God's command. By the heavens enclosing the whole world, this means that God's Providence is universal, and suggests that a science like astrology can be used to interpret that Providence. In terms of how the stars produce their changes, in one work al-Kindī says that the motions of the stars produce generation and corruption in the sphere below the Moon (our world) through friction that is physically communicated to our lower regions. But in the work on the stellar rays mentioned above, the stars influence matters through their geometric rays.

In this very brief description of his general astrological attitudes, we can discern two sets of classical conflicts in astrology and traditional philosophy. First, note the strain between reasoning and commanding: if the stars (or perhaps their souls) were rational, they would not need to be commanded; or

---

such a short time. My sense is that these charts were either cast by him as theoretical examples, or inserted by someone else.

[10] Al-Bīrūnī 1983, pp. 29-31.

[11] See Burnett 1993, p. 92 and al-Rijāl II.2. Nevertheless, I will be translating much of Abū Ma'shar for upcoming works on elections and mundane astrology.

[12] The only full English translation I am aware of, is by Robert Hand and Robert Zoller in an out-of-print edition for Project Hindsight (1993). I will produce my own translation and commentary in 2012-2013.

rather, if God were also rational, then by their rationality the stars would understand what God or goodness required, and act voluntarily[13]—but the need to be commanded suggests that God is either not rational (in a recognizable sense), or is somehow beyond reason (in which case one wonders how the stars benefit by being rational).[14] Next, there is also a strain in his understanding of what astrology is. The friction-based view falls squarely into the Ptolemaic-Aristotelian picture of astrology as a subdivision of physics, but his account of interpretation and Providence is closer to the Stoic conception of astrology as an interpretive discipline, which applies rational rules to the appearances of the heavens in order to discern the Providence and intentions of Cosmic Reason or the Divine Mind. We should not really blame al-Kindī for these internal conflicts in his thought: they appear again and again throughout the history of Western astrology, with individual astrologers frequently believing both sides of each conflict at the same time.

Following are some notable astrological works by al-Kindī:[15]

- *The Book of the Judgments of the Stars*, that is, *The Forty Chapters*, on questions and elections.
- *On the Rays of the Stars* (or *On the Stellar Rays*), on a theory of magic and astrology.
- Several letters on weather and meteorology, of which the two found in separate Hebrew translations were combined in the well-known Latin version, *De mutatione temporum*, *On the Changing of the Weather* (or: *On the Changing of Seasons*).
- *Treatise on the Judgment of Eclipses.*
- *Treatise on the Dominion of the Arabs and its Duration.* This was the book used to predict the end of Arab rule above.
- *The Choices of Days*, on elections.
- *Essay on the Revolutions of Years.* This is probably a mundane work, but may include natal revolutions.
- *De signis astronomiae applicatis ad medicinam*,[16] *On the signs of astronomy as applied to medicine.* This is possibly the well-known medical work on the "degrees" of medicinal combinations mentioned above.

---

[13] Classically, reason is closely associated with the Good, so someone who is rational is also impelled to do the Good.
[14] I explore this problem further in my *Logos & Light* audio lectures (www.bendykes.com).
[15] Sezgin pp. 131-34 lists several others.
[16] This seems to be only in Latin.

• *Treatise on the Spirituality of the Planets.* This could be the work in which he suggests that the soul is associated with one of the planets after death.

Although al-Kindī enjoyed popularity and esteem for many years, his relations with the court were not as close under al-Mu'tasim's son al-Wāthiq (r. 842-847). They improved somewhat under his brother, al-Mutawakkil (r. 847-861), but al-Kindī soon met with disfavor from rivals, and also probably because of his association with a certain group of theologians called the Mu'tazilites, whom the Caliph was persecuting. Among other beliefs, the Mu'tazilites argued for atomism in their physics (with which al-Kindī disagreed), and an absolute unity of God and the inseparability of His attributes (with which he agreed). He was perhaps beaten by the authorities, and his library was taken away for a time. In fact, his prologues sometimes make it seem as though he has to struggle with an unfavorable readership. He died more or less in obscurity in about 870 AD.

However, al-Kindī's astrological story does not end there. For, apart from the translations of *Forty Chapters* by Hugo and Hermann, al-Kindī's material was adopted in widespread ways by al-Rijāl, al-Qasrānī, by Hugo in the *Book of the Three Judges*[17] and *The Book of the Nine Judges*, William Lilly, and to a lesser extent al-Qabīsī. But first, let us turn to *Forty Chapters* itself.


### §3: The Forty Chapters

*Forty Chapters* is a no-frills book on horary and electional astrology, with virtually no philosophical reflections.[18] But this mixture of questions and elections is important for two reasons. First, in a sense it reflects astrological history itself, since some late ancient and early medieval horary material is really electional material rewritten in the form of a question. As Pingree has pointed out,[19] instructions that describe *when* to do something are sometimes rewritten as *whether* something will happen if a horary chart contains those

---

[17] The precursor to *The Book of the Nine Judges*: it contains translated excerpts from *Forty Chapters* (by Hugo of Santalla), a horary work by 'Umar al-Tabarī (by Hugo), and Sahl's *On Questions* (by Hermann of Carinthia). These three texts were supplemented with excerpts from other Arabic authors (and with Sahl's material being reworked by Hugo), for the *Book of the Nine Judges*.

[18] For such reflections, see Bonatti's *Book of Astronomy* Tr. 6 and Sahl's *On Quest.*, parts of which I have included as Appendices in *Judges*.

[19] Pingree 1997, p. 47.

same configurations. In a similar way, the material on laying foundations in Ch. 15 is really indistinguishable from an election, apart from the single mention of the word "question" in the first sentence. Al-Kindī himself does not even distinguish conceptually between an election and question, simply glossing the whole book as being about "judgments" in his Arabic title.

Second, it means that we should not take Chs. 1-3 as being an exhaustive introduction to astrology, but only as listing the necessary points for making judgments about questions and elections. For example, Ch. 2 looks like it is on definitions of planetary configurations, much like *ITA* III; but the chapter really focuses narrowly on configurations which can lead to the completion of failure of a matter (as its title suggests):[20] al-Kindī does not distinguish pushing power from pushing nature (and so on), or other configurations such as bodyguarding—much of which would have been readily available from other Arabic and Greek texts (such as those by Porphyry, Rhetorius, and Sahl).[21] Likewise, in §82 he does not define "assembly" and whole-sign aspects as a whole, but assemblies and regards *with benefics*. Thus, an understanding of those definitions (such as in *ITA* III) is still necessary for practicing astrology generally.

Apart from excerpts here and there in other authors, only three versions of *The Forty Chapters* survive: a single Arabic manuscript, and the two Latin versions by the 12th-Century translators and colleagues, Hugo of Santalla and Robert of Ketton.[22] Robert's translation was produced in the late 1130s-early 1140s at the request of Robert's friend Hermann of Carinthia, who said that al-Kindī was the most "agreeable and truthful" of the astrologers.[23] Hermann then promptly used some passages from Robert's translation in his own *Search of the Heart*.[24]

This English translation is primarily of Hugo's version, but I sometimes add or substitute Robert's corresponding paragraphs for the sake of clarity or completeness. I have used Burnett's parallel edition of these Latin works, but

---

[20] In horary astrology this is frequently called "perfection."

[21] Al-Kindī mentions only Dorotheus as a source (§244), but surely he must also have drawn on Theophilus for his war material.

[22] Neither Hugo nor Robert divide the book into the same chapters as the Arabic does; I have mainly followed the Arabic in the forty primary chapter headings, and have added my own subchapter and section divisions to help the reader.

[23] *Commodissimum et veracissimum.* See Burnett 1993, p. 106. As Burnett points out (p. 97), Robert's version was never printed; this is probably precisely because Hugo's (more readable) version was already part of the more famous *Judges.*

[24] For example, the material on finding hidden treasure, Ch. II.2.3.

have occasionally found it useful to refer to the 1509 printed edition of *Judges* to correct a few things here and there. I have also consulted additional articles on the texts or its content to provide some corrections and clarity. All diagrams are my own.

Earlier I mentioned that *Forty Chapters* was important for a number of influential astrologers, such as al-Rijāl. Al-Rijāl generally praises al-Kindī as someone who "surpasses everybody in judicial astrology,"[25] pointing out that both he and Ptolemy (!) were also Muslims.[26] Many sections in his material on questions and elections are taken verbatim from *Forty Chapters*, to the extent that I was able to use the Latin al-Rijāl as a check on Robert and Hugo, following them sentence-by-sentence. In the chapters below, I indicate what material is obviously found in al-Rijāl, though I may have missed small passages here and there. Some of the longer passages include the material on theft and fugitives, travel, electing by the *bust* or scorched hours, seeking wealth, the safety of ships, engagement and marriage, children, seeking friendships, buying and selling animals and slaves, and news and rumors.

As for al-Qabīsī, it is evident that his material on the lords of houses in other houses (*ITA* I.15) is a curtailed and less informative version of *Forty Chapters* Ch. 2.3, and his material on phases of Mercury and the Moon (*ITA* V.6-7) are taken from Ch. 1.3. In fact, al-Qabīsī's statement that "this whole 'pushing' is called 'reception'" (*ITA* III.25) probably stems from al-Kindī's tendency to treat various forms of pushing[27] under the umbrella of reception—by which he really means *receiving an aspect from* another planet (Chs. 2.1.6-1.8). Other passages with more than a passing relation to al-Kindī include his victor material (*ITA* I.18, VIII.1.4), which allows us to see something potentially important: in al-Kindī and *Search*, the victors over topics and over the querent or chart are primarily used for thoughts and questions, but in al-Qabīsī the victor over the querent or chart is applied without comment to nativities. In my Introduction to *Search*, I make some proposals about the relation between victors, questions, and nativities. Al-Qabīsī[28] probably gets his orb of 6° from §90 of *Forty Chapters*.

The case of Lilly is interesting and complicated, and helps us understand better what kind of book *Christian Astrology* is. In his Letter to the Reader p.

---

[25] Burnett 1993, p. 90.
[26] Burnett 1993, p. 92.
[27] For example, pushing power, pushing nature, etc.: see *ITA* III.15-18.
[28] *ITA* III.7.

*xiv*, Lilly discusses some of his preferred source texts, and sniffs that the authors of *Judges* and "other pieces of Alkindus" understand neither astrology nor its terminology.[29] The primary translator and compiler of *Judges* was of course Hugo, and the only other author Lilly could mean was Robert, a copy of whose translation is listed in Lilly's bibliography. From this, one might assume that al-Kindī is not well represented in *CA*.

But not only did Hugo and Robert do very well in translating al-Kindī, it is absolutely clear that Lilly used both al-Rijāl's al-Kindī passages, as well as some of Robert's translation, though he rarely flags either one as belonging to al-Kindī.[30] One lengthy set of passages is in Lilly's Ch. L (pp. 319ff), which proceeds to follow *Forty Chapters* Ch. 7 virtually sentence-by-sentence (beginning with §249), from the 1571 Latin al-Rijāl, Book II.33.[31] We can be certain it is from this edition of al-Rijāl, because Lilly copies an error from the 1571 edition, which he then uses to gloss the opening paragraph as being about strayed beasts. Now, the opening parts of *Forty Chapters* Ch. 7 is on the subject of lost *inanimate* objects, and both Robert and Hugo and the 1485 al-Rijāl state that the lord of the *second* is one of the significators; only later in §266 does al-Kindī say that some of the same rules may apply to non-human living property (such as animals). But in the 1551/1571 al-Rijāl, the lord of the *twelfth* is given instead. And so, taking the twelfth for large animals, Lilly inserts a marginal note that "This principally concerns Cattle strayed": thus much of the chapter looks like a treatment of animals, when in fact it principally concerns goods and objects and fugitives.[32]

One other al-Kindī passage in *CA* is worth noting. Sometimes, Lilly feels obliged to report what his predecessors have instructed, but then offers his own view. And on pp. 193-94, Lilly presents a summary of rules about the truth and falsity of messengers' reports: in al-Rijāl this is clearly labeled as being al-Kindī, but Lilly credits "the Ancients." At first it would seem he

---

[29] That is, they "did not understand the Arte or the Termes thereof."
[30] Another example of such an uncredited adoption of much older text is *CA* p. 341, in which Lilly credits certain "modern Professors" with trying to find the "Christian name" of the thief using a certain method. But as *Judges* §§7.134-39 show, such methods were explicitly described by the early medieval Persians. I hope that these horary volumes of my *EMA* give a more accurate picture of the richness in Persian and Arabic astrology, and later astrologers' indebtedness to it.
[31] I have used the 1551 edition, but they must be identical. Also, the al-Rijāl passage clearly credits al-Kindī, but Lilly omits the reference.
[32] For example, in *CA* p. 321, Lilly addresses whether "the Beast" has strayed by itself or someone has taken it; in *Forty Chapters* §§267-68, this is really about a missing human or fugitive.

disagrees with the al-Kindī passage, because on pp. 192-93 he reports his preferred approach. But a few pages later, Lilly does indeed largely adopt the attitude of the al-Kindī instructions when looking at an actual chart.

Given these facts, it is difficult to gauge exactly what Lilly thought about al-Kindī, to the extent that he realized he was using al-Kindī. None of this detracts from Lilly as an astrologer, but it does remind us that tracing the influence of texts and their appropriation is a complicated business that is an important part of our uncovering and unraveling of the full complexity of traditional astrology.

## §4: Notable features of *The Forty Chapters*

*1. The conjunction/opposition prior to the chart.* In certain traditional techniques, the conjunction ("assembly") or opposition of the luminaries which most recently preceded the birth, is considered important. This interest is much more widespread in al-Kindī, who is interested in this lunation prior to *every* kind of chart: questions, elections, and mundane revolutions and ingresses. Al-Kindī was assuredly not the first person to emphasize its importance, but it is unfortunate that he does not name his sources (except for a reference to Dorotheus in §244).

*2. Emphasis on authority figures and war.* Approximately 20% of the interpretive material in *Forty Chapters* reflects the concerns of authority figures: war, sieges, treason, and royal undertakings. This is a higher percentage than in many other horary texts, and may reflect al-Kindī's sources—which probably includes Theophilus of Edessa, due to his well-known contributions to military astrology—but until we have a translation of Theophilus, we do not know.

*3. The Ascendant signifies the topic and especially an agent.* For the most part, in horary we expect the Ascendant and its lord to signify the person asking the question (or the person on whose behalf someone asks), while some other house and its lord signify the person or matter asked about. So, in a question about a prisoner, we would expect the Ascendant and its lord to signify the querent, and the twelfth and its lord the prisoner; or if the querent were a mother asking about her child in prison, we might expect the Ascendant to represent the mother, and the fifth and its lord to represent her child. But al-Kindī does not take this approach. First of all, in some questions he assigns the Ascendant to the person asked about, regardless of how they are related to the querent. For example, if someone asks about a prisoner, the Ascendant indicates the prisoner (Ch. 23); likewise about an absent person (Ch. 25) or a messenger (Ch. 29) or a sick person (Ch. 31) or a besieged city (Ch. 10). To me, this suggests that al-Kindī is more concerned with the chart as a whole and as treating the Ascendant as objectively representing the question itself, rather than with assigning house-based significators to every party involved.

But on the other hand, al-Kindī also emphasizes (§150) that the Ascendant especially signifies the *initiator* of an action, no matter who is actually asking the question. For example, in questions about rebellions against the government, al-Kindī gives the Ascendant to the rebel, since the rebel is the presumptive initiator of action (namely, the rebellion). He does, however, partly give the Midheaven for royal querents (Ch. 9.3). Even in Ch. 6 (on theft), the Ascendant signifies the owner of the goods and not the thief that causes the trouble, but probably because the owner is initiating a *search for* the thief.

*4. Al-Kindī's naturalism.* In keeping with his Aristotelian sympathies and naturalized theory of planetary influence (see above), al-Kindī departs from the simpler and older way of associating aspects, domiciles, and planetary natures in the Thema Mundi.[33] In that older approach, the basic meaning of aspects derives from the planets and the aspects their domiciles make to those of the Sun and Moon. For example, Mars is the domicile lord of Aries and Scorpio, both of which make square aspects to Cancer (the domicile of the Moon) and Leo (the domicile of the Sun), respectively: so, the meaning of the square can be understood as being analogous to Mars. Likewise, the domiciles of Jupiter make trine aspects to Cancer (from Pisces) and Leo (from Sagittarius), so the meaning of the trine can be made analogous to Jupiter. But al-Kindī wants to make the aspects depend on the relationship between the *elemental qualities* of these signs. As I show below in Figure 13, al-Kindī uses the sharing of active (hot, cold) and passive (wet, dry) qualities to explain how the natures of the planets and the aspects harmonize together. Unfortunately, the pattern breaks down with Saturn's domiciles and the opposition, since his domiciles share the active quality but not the passive quality, and so are identical to the signs of Venus and the sextile. That is, al-Kindī's scheme generally suggests that signs sharing the active qualities with

---

[33] See Ch. 1.1.8 and my footnotes to it.

Cancer and Leo indicate benefic planets and aspects, while not sharing them indicates malefic ones. So, the domiciles of Venus, which are in a sextile to Cancer and Leo, share their active quality (Taurus and Cancer share cold, Libra and Leo share hot); just so, those of Mars do not share in the primary quality (Aries and Cancer disagree in hot and cold, and so do Scorpio and Leo). But the signs of Saturn do share in the primary quality, and so according to his scheme they should be benefic: Capricorn agrees with Cancer in coldness just as much as Taurus did for Venus, and Aquarius agrees with Leo in hotness just as much as Libra did for Venus. And so, al-Kindī must import pre-existing notions of Saturn and the opposition in order to say that the opposition has negative qualities. Still, it is perhaps worth considering what could be done with this scheme in chart interpretation.[34]

5. *The importance of aspecting domiciles.* As I pointed out in §3 of my Introduction to *WSM*, medieval astrologers were very interested in whether or not a domicile lord aspected that domicile. If a house is regarded by its lord, then it suggests consistency and security in producing the matters of that house; if not, it suggests inconsistency and sluggishness—and, I would add, disruptions and breaks in that matter. Al-Kindī builds upon this idea, and in numerous sections he notes that what a planet conveys in a situation will depend upon the house position of that one of its domiciles which it aspects best and most strongly (or perhaps, at all).[35] So for example, suppose Leo were rising, and Venus were a planet of interest in a chart. If she were in Cancer, then she would aspect Taurus (in the 10th house) from a sextile, and Libra (in the 3rd house) from a square. Since a square is a stronger and more intense aspect than a sextile, she would probably introduce 3rd house matters into the equation, more readily than she would 10th house matters.

6. *"Reflection" and "transfer/collection" of light.* Readers of *ITA* will know that Abū Ma'shar distinguishes two kinds of scenarios in which a third planet helps to connect two others. The first kind involves planets which are already configured to each other by sign, but are not in a position to complete their connection by degree: and so, the third planet either transfers or collects their light, connecting them indirectly through itself. For instance, if Venus is in a trine relationship to Jupiter by sign, but she is not yet connected with him or will not be able to do so before he leaves his sign, then a third planet

---

[34] Mercury presents a special case, which I discuss briefly in my footnote to §18.
[35] See §§127a, 307, 364, 419, 614-15, and 619. Possible references are also in §§246, 340, and 465. §500 says that aspecting the domicile is important, but does not mention its house position.

whose degree is between them might transfer the light from Venus to Jupiter (*ITA* III.11), or Saturn in yet a later degree (and in a sign-based relationship to both) might collect their light together (*ITA* III.12). But the second kind of scenario involves planets which are in aversion to each other:[36] in that case, a third planet which can see both of them by sign acts as a kind of mirror and "reflects" their light (*ITA* III.13), allowing them to see each other in the way a mirror allows us to see something hidden from direct view. One kind of reflection mimics the transfer of light, while the other mimics the collection of light, but the point is that reflection requires that the two planets to be connected are in aversion, while transfer and collection proper require that they regard each other by sign.

But al-Kindī, perhaps drawing on the example of transfer in Sahl's *Introduct.* §5.5, does not distinguish the situations in this way.[37] Instead, for al-Kindī (and apparently for Sahl), transfer and collection are *only* possible from positions of aversion: there is not one kind of transfer and collection for planets already regarding one another, and then a special "reflection" version for planets in aversion. Indeed, this could have been the original viewpoint of the Persian astrologers, which suggests two things: (1) al-Kindī, and possibly many other Persian astrologers, believed that in many cases a planetary aspect by sign alone is enough to ensure perfection, even if a close application by degree is best; (2) Abū Ma'shar or those around him might have been responsible for this distinction between two kinds of transfer and collection—one for planets regarding each other by sign, and another for those in aversion.

7. *General instructions on perfection.* Speaking of perfection (that is, the conditions of indicating that something will be brought about), al-Kindī has a number of short sections and chapters which offer general advice. This is especially valuable because traditional astrologers do not always explicitly step back and reflect on their own methods. Readers should consult the following: §§81, 132-33, 141, 458, Chs. 2.1 and 2.5, and Chs. 4 and 22.3 (for elections in particular). Here I would simply like to comment on §§81 and 141, which explicitly mention Lots. Al-Kindī recommends that the house for a topic, and the relevant Lot, be aspected[38] by (or be in the same sign as): (1) the sect light, (2) its own domicile lord, and (3) the natural significator of the

---

[36] That is, they cannot regard each other by sign, such as one planet in Gemini and another in Capricorn.
[37] See Chs. 2.1.3-1.4.
[38] I take this to mean a whole-sign aspect.

matter. For example, in a question about money in a nocturnal chart, suppose the second house were Gemini, and the Lot of money was in Capricorn. Al-Kindī is suggesting that the second house should be aspected by the Moon (the nocturnal sect light), Mercury (the domicile lord), and Jupiter (the natural significator); likewise the Lot of money should be aspected by the Moon, Saturn (the domicile lord of the Lot), and Jupiter. But why is this important? I think al-Kindī's statement goes beyond the usual type of instruction, in which we are told to heap together as many benefics, angular planets, and trines and sextiles as possible, with everything being highly dignified, and so on. Instead, al-Kindī seems to mean that each factor plays a different role in the perfection of something. I suggest that (1) the aspect from the sect light gives the matter a kind of authority to move ahead, such as when one is told "the President is behind this," even though the President is not personally making it happen. Likewise, (2) the aspect from the domicile lord provides a kind of consistency and steadiness in the management of the event. Finally, (3) the aspect from the natural significator helps ensure that the quality of the event is in harmony with the basic principles of the matter, so that it is not handled by a planet or sign out of synch with the topic. For example, Mars is not normally considered a financially helpful planet, and even if he is the domicile lord of the second or of the Lot, and aspects it well, he will still try to indicate or produce money in a Martial way. But if Jupiter is able to aspect the house or Lot (or both), perhaps Jupiter can provide the qualitative push that aids Mars in bringing about wealth in a more appropriate way.

8. *The use of victors.* In *Search* I have discussed the topic of victors (also known as *almutens* or *mubtazz*) thoroughly.[39] Here I would like to describe the ways in which al-Kindī uses them. The first thing to say is that al-Kindī formally endorses three kinds of victors, but in practice also endorses a fourth, and also uses some candidate victors individually.

(1) In Ch. 3.1, al-Kindī introduces a victor for a particular house topic, taken from the planet which has more powers in the relevant house, its Lot, the natural significator, and the lord of the hour. In the case of a question about money, this would involve whatever sign was on the second house, the Lot of money,[40] Jupiter, and whatever the lord of the hour was. Al-Kindī does not tell us whether the various rulers of these places are counted equally

---

[39] See the glossary in §6 of the Introduction, below.
[40] But probably the Lot of Fortune would be considered, too.

or in a weighted fashion (see below), but I suspect he favors a weighted count. It is also likely that the easternness of the candidate victors (i.e., their relation to the Sun) also matters, as he suggests in §130. This kind of victor is explicitly endorsed in Ch. 9 (§320),[41] Ch. 30 (§611),[42] and is implied in Ch. 13.3 (§460).[43] It seems to be the basis of al-Qabīsī's victor for a topic in *ITA* I.18, though al-Qabīsī omits the lord of the hour. It is probably the basis for the victor for a topic in *Search* III.1.3.

(2) In Ch. 3.2, al-Kindī describes a weighted victor for the querent, but this should rather be considered a victor for the whole chart. This victor is the most authoritative of: the Sun, Moon, Ascendant, Lot of Fortune, and the degree of the assembly/opposition prior to the chart. It is notable that al-Kindī's weighted system favors the bound lord, giving the bound lord 3 points and the primary triplicity lord 2 points: authors like ibn Ezra and al-Qabīsī do the reverse. An example of this victor might be in Ch. 30 (§611).[44] If we added house strengths to the equation, it would be roughly the same as the victors which act as significators of thoughts or the chart from *Search* I.3.4 and III.1.1-1.2, and in ibn Ezra pp. 13-14.

(3) In Ch. 3.3, al-Kindī outlines his version of finding the longevity releaser and its associated *kadukḥudhāh*.[45] This is important because the releaser is normally only used in *natal* astrology, which al-Kindī explicitly recognizes—but then he says that "by it a similar judgment can also come to be with the rest of matters and their beginnings" (that is, questions and inceptions or elections). He does not seem to explicitly use this victor in *Forty Chapters*.

(4) In the al-Kindī passages of the Latin al-Rijāl (but consistent with Hugo and Robert in §311), al-Kindī changes his victor for the querent/whole chart slightly, and treats it as a significator of the topic itself. Instead of applying weighted dignities and taking the planet which has the most in all of the places taken together, we are supposed to choose the best one *from among* the five candidates, taken individually. Moreover, instead of using the degrees of the Lot of Fortune, and of the Ascendant, and of the degree of the assembly/opposition, he has us use their lords. So, we must compare each of the following individually, and choose the best one: the Sun, Moon, lord of

---

[41] The "victor…for the Ascendant, and [the victor for] the Midheaven."
[42] The "victor of the matter."
[43] The "significator of money."
[44] The "victor over the five releasers."
[45] For longevity material, see the associated natal material in *Persian Nativities I-II*.

the Ascendant, lord of the Lot of Fortune, and the lord of the assembly/opposition.

(5) Finally, al-Kindī again has us substitute the lords of three of the releasing places for the degrees themselves, and evaluate each place individually and separately—without choosing the victor among them. For example, in Ch. 8.1, we are to examine the position of each of the following, and use that assessment to get a general impression about the topic of travel: the Sun, Moon, lord of the Ascendant, lord of the Lot of Fortune, and the lord of the assembly/opposition.[46]

To make some of this clear, consider the chart below[47] and each kind of victor, and assume it is a question about money. The lord of the hour is Mercury, the degree of the assembly prior to the chart was at 13° 55' Pisces, and the Lot of money is at 26° 24' Taurus. I use only Egyptian bounds, the traditional "Chaldean" decans or faces, and the primary triplicity lord in each case.

---

[46] Lilly uses material from Ch. 8 in *CA* pp. 423ff, but omits any mention of these releasers.
[47] I have used Regiomontanus houses under the assumption that al-Kindī favors those (see below).

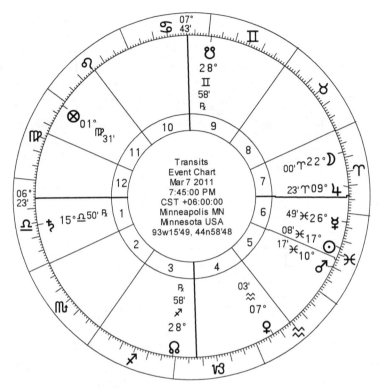

**Figure 1: Example chart for al-Kindī's victors & releasers**

(1) The victor over the topic. I will calculate this first using equal points for each dignity, then using the weighted system from Ch. 3.2. Mars is clearly the victor in each case.

| | ♄ | ♃ | ♂ | ☉ | ♀ | ☿ | ☽ |
|---|---|---|---|---|---|---|---|
| 2nd house (0° ♏) | | | xxxx | | | | |
| Lot of money | xx | | | | x | | xx |
| ♃ | | x | xx | x | x | | |
| ☿ | | x | xxx | | x | | |
| **Totals:** | 2 | 2 | **9** | 1 | 3 | 0 | 2 |

**Figure 2: Example of victor for topic (equal points)**

| | ♄ | ♃ | ♂ | ☉ | ♀ | ☿ | ☽ |
|---|---|---|---|---|---|---|---|
| 2nd house (0° ♏) | | | 5,3,2,1 | | | | |
| Lot of money | 3,1 | | | | 5 | | 4,2 |
| ♃ | | 2 | 5,1 | 4 | 3 | | |
| ☿ | | 5 | 3,2,1 | | 4 | | |
| **Totals:** | 4 | 7 | **23** | 4 | 12 | 0 | 6 |

**Figure 3: Example of victor for topic (weighted points)**

(2) Victor over the querent/chart. Mercury is the victor.[48]

| | ♄ | ♃ | ♂ | ☉ | ♀ | ☿ | ☽ |
|---|---|---|---|---|---|---|---|
| ☉ | | 5,1 | 2 | | 4 | 3 | |
| ☽ | | 2 | 5,3 | 4 | 1 | | |
| Ascendant | 4 | | | | 5 | 3,2 | 1 |
| ⊗ | | | | 1 | | 5,4,3 | 2 |
| Assembly | | 5,3,1 | 2 | | 4 | | |
| **Totals:** | 4 | 17 | 12 | 5 | 14 | **20** | 3 |

**Figure 4: Example of victor over the querent/chart**

(3) The longevity releaser and its *kadukḫudhāh*. Al-Kindī's stated method should be viewed with caution, because it omits the fact that (a) the releaser is normally only allowed to be in certain houses of the chart, and (b) there is often a preferred ranking of aspecting rulers. But here is my tentative take on it: it is a nocturnal nativity; the Moon is in a feminine quadrant; she is regarded (by whole sign) by her decan lord Venus, and in an assembly in the same sign with her triplicity lord, Jupiter. The triplicity lord is more important than the decan lord, so the Moon is the releaser and Jupiter is her *kadukḫudhāh*.

---

[48] Note that being a victor by dignities like this is a question of *authority*, not goodness or strength: just as one's boss may be venal and weak, so a planetary victor might be weak and in fall, as is the case here.

(4-5) Evaluation of individual releasers (from modified releaser list). To my mind, Venus seems like the best of the five.

| | |
|---|---|
| ☉ | Retreating (cadent), peregrine, sextiles Lot of money and 2nd but burning up the lord of 2nd (Mars). Possibly considered received by bound lord (Mercury) |
| ☽ | Pivotal (angular), increasing in light, in an assembly with Jupiter, in her own *halb*. Separating from an opposition with a powerful Saturn. Suggests prosperity, although she is also peregrine and empty (void) in course by medieval standards, and aspects neither the Lot of money nor the 2nd. |
| Lord of Asc (♀) | Pivotal, in an applying mutual reception with an exalted Saturn, and in an application with an angular and benefic Jupiter.[49] Aspects both the 2nd and the Lot by a strong aspect, and is the lord of the Lot. |
| Lord of ⊗ (☿) | Retreating, under the rays, in detriment and fall. |
| Lord of assembly (♃) | Peregrine (or at least not the primary triplicity lord), western and close to entering the rays, applying to an opposition without reception with a powerful malefic Saturn. In aversion to both the Lot and the 2nd. |

*9. Al-Kindī's house system.* House division was already a somewhat vexed question by al-Kindī's time. On the one hand, some authors straight-forwardly assume (or do not explicitly depart from) whole-sign houses and their associated concepts, in which each sign itself constitutes a house. So for example, if the degree of the Ascendant is on Gemini, then all of Gemini—whether above the horizon or below it—is the first house, and any planet in it has first-house meanings; just so, all of Cancer is the second house, and so on.

On the other hand, there were already several quadrant-based house systems which posit cusps falling in various places, such as the Porphyry or Alchabitius Semi-Arc systems. Over the next few centuries, yet more would

---

[49] This could be considered a transfer of light by Abū Ma'shar's standards.

appear. For reasons I will not get into here,[50] there are also hybrid positions which may have represented the majority of astrological practice: for example, using whole signs for topics, but quadrant divisions to measure dynamic "strength."

Al-Kindī follows something of a hybrid approach. In terms of his quadrant house system, in Ch. 1.3.5 he describes a quadrant-based approach for topics, and I have no real reason to doubt that he also uses them for his theory of advancement and retreat (i.e., angularity and cadency) in §37. In Ch. 1.3.5, al-Kindī instructs us to begin from the degree on the horizon (which probably means the equatorial degree), and to divide the celestial equator into equal 30° increments from there.[51] According to Gansten, al-Kindī is probably advocating Regiomontanus houses: if so, then it pushes the use of Regiomontanus back by over a century, since it is normally associated with an Ibn Mu'ādh al-Jayyānī (989 – ca. 1079 AD).[52]

But how is al-Kindī's approach a hybrid of whole signs and quadrant divisions? Well, on the one hand (1) he still recognizes something of the whole-sign approach to advancement and retreat (at least by analogy); on the other, (2) some of his statements suffer ambiguity because they apply whole-sign notions to his quadrant houses.

(1) As for recognizing the analogical relevance of whole signs, al-Kindī warns in §477 that when we elect a time to lay the foundation of a building, the degree of the Midheaven should *not* fall on the ninth sign: instead, it should be in the eleventh or the tenth signs. So for example, in Figure 1 above, the Ascendant is on Libra. Normally we would expect the Midheaven to be in the tenth sign, and so it is. But depending on what sign and degree is rising and what one's latitude is, we know that the Midheaven often floats around anywhere between the ninth and eleventh signs: al-Kindī would not want the election to have the Midheaven on Gemini, but rather on Leo or Cancer. Now, this kind of statement only makes sense against the backdrop of a whole-sign theory of advancement and retreat, since in whole signs the ninth sign is by definition cadent, while the eleventh and tenth are advancing. In a *fully* quadrant-based system, the signs would not matter like this at all. So, al-Kindī's assignment of house topics still takes into account the

---

[50] See my Introduction to *ITA*.
[51] I am grateful to Martin Gansten for his help in looking at this passage.
[52] See Kennedy, article XIX p. 543.

categorizing of the signs as pivotal (angular), succeedent, and remote (cadent).

(2) As for ambiguity, there is an important area in which statements by al-Kindī only make full sense in a whole-sign context, but they have been pressed into service for quadrant divisions: that is, the issue of a planet aspecting its own house—or indeed, for any planet aspecting any house. As I showed above, al-Kindī is very interested in which of its own domiciles a planet aspects, and generally what planets aspect a house.

In a whole-sign approach, this matter is straightforward. The signs are the basis of aspects, not purely mathematical degrees, and so by definition any planet will always be in one sign, aspect seven others, and be in aversion from four: there are no out-of-sign aspects.[53] In some cases, a planet will be in aversion to its sole domicile (such as the Moon in Gemini), and in others a planet will be in aversion to one of its two domiciles (such as Venus in Gemini, which trines Libra but is in aversion to Taurus). Likewise, no planet in the first house can aspect or "see" anything in the twelfth house, which makes some philosophical sense for a house that normally indicates obscurity, institutions, secret enemies, and so on.

But in a fully quadrant-based approach, houses tend to be identified particularly with the cusps, whose positions float around: sometimes with more than one cusp on a sign, and with "intercepted" signs. In this approach, it is possible for a planet can aspect *both* of its houses even if they are in aversion by sign, or even aspect *none* of its houses. In the first case, suppose Venus were in the last few degrees of Gemini, but a cusp fell in the first few degrees of Taurus: if we factor in her orb of influence (usually taken to be 7°), then she could actually aspect her "house" in that adjacent sign, even though the signs are in aversion. But in the second case, it would be possible for Venus to aspect *none* of her houses: perhaps Libra is fully intercepted between cusps (and so has no cusp to aspect), while Venus cannot aspect some cusp on Taurus within the required orb. In that case, what can we say about al-Kindī's insistence that Venus will convey the meanings of the house she aspects best? The only recourse I see is to invent a new theory, in which intercepted signs become "secondary" houses: so for instance, if a house cusp falls somewhere in late Virgo—and so is ruled by Mercury—and Libra is intercepted, then Libra and Venus have an unspecified "secondary" influence in that house. This is in fact the solution

---

[53] But Sahl does seem to allow out-of-sign conjunctions in *On Quest*. §5.3.

advocated by later astrologers such as Morin and Lilly, but one can see that it arises precisely because aspects have been detached from their basis in signs, and houses have been identified with cusps. Thus, certain statements by early authors like al-Kindī are ambiguous, because one does not always know exactly how *they* conceived of what they were doing or how each one navigated this tangle of signs, aspects, topics, and strength.

## §5: The Latin translators & their texts

As already mentioned above, this edition is based primarily upon the two 12th-Century Latin versions of Robert of Ketton and Hugo of Santalla, and between them I have relied most on Hugo. Readers should be aware that neither Hugo's nor Robert's language is easy.

In the first place, some of their vocabulary does not match what most astrologers are used to, because since the High Middle Ages the easier style and vocabulary of John of Spain has reigned supreme. For example, when John translated his Arabic texts, he said that Aries is the "exaltation" (*exaltatio*) of the Sun; but Robert and Hugo prefer to say it is the "supremacy" or "kingdom" of the Sun (*regnum*). When two planets are in the same sign, John prefers to call it a "conjunction" (*coniunctio*), while Robert and Hugo call it an "assembly" (*conventus*). In some cases, Robert and Hugo have preferable readings of the Arabic, and in *ITA* III I have compared John's vocabulary to theirs and the Arabic originals, sometimes preferring Robert and Hugo.

Also, their sentence structure is very different from John's, whose style is very much like modern Western languages as well as Arabic: so, the reader must slow down. For example, John might say, "If the Moon and the lord of the second are of a good condition, then the querent will obtain wealth." This is a straightforward, if-then statement that matches Arabic sentence structure well. But Hugo would be bored with this style and want something that sounded more fancy: so he would more likely say that "The favorable bearing of the Moon, and no less the lord of the second, supports a judgment of wealth." Both sentences say essentially the same thing, but Hugo's style demands a bit more concentration. (Sometimes Hugo's sentences are downright irritating.) So while their vocabulary and style are different, Robert and Hugo do know what they are talking about. But an impatient reader, or one unfamiliar with their style, might think they misunderstand astrology (as Lilly did).

In some cases, I have substituted Robert's passages for Hugo's. In general, Robert's Latin is extremely concise (as was his intention),[54] but sometimes he omits details and nuances. Indeed, it would be hard to understand some nuances of the text well using only his translation.

On the other hand, Hugo affects his own idea of a cultured Latin style, which means he sometimes says too much, inserts double negatives, ponderous literary curlicues, and unnecessary variations on words—a sign, as Burnett rightly notes, of his boredom with the repetitive instructions by al-Kindī and what he took to be dullness and inferiority of Arabic style.[55] I will simply point out one type of awkwardness in his style, a certain way of using genitive clauses. Sometimes at the end of sentences, al-Kindī simply means to say something like "the querent will fare badly," or "the result will be unsteady." But Hugo decides to double up on the terms involved, and so he will speak redundantly of "the difficulty of faring badly" (§556b) or "the unsteadiness of fragility" (§480). In his own mind, I'm sure he believed he was creating interesting and thoughtful imagery or turns of phrase; but it does not benefit the astrology at all. The reader must be on the lookout for these phrases and understand them for what they are; in one case (§261) I simply separate the terms, reading "sexual immorality [or] longing" for Hugo's somewhat ridiculous "sexual immorality *of* longing."

## §6: Glossary

The following glossary of terms is partly relevant to traditional astrology in general, but especially includes terms favored by Hugo and Robert in their Latin renderings of al-Kindī's text.

- **Advancing**. Normally, when a planet is in a **pivot** or succeedent. But al-Kindī treats only succeedent places as advancing. See Ch. 1.2.3 and *ITA* III.3.
- **Apogee.** The point at which a planet is furthest from the earth while on its deferent circle, and appears faintest and slowest. See *ITA* II.1.

---

[54] See Burnett 1993, p. 106.
[55] Burnett 1993, p. 96.

- **Assembly.** When two or more planets are in the same sign, and more intensely if within 15°. See Ch. 2.11 and *ITA* III.5. But it also refers to the conjunction of the luminaries (the New Moon), especially before a birth or the chart of an election, question, or revolution.
- **Aversion.** Being in the second, sixth, eighth, or twelfth sign from a place. For instance, a planet in Gemini is in the twelfth from, and so in aversion to, Cancer.
- **Bearing** (Lat. *habitudo*). Usually, any kind of planetary configuration as described in Ch. 2 (or *ITA* III). But in Ch. 1.3.2, Hugo also uses it to describe *ḥalb* or **domain**.
- **Cadent** (Lat. *cadens*, lit. "falling"). Cadency is meant in three ways. (1) If a planet is cadent by sign from the angles or **pivots**, then it is in the twelfth, ninth, sixth, or third sign. (2) If a planet is cadent from the angles or pivots in terms of quadrant-based **houses**, then it is in the twelfth, ninth, sixth, or third houses, but not necessarily in those corresponding *signs*. For the difference between these, see the Introduction to *ITA* and §4 of this Introduction. (3) If a planet is cadent from the Ascendant (i.e., the rising sign) or from any specifically-named planet or place, then it is in **aversion** to it, namely, in a sign which cannot aspect the rising sign or planet or place: by definition this will always be the second, sixth, eighth, and twelfth signs from a given sign. For example, if a planet is cadent from the Ascendant, it is in the twelfth, eighth, sixth or second signs, since these cannot make a classical aspect into the rising sign.
- **Cleansed.** When a planet is in **aversion** to the malefic planets (the **infortunes**).
- **Convertible.** Equivalent to "movable": see **Quadruplicity**.
- **Domain** (Ar. *ḥayyiz*). Normally a gender-intensified condition of *ḥalb*. See §68 and *ITA* III.2.
- **Drawn down from** (Lat. *reductus*). See **Cadent**.
- **Estranged** (Lat. *alienus*). Equivalent to **Aversion**.
- **Foreign** (Lat. *alienus, peregrinus*). Equivalent to **Peregrine**. But in one instance (§131) it might mean being in **aversion**.
- **Fortunate.** Normally, any planet which is in a good condition or **supported** by a benefic planet or one in a good condition. But sometimes, equivalent to a **fortune/lucky** planet.

- **Fortune/lucky.** Normally, one of the two benefic planets (Venus, Jupiter), but perhaps a planet such as Mercury or the Moon if in a good condition.
- **Ḥalb.** Probably Pahlavi for "sect," but normally describes a planetary rejoicing condition. Hugo often calls this a planet's "fortification" (Lat. *munimentum*). See §68 and *ITA* III.2.
- **Hexagon.** Equivalent to "sextile," one of the aspects.
- **House** (Lat. *domus*). "House" is meant in two ways. (1) The sign which is the domicile or rulership of a particular planet: Aries is the house or domicile of Mars, who rules it (see Figure 10). (2) A place in the chart signifying a particular topic in life: the second house indicates wealth, goods, allies, and so on (see Ch. 1.3.5 and *ITA* I.13). But there are two ways of determining what such places are. (2a) "Whole-sign" houses use each domicile as a house: for example, if Leo is rising, then all of Leo—both the parts above the horizon or degree of the Ascendant, and those below it—is the first house, all of Virgo is the second house, and so on. (2b) Quadrant-based houses use the circles of the horizon and meridian to determine the house divisions, sometimes based on rising and culmination times, sometimes based on divisions of the celestial equator. In quadrant-based houses, the divisions between houses are called "cusps" and may fall anywhere on a sign. Historically, whole-sign houses and quadrant houses were used either separately or in concert (for example, using whole-sign houses for topics, but using the quadrant divisions to measure a planet's "strength"). Al-Kindī uses quadrant-based houses for topics, but recognizes that signs do have some integrity in terms of being **pivotal** (angular), succeedent or **cadent** (such as in §477). For more on al-Kindī's house system, see §4 of this Introduction.
- **Inceptor.** The person who undertakes an action (from Lat. *incipio*).
- **Infortune/unlucky.** Normally, one of the two malefic planets (Mars, Saturn), but perhaps a planet such as Mercury or the Moon if in a bad condition.
- **Kadukhudhāh** (From the Pahlavi for "domicile master"). One of the lords of the longevity **releaser**, preferably the bound lord. It is also equivalent to the distributor when directing any releaser through the bounds. See Ch. 3.3 and *ITA* VIII.1.3.
- **Latitude.** A planet's distance north or south of the ecliptic.
- **Led down from** (Lat. *deductus*). See **Cadent**.

- **Partner** (Ar. *ṣāḥib,* "associate, owner"). Usually, one of the lords of a place. But sometimes, a planet in some configuration with another, and so having a partnership with it (see §312).
- **Peregrine**. When a planet is not in one of its five **dignities**. But sometimes al-Kindī considers being peregrine only in terms of not being in one's domicile or exaltation. See *ITA* I.9.
- **Perverse, wicked, turned awry** (Lat. *perversus*). "Perverse" is meant in three ways. (1) A perverse *place* is one in **aversion** to the Ascendant.[56] (2) A perverse *aspect* is a "bad" aspect or **regard**, namely the square or opposition (whether by sign alone or by a certain number of degrees).[57] (3) A perverse *planet* is an **infortune** (Mars or Saturn).[58]
- **Pivot** (Lat. *cardo*). A synonym for "angle," but ambiguous as to whether it means an angular sign, the degree of an axis (such as the Midheaven), or a quadrant-based house or region of power.
- **Possess, hold onto** (Lat. *possideo, obtineo*). Equivalent to a planet being "in" a house or sign.
- **Quadruplicity**, often called a "mode" in modern astrology. A group of four signs having a similar style: the movable/convertible/turning signs are Aries, Cancer, Libra, Capricorn; the firm/fixed signs are Taurus, Leo, Scorpio, Aquarius; the common/double-bodied signs are Gemini, Virgo, Sagittarius, Pisces. See Chs. 1.1.4 and 2.6, and *ITA* I.10.5.
- **Regard** (Lat. *respectus*). An aspect, whether by sign alone or within a certain number of degrees. See Ch. 2.1.1 and *ITA* III.6.
- **Releaser** (Ar. *hīlāj*). The point which is the focus of a primary direction. In determining longevity, it is the one among a standard set of possible points which has certain qualifications (see Ch. 3.3 and *ITA* VIII.1.3), and is directed for purposes of predicting life expectancy. But in *Forty Chapters* and *Search* (III.2), it is recommended that the releaser be used interpretively (and perhaps predictively) even in the charts of questions on other topics. See §4 of the Introduction, above.
- **Remote** (Lat. *remotus*). Normally, equivalent to **retreating**, but in some cases perhaps equivalent to **aversion**.
- **Retreating**. When a planet is **cadent** from a **pivot** (angle), namely in the twelfth, ninth, sixth or third **houses**. See Ch. 1.2.3 and *ITA* III.4.

---

[56] See §425.
[57] See §§103, 316, 360a, 384, 388, 443.
[58] This use of "perverse" is found in Māshā'allāh's *Book of Aristotle* (translated from Arabic by Hugo), but is not used in *Forty Chapters*. It is found in my *PN I*.

- **Shift** (Ar. *nawbah*). The role taken by a luminary as the sect light: the Sun in the day, or the Moon at night. Al-Kindī defines day and night as the moments when the center of the Sun's body is on the horizon (Ch. 11.7).
- **Sovereignty** (Lat. *regnum*). Equivalent to exaltation.
- **Support/favor**. A helpful aspect from another planet, whether from a **fortune** or **infortune**. For support from malefic planet, see §160.
- **Tetragon.** Equivalent to "square," one of the aspects.
- **Trigon**. Equivalent to "trine," one of the aspects.
- **Triplicity**. A group of three signs of the same element, and arranged in a triangular relationship. The fiery triplicity is Aries, Leo, Sagittarius; the earthy triplicity is Taurus, Virgo, Capricorn; the airy triplicity is Gemini, Libra, Aquarius; the watery triplicity is Cancer, Scorpio, Pisces. See Ch. 1.1.3 and *ITA* I.7.
- **Turning.** Equivalent to "movable": see **Quadruplicity**.
- **Unfortunate**. Normally, any planet which is in a bad condition or harmed by a malefic planet or one in a good condition. But sometimes, equivalent to an **infortune/unlucky** planet.
- **Victor** (Ar. *mubtazz*, "the winner, victor"). A planet which is the most authoritative (or "strong," etc.), from among several rulers of a place, or several other candidate planets. Victors are used as high-level proxies for a topic or person or chart, and are also used in the interpretation of thoughts (such as in *Search*). See Ch. 3, and §4 of this Introduction.

# CHAPTER 1: ON THE FORTUNES OF THIS WORLD & THE GREAT IMPORTANCE ATTACHED TO THEM

## Chapter 1.1: Signs & triplicities

### *Chapter 1.1.1: The ecliptic and equator; northern and southern signs*

§1. The spherical shape of the celestial circle holds the same center as the earth does. But it is divided into twelve parts, which the astrologers call "signs." There even comes to be another, two-fold division of them, one part of which deviates into the south, the other into the north.[1] For this greatest circle [of the ecliptic], principally designated in the sphere itself, splits the equinoctial circle[2] crosswise. [The equinoctial circle's] distance from each pole is equal to the east and the west, [and] the constant and tireless motion of its revolution exists unchangeably above those [poles]. The southern part [of the ecliptic] gets six signs, [and] the northern one the same amount, of which each [half] gains 180 equal parts (or rather, "degrees"). For the 360 equal degrees establish the completed zodiac; the individual signs even claim 30° for themselves.

§2. Also, Aries particularly preserves the beginning of these signs for itself. In fact, once the beginning has been taken up, it goes into the north from the equinoctial line. Taurus follows it, and [then] the rest in order: namely Gemini, Cancer, Leo, Virgo, Libra, Scorpio, Sagittarius, Capricorn, Aquarius, Pisces. But Libra possesses a second beginning, in a secondary way: because the dignity of the first beginning [from Aries] is a deviation from the equator[3] into the north. Indeed the effectiveness of the stars is made more robust in this [northern] part, [because] it is made closer to us, [and] advances upon us in a familiar way; but it is made more feeble in the south. Whence Aries takes the beginning of the whole, [but] Libra [makes] a start in a secondary way, into the southern [half].

---

[1] The signs of northern and southern declination: see the figure below, and *ITA* I.10.1.
[2] That is, the celestial equator.
[3] Reading for *isimerino* (which Hugo tends to use for "ecliptic").

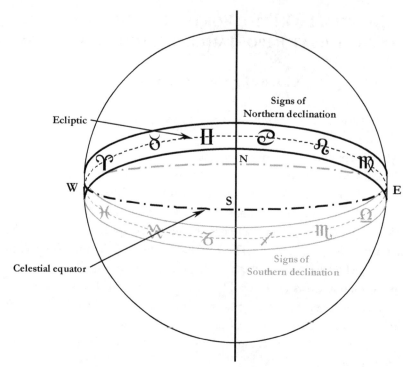

**Figure 5: Celestial equator, ecliptic, zodiac**

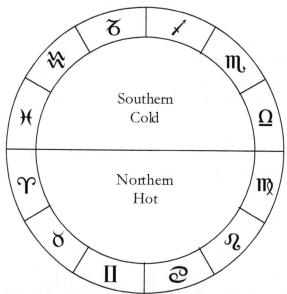

**Figure 6: Hot/cold, northern/southern signs**

*Chapter 1.1.2: The signs and the human body*

§3-4a. Also, in this manner, the distribution of the limbs of the human body which is made [in this manner] ascribes the head to Aries. But Taurus is allotted the neck. Gemini, the shoulders and hands. Cancer, the chest and lungs. Leo, the stomach and the vital organs.[4] Virgo, the back and sides. But this half of the human body is terminated in the top part.

§4b. Following this, Libra (claiming the kidneys) is made the beginning of the rest which follow in descending [order]. Scorpio makes for himself the places of longing (both the male and the female). Also, Sagittarius [claims] the buttocks and those [parts] through which nature releases [itself] downwards.[5] Capricorn, the knees and lower half of the legs. Aquarius, the shins. But they left the feet to Pisces. If therefore something is sought from one of the signs, it shows a definite signification in the limbs dedicated to it.

|  | Body part |
|---|---|
| ♈ | Head |
| ♉ | Neck |
| ♊ | Shoulders, hands |
| ♋ | Chest, lungs |
| ♌ | Stomach, vital organs |
| ♍ | Back & sides |
| ♎ | Kidneys |
| ♏ | Genitals |
| ♐ | Buttocks and anus |
| ♑ | Knees |
| ♒ | Shins |
| ♓ | Feet |

**Figure 7: Al-Kindī's sign-limb correspondences[6]**

---

[4] *Exta.*

[5] Reading *dimittit* for *demittit.* That is, excretion. Robert politely says, "the buttocks and what lies between them."

[6] See also a slightly different list in *ITA* I.3.

*Chapter 1.1.3: The triplicities*

§5. Moreover, there is a four-fold division of these, according to the four natures of the elements. For certain ones of them (the hot and dry) follow the nature of fire; but others (the cold and dry) imitate the nature of earth; others (the hot and moist) are united to the airy nature; but others (the cold and moist) are joined to the watery nature.

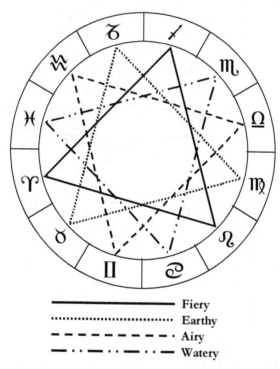

———————— Fiery
·················· Earthy
— — — — — · Airy
— · · — · · — · · — Watery

**Figure 8: Signs related by triplicity**

*Chapter 1.1.4: The quadruplicities and the seasons*[7]

§6. A three-fold distribution of them even follows, according to the *effects* of the natures. For certain ones are called "fixed" on account of the persistence of [the effect's] time in that nature. Others are "double-bodied"[8] on account of sharing that time in a two-fold nature of elements. Others are "turning"[9] on account of the change of that season from one [quality] into the other quality of the following element.

§7. But among them there is a certain shared quality. Therefore, the beginning of the signs (which is Aries) is "turning," on account of the changing of the season of winter (namely from the nature of water, for winter is cold and moist), to the airy one (namely of spring): for spring and winter are partners in moisture, but they differ in the quality of heat and cold. But Taurus is called a fixed sign on account of its steadiness in that same nature of spring. But Gemini is designated as being among the double-bodied [signs] on account of the common quality of spring and summer. Cancer is convertible, for air—giving up the hot and moist nature of spring—approaches the hot and dry quality of summer. But Leo is said to be firm because it demonstrates the steadfastness of the nature of summer. Virgo takes on the nature of summer and autumn in a shared way, because the atmosphere of each is made common.

§8. But Libra is called convertible on account of the changing of the atmosphere from summer to autumn. The sign of Scorpio is made firm in the steadiness of autumn. But Sagittarius, being a partner in the nature of autumn and winter, signifies the common quality of the atmosphere in each. Also Capricorn, making the difference between autumn and winter, is called convertible. The firmness of Aquarius designates the steadiness of winter in that same nature. Pisces is named as being of the common or twin substance, because it embraces the quality of winter and the spring-like [quality].

---

[7] For various views on the particular effects these create, see Addition 1 below and *ITA* I.10.5. Al-Kindī's explanation of the quadruplicities in terms of seasons derives from Ptolemy's naturalistic account, according to which the quadruplicities mimics the seasonal changes when the Sun is in the respective signs (see *Tet.* I.12). So, movable signs indicate swift changes (as at the beginning of each season); fixed signs indicate persistence and intensity and depth (as in the middle of each season); common signs indicate wavering, repetition, and back-and-forth activity (as when the current season is ending and qualities of the next one are introduced).

[8] Also known as "common" signs.

[9] Or, "tropical." These are also called the "movable" and "convertible" signs in medieval texts.

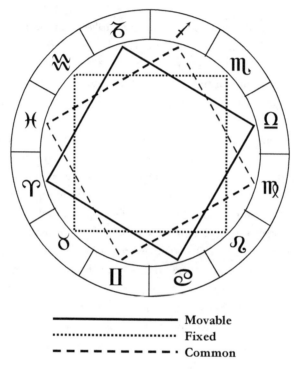

Movable ——————
Fixed ··············
Common — — — — —

**Figure 9: Quadruplicities**

*Chapter 1.1.5: The cycle of seasons, elements, and human life*

§9. Nevertheless, the distinction in these seasons makes a start from spring, for [spring] has a certain appropriateness in a two-fold birth—namely of seeds and animals.[10] But vital heat and moisture offer the beginning of subsistence to these two [types of life]. Once the period of their virtue is strengthened in further parts of life, heat and dryness are displayed. But then dryness[11] thrives with coldness in its own time. At last, moisture joined with pronounced coldness swallows [them] up,[12] with no solace of heat or dryness; [and] what is remaining in the [body][13] is corrupted and putrefies.[14]

---

[10] Ar.: "agriculture and reproduction."
[11] Reading with the Ar. and Robert, for Hugo's "heat."
[12] Reading as active instead of passive.
[13] Reading *in corpore* with the Ar. and Robert for Hugo's "womb."
[14] Note the relation between this paragraph and *Tet.* I.10.

*Chapter 1.1.6: Elemental qualities of the equinoctial and solsticial signs*

§10. Again, they ascribed Aries (the beginning of the signs) to fire, which possesses first place among the elements. Moreover, they arranged the solsticial [sign] which follows it (namely, Cancer) as being watery and the opposite of the first [sign]. Likewise they decreed the equinoctial [sign] which follows that (namely, Libra) as being airy and the opposite to it (for Cancer and Libra are connected by the agreement of moisture, though they differ in coldness and heat).

§11. But they call the solsticial [sign] which succeeds Libra (namely, Capricorn) earthy and an opposite to Libra. Finally, the equinoctial [sign] placed after Capricorn (namely, Aries), [is] fiery and an opposite to it. For Aries and Capricorn have an agreement in dryness, [but] their heat and coldness is in opposition. And so, these convertible signs claim the beginnings of the seasons, and are decreed as being more worthy in the order of signs—wherefore, these four deserve to be in charge of the loftinesses and sovereignties[15] of the four superior planets.[16]

---

[15] That is, the exaltations.
[16] The exalted lord of Aries is the Sun; of Cancer, Jupiter; of Libra, Saturn; of Capricorn, Mars.

| | Domicile | Detriment | Exaltation | Fall |
|---|---|---|---|---|
| ♈ | ♂ | ♀ | ☉ (esp. 19°) | ♄ (esp. 21°) |
| ♉ | ♀ | ♂ | ☽ (esp. 3°) | |
| ♊ | ☿ | ♃ | | |
| ♋ | ☽ | ♄ | ♃ (esp. 15°) | ♂ (esp. 28°) |
| ♌ | ☉ | ♄ | | |
| ♍ | ☿ | ♃ | ☿ (esp. 15°) | ♀ (esp. 27°) |
| ♎ | ♀ | ♂ | ♄ (esp. 21°) | ☉ (esp. 19°) |
| ♏ | ♂ | ♀ | | ☽ (esp. 3°) |
| ♐ | ♃ | ☿ | | |
| ♑ | ♄ | ☽ | ♂ (esp. 28°) | ♃ (esp. 15°) |
| ♒ | ♄ | ☉ | | |
| ♓ | ♃ | ☿ | ♀ (esp. 27°) | ☿ (esp. 15°) |

**Figure 10: Table of major dignities & corruptions/debilities[17]**

*Chapter 1.1.7: Solar and lunar halves of the zodiac*

§12. Moreover, they divided the circle into two parts, of which they give one (from the beginning of Leo to the end of Capricorn) to the Sun, and from the beginning of Aquarius to the last parts of Cancer, to the Moon. The six signs of this partitioning which follow the distribution of the Sun, use up more than 180° in ascensions. But the leftover ones (namely those which the lunar partitioning takes up) are ended in less than 180° in ascensions. Whence they said this [lunar] half is lesser, but the one which belongs to the Sun is greater.[18]

§13. Moreover, the Sun is effective in the individual signs of his portion, [and is] a partner with their lords; but it is claimed no less with the Moon in her own division.

---

[17] In traditional texts there is widespread inconsistency between cardinal and ordinal numbers. For example, the exaltation of the Sun is variously given as "nineteen" degrees (19°), and the "nineteenth" degree (18°). My sense is that the authors probably meant "at the end of the nineteenth degree, namely at 19°."

[18] This seems not to be true just on the equator, but the Sun's half increases dramatically in ascensions the further north one is. But the reverse should be true in southern latitudes (i.e., the Lunar half increases in ascensions).

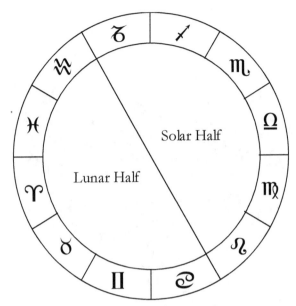

**Figure 11: Solar *&* lunar signs**

*Chapter 1.1.8: Relationships of domiciles, planets, and aspects*

§14. Furthermore, since Saturn's signs are arranged opposite the Sun and his house, they call [Saturn] the adversary of the Sun (and of the Moon, in the same way). For one house of his, namely Aquarius, which occupies the first position in the lunar partition,[19] is in the opposite of the solar domicile (which is Leo). But the other one, which is Capricorn, being the last in the order of the solar distribution, is found to be opposite the lunar lodging-place (namely Cancer). This explanation makes it necessary that he be called an "adversary" and "corruptor."[20]

---

[19] That is, moving clockwise in the zodiac: see the figure above.

[20] Note the similarity between Saturn (as the opposite of the lights) and Satan (the opposite of God), whose name means "adversary" in Hebrew, and is known as a corruptor.

**Figure 12: The Hellenistic Thema Mundi & aspects[21]**

| | Aspect | Qualities shared with domiciles of luminaries? | |
|---|---|---|---|
| | | Active/primary (hot/cold) | Passive/secondary (dry/wet) |
| ♄ | Opp. ☍ | Y | N |
| ♃ | Trine △ | Y | Y |
| ♂ | Square □ | N | N |
| ♀ | Sextile ✳ | Y | N |
| ☿ | Assembly[22] ☌ | N | Y |

**Figure 13: Al-Kindī's relation of planets, aspects,**
**& elemental qualities[23]**

---

[21] The Thema Mundi ("Chart of the World") is a Hellenistic teaching tool supposed to represent the creation of the world, in which Cancer rises and all of the planets are in their own domiciles between Cancer and Capricorn. House meanings and the significations of planets can be related to the domicile and exaltation rulerships, and the meanings of aspects can be associated with the planets by their relation to the luminaries, in a way similar to how al-Kindī explains here (such as Mars and the square having a similar meaning due to the square relation of Aries and Scorpio to Cancer and Leo). For more on this, see *ITA* III.6.2, and Firmicus Maternus's *Mathesis* III.1.

[22] Otherwise known as a bodily conjunction or bodily connection.

[23] Note that Saturn's domiciles are similar to those of the luminaries in just the way Venus's are. This shows that al-Kindī has to presuppose the meaning of the opposition to

§15. Also, since Jupiter's houses are situated in the trigon of the Sun and Moon (for his domicile Sagittarius is in the trigon of the Sun, also Pisces does so in a trigonal way from the Moon's house), [and] moreover since the lunar lodging-place agrees with the nature of the jovial house,[24] he appears as "one who makes fortunate" or "one who invites."[25]

§16. Mars, an unlucky [planet], [is] a corruptor of [the domiciles] of the lights, because we have his houses disposed in a tetragon of the houses of the Sun and Moon. For Scorpio, which is his house, possesses the tetragon of the solar domicile. And the second one (which is Aries, namely a fiery one) [has] the tetragon of the lunar lodging-place—whence [Aries] is adverse to the house of the Moon, namely a watery one. And because his houses are more distinctly adverse to the lodging-places of the Sun and Moon,[26] they say he corrupts more readily[27] than Saturn.

§17. But since the Venusian houses are placed in a hexagon from those of the Sun and Moon, the regard of the hexagon is of half-friendship,[28] because [that regard] proceeds from signs of that same figure and proper quality. For her lodging-place Libra (a hot and moist [sign]), being in a hexagon from the house of the Sun, agrees in heat with Leo (namely the solar lodging-place), but differs in the dry and moist. But that which has a hexagon with the lunar house (Taurus, being cold and dry), concedes coldness to Cancer (which supplies the lodging-place of the Moon), [and] disagrees in the dry and moist. Wherefore they decreed that she is fortunate and lucky. But her luckiness is less than the jovial [kind], for Jupiter agrees with the domiciles of the lights in both qualities.

§18. But the houses of Mercury follow [next to] the lodging-places of the Sun and Moon. For Virgo succeeds Leo (the [house] of the Sun), agreeing with it in the passive quality [of dryness], but it disagrees with Leo in heat

---

support his scheme, otherwise the sextile and Venus would be the same as the opposition and Saturn.

[24] Pisces is a watery sign (as Sagittarius is a fiery sign, agreeing with Leo).

[25] *Vocator.* This can also mean "host."

[26] Elementally, Aries (hot and dry) is totally different from Cancer (cold and moist); likewise Scorpio (cold and moist) with respect to Leo (hot and dry). The domiciles of Saturn share one quality with those of the luminaries: Capricorn shares the cold with Cancer, Aquarius the hot with Leo.

[27] Reading with Robert for Hugo's "more quickly" (*celerius*).

[28] Half, because unlike the domiciles of Jupiter (which fully agree with the luminaries' qualities), those of Venus agree in only one.

and coldness. But the [house] which adheres[29] to Cancer [is] namely Gemini: it and Cancer share in moisture, but they differ in heat and coldness. Whence, they say [Mercury] is more weakly a fortune than Venus is.

### Chapter 1.1.9: Rulerships and quadruplicities

§19. But because [Mercury's] signs are double-bodied, [and] resemble[30] the houses of the Sun and Moon in the lesser quality, he is made lucky with fortunate [planets], [and] wicked with infortunes. However, Jupiter's signs [are] likewise double-bodied, each one of which regards the houses of the Sun and Moon by a lucky and friendly aspect (and the greater one [is] from the trigon of the Sun);[31] but since they conquer in a shared quality, they never vary from fortune into the contrary.

§20. The remaining stars (namely Saturn, Mars and Venus) divide up the firm and convertible signs (except for the lodging-places[32] of the lights), and each one of them obtains a firm lodging-place and a turning one. For Saturn takes Aquarius (a firm one from the Moon's part[33] [of the zodiac]) and also a convertible one (namely Capricorn, from the Sun's part). Also, to Mars they grant Scorpio (which is firm and from the Sun's part) [and] Aries (a convertible one, from the lunar partition). Likewise Venus obtained Taurus (namely, a firm one from the Moon) and a convertible one (Libra, from the solar[34] distribution).

---

[29] This term (Lat. *adhaeret*) helps to express a bodily connection or conjunction, which is normally called ʾittiṣāl in Arabic, but in Greek is kollēsis, "adherence" (see Schmidt 2009, p. 161). This is important because it helps draw a parallel between Mercury's domiciles being adjacent to and abutting those of the luminaries, the meaning of the bodily conjunction as two planets connected directly together, and Mercury's meaning of juxtaposing and connecting different things (for example, Mercury is a significator of sewing, in which two pieces of fabric are externally stuck together by needle and thread).
[30] Reading *accedunt* for *accidit*.
[31] Robert omits this. Hugo must mean that the regard from Jupiter to the Sun is greater because they are both rulers of the fiery triplicity: see Ch. 1.3.2 below.
[32] That is, the sign in which they are.
[33] Throughout this paragraph, Robert reads *haiz* ("domain"). This is normally a sect-based rejoicing condition (see *ITA* III.2). But since it has connotations of taking sides, al-Kindī evidently feels justified in using it here in the division of the zodiac into lunar and solar halves.
[34] Reading *solari* for *lunari* with Robert, and following the logic of the paragraph.

*Chapter 1.1.10: Hot and cold halves of the zodiac*

§21. Likewise, a two-fold division of the circle takes place: the first part [is] hot, from the beginning of Aries to the beginning of Libra; but the other [is] cold, [and reaches] from the beginning of Libra [until it] touches the end of Pisces.[35]

*Chapter 1.1.11: Signs of straight and crooked ascension*

§22. Likewise, it pleased them to name one part of the circle (namely from the beginning of Cancer and summer's turning up to the beginning of Capricorn, I say the winter solstice), "complete" and "straight." For the individual signs of its partition expend more than two hours in their own ascension. But from the beginning of Capricorn to the end of Gemini they judge it "incomplete,"[36] because the ascension of the signs of its part require less than two full hours.[37]

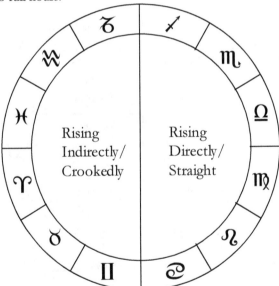

**Figure 14: Signs ascending directly/indirectly (northern hemisphere)**

---

[35] See above, §1.1.1.
[36] More often, "crooked."
[37] This is the scheme for births or events in the northern hemisphere. In the southern hemisphere it is reversed, so that the signs of straight ascension are from Capricorn to Gemini, and the crooked ones Cancer to Sagittarius.

*Chapter 1.1.12: Quarters of the zodiac*

§23. On the other hand, a four-fold division of the circle must be made. For the first one is measured from the beginning of Aries to the beginning of Cancer, and it is called "childlike, arising, hot and moist, spring-like, sanguine." The next one, from the beginning of Cancer, touches the beginning of Libra: this one is called "youthful, increasing, hot and dry, summery, choleric." The next is measured from the beginning of Libra to the beginning of Capricorn, but this one is said to be "the beginning of failure, and entering the manly years, cold and dry, melancholic, autumnal." Likewise a quarter comes after that from the beginning of Capricorn [to] the starting points of Aries: the title of this one is, "declining, old, ending, cold and moist, wintry, phlegmatic."

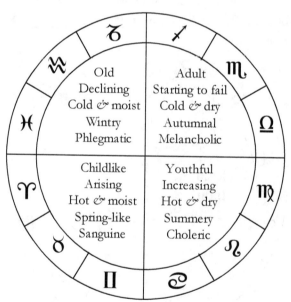

**Figure 15: Quarters of the zodiac**

## Chapter 1.1.13: The decans or faces

§24. The individual [signs] of these partitions [each] receive a division into three parts, each of which gets 10°. These are called "faces," because they seem to signify the faces of animals.[38] And so, very many [authorities] give the first face of Aries to Mars, the second to the Sun, the third to Venus, and thenceforth [following] in the order of [planetary] circles, until the last face of Pisces yields to Mars. This distribution seems incongruous, though, because the last face of Pisces is followed by the first one of Aries in order—whence the same star takes two successive [faces] inappropriately.

§25. Therefore,[39] in our own case the distribution that seems better than the prior [version], and [more] fitting than it, is the one which we have stated in our greater book entitled *On the Secrets of the Stars*.[40] For there, describing the faces in terms of the order of the signs, we gave the first [face] of Aries to Mars, the lord of that same sign. The second one is left for Venus, who possesses the rulership of Taurus. Also Mercury, the ruler of Gemini, retains the third. Whence it happens that the last [face] of Cancer is finally left for Jupiter, the lord of Pisces (the last in the order of signs).

§26. Again, [al-Kindī] transferred the first face of the second fiery sign over to Mars, continuing with the rest in order, up to where the last [face] of Scorpio likewise yields to Jupiter, who rules Pisces. Moreover, Mars takes the first [face] of the third[41] fiery [sign], [and] from thence until the last [face] of

---

38 In Egyptian religion the faces or decans were attributed to special gods, many of which obviously had animal forms. The planetary attributions must have come later.

39 In a discussion of this passage, al-Rijāl (II.2) points out that al-Kindī's proposed faces are subject to exactly the same criticism as was just stated, namely that the traditional system yields a case of the same ruler twice in a row (Mars, ruling the last face of Pisces and the first of Aries). Al-Kindī arranges the rulership of his faces according to zodiacal order, but since Saturn rules adjacent signs (Capricorn, Aquarius), al-Kindī's faces will contain *three* instances of the same ruler appearing twice in succession: once in Cancer, once in Scorpio, and once in Pisces (see table). While it is true that al-Kindī's version contains a repeated ruler (Saturn), at least Saturn already appears repeated in the zodiac, and the cycle of planets and signs fit neatly into the faces. But the repetition of Mars seems inadvertent and inappropriate. At any rate, the faces are rarely considered important in traditional astrology, and I am doubtful of the assignment of planets to them, since they originally depicted individual deities.

40 Burnett (1993, p. 85 and n.21) thinks this might refer to a letter attributed to al-Kindī, addressed to a student "on the secrets of the stars and the instruction on the commencements of actions."

41 Reading *tertii* for *ternarii*, following Robert.

Pisces is conceded to Jupiter, who possesses its rulership. Finally, a return is made to the first face of Aries.[42]

| ♈ | ♂ 0°-9°59' | ♀ 10°-19°59' | ☿ 20°-29°59' |
|---|---|---|---|
| ♉ | ☽ 0°-9°59' | ☉ 10°-19°59' | ☿ 20°-29°59' |
| ♊ | ♀ 0°-9°59' | ♂ 10°-19°59' | ♃ 20°-29°59' |
| ♋ | ♄ 0°-9°59' | ♄ 10°-19°59' | ♃ 20°-29°59' |
| ♌ | ♂ 0°-9°59' | ♀ 10°-19°59' | ☿ 20°-29°59' |
| ♍ | ☽ 0°-9°59' | ☉ 10°-19°59' | ☿ 20°-29°59' |
| ♎ | ♀ 0°-9°59' | ♂ 10°-19°59' | ♃ 20°-29°59' |
| ♏ | ♄ 0°-9°59' | ♄ 10°-19°59' | ♃ 20°-29°59' |
| ♐ | ♂ 0°-9°59' | ♀ 10°-19°59' | ☿ 20°-29°59' |
| ♑ | ☽ 0°-9°59' | ☉ 10°-19°59' | ☿ 20°-29°59' |
| ♒ | ♀ 0°-9°59' | ♂ 10°-19°59' | ♃ 20°-29°59' |
| ♓ | ♄ 0°-9°59' | ♄ 10°-19°59' | ♃ 20°-29°59' |

Figure 16: Al-Kindī's proposed decans or faces

§27. The [traditional] faces of [all] the planets:[43]

| ♈ | ♂ 0°-9°59' | ☉ 10°-19°59' | ♀ 20°-29°59' |
|---|---|---|---|
| ♉ | ☿ 0°-9°59' | ☽ 10°-19°59' | ♄ 20°-29°59' |
| ♊ | ♃ 0°-9°59' | ♂ 10°-19°59' | ☉ 20°-29°59' |
| ♋ | ♀ 0°-9°59' | ☿ 10°-19°59' | ☽ 20°-29°59' |
| ♌ | ♄ 0°-9°59' | ♃ 10°-19°59' | ♂ 20°-29°59' |
| ♍ | ☉ 0°-9°59' | ♀ 10°-19°59' | ☿ 20°-29°59' |
| ♎ | ☽ 0°-9°59' | ♄ 10°-19°59' | ♃ 20°-29°59' |
| ♏ | ♂ 0°-9°59' | ☉ 10°-19°59' | ♀ 20°-29°59' |
| ♐ | ☿ 0°-9°59' | ☽ 10°-19°59' | ♄ 20°-29°59' |
| ♑ | ♃ 0°-9°59' | ♂ 10°-19°59' | ☉ 20°-29°59' |
| ♒ | ♀ 0°-9°59' | ☿ 10°-19°59' | ☽ 20°-29°59' |
| ♓ | ♄ 0°-9°59' | ♃ 10°-19°59' | ♂ 20°-29°59' |

Figure 17: Traditional system of decans or faces

---

[42] Another version of these planetary rulerships is called the *darījān*, attributed to the Indians (*ITA* VII.6). What these conflicting systems suggest to me is that the decans or faces were attributed to gods and images first (such as by the Egyptians and others), but were later overlaid with planetary rulerships so as to incorporate them into Hellenistic astrology. Fortunately, the faces are rarely used. For one use, see Sahl's *On Questions* §7.22 (in *WSM*).

[43] From Robert.

*Chapter 1.1.14: Ninth-parts*[44]

§28. Likewise follows a two-fold partitioning of the twelve signs: the first is bequeathed to the lord of the house, the second to the lord of the ninth-part.[45] But the astrologers of the Indians follow this [second partitioning]. Moreover, the experts among the Indians divide the individual signs into nine parts. Of these, each part (containing 3 1/3 degrees) grants the first [ninth-part] to the lord of the [movable] sign [of that triplicity],[46] the second one to that of the following sign.

| | 0°00'-3°20' | 3°20'-6°40' | 6°40'-10°00' | 10°00'-13°20' | 13°20'-16°40' | 16°40'-20°00' | 20°00'-23°20' | 23°20'-26°40' | 26°40'-30°00' |
|---|---|---|---|---|---|---|---|---|---|
| ♈ | ♂ | ♀ | ☿ | ☽ | ☉ | ☿ | ♀ | ♂ | ♃ |
| ♉ | ♄ | ♄ | ♃ | ♂ | ♀ | ☿ | ☽ | ☉ | ☿ |
| ♊ | ♀ | ♂ | ♃ | ♄ | ♄ | ♃ | ♂ | ♀ | ☿ |
| ♋ | ☽ | ☉ | ☿ | ♀ | ♂ | ♃ | ♄ | ♄ | ♃ |
| ♌ | ♂ | ♀ | ☿ | ☽ | ☉ | ☿ | ♀ | ♂ | ♃ |
| ♍ | ♄ | ♄ | ♃ | ♂ | ♀ | ☿ | ☽ | ☉ | ☿ |
| ♎ | ♀ | ♂ | ♃ | ♄ | ♄ | ♃ | ♂ | ♀ | ☿ |
| ♏ | ☽ | ☉ | ☿ | ♀ | ♂ | ♃ | ♄ | ♄ | ♃ |
| ♐ | ♂ | ♀ | ☿ | ☽ | ☉ | ☿ | ♀ | ♂ | ♃ |
| ♑ | ♄ | ♄ | ♃ | ♂ | ♀ | ☿ | ☽ | ☉ | ☿ |
| ♒ | ♀ | ♂ | ♃ | ♄ | ♄ | ♃ | ♂ | ♀ | ☿ |
| ♓ | ☽ | ☉ | ☿ | ♀ | ♂ | ♃ | ♄ | ♄ | ♃ |

[44] For more on these, see *ITA* VII.5 and *Persian Nativities 3*, III.9-10.

[45] Reading *novenae* with Robert for *noni*.

[46] Adding material in brackets and reading *mobilis* for *primi*. But Hugo's wording almost sounds like an alternate (and perhaps mistaken?) version of the ninth-parts described by Hermann in *Search* Ch. I.9.3.

## Chapter 1.1.15: Planetary hours

§29. Moreover, [now] follows a partition of the [diurnal] circle made into twelve parts, all of which take the name of an individual hour. Moreover, they distribute these hours into days. And so, they ascribed the first hour of the first day[47] to the Sun, the second one to Venus, the third to Mercury, just as the order of [planetary] circles shows, until the lord of the original hour once more takes the eighth hour. From this order it happens that the first hour of the second day is conceded to the Moon, the first one of the third [day] to Mars, the first one of the fourth [day] to Mercury. Jupiter claims the first one of the fifth [day], Venus the principal one of the sixth [day], Saturn the first one of the seventh [day]. After that, the Sun likewise assumes the first [hour] of the Lord's day.

§30. For every star having power over the principal hour of the day, manages the entire day, and it takes the lords of the individual hours of that day (belonging to its management)[48] as partners with their own times. For example, Venus rules over the second hour on the first day: but that second hour tempers the diurnal management with the Sun. Likewise, Mercury as the ruler of the third [hour] happens to be the partner of the shared management with the Sun. The rest are disposed in this order. But the lord of the day does not care to take on any partner in its own hour.

|    | Sunday | Monday | Tuesday | Wednesday | Thursday | Friday | Saturday |
|----|--------|--------|---------|-----------|----------|--------|----------|
| 1  | ☉ | ☽ | ♂ | ☿ | ♃ | ♀ | ♄ |
| 2  | ♀ | ♄ | ☉ | ☽ | ♂ | ☿ | ♃ |
| 3  | ☿ | ♃ | ♀ | ♄ | ☉ | ☽ | ♂ |
| 4  | ☽ | ♂ | ☿ | ♃ | ♀ | ♄ | ☉ |
| 5  | ♄ | ☉ | ☽ | ♂ | ☿ | ♃ | ♀ |
| 6  | ♃ | ♀ | ♄ | ☉ | ☽ | ♂ | ☿ |
| 7  | ♂ | ☿ | ♃ | ♀ | ♄ | ☉ | ☽ |
| 8  | ☉ | ☽ | ♂ | ☿ | ♃ | ♀ | ♄ |
| 9  | ♀ | ♄ | ☉ | ☽ | ♂ | ☿ | ♃ |
| 10 | ☿ | ♃ | ♀ | ♄ | ☉ | ☽ | ♂ |
| 11 | ☽ | ♂ | ☿ | ♃ | ♀ | ♄ | ☉ |
| 12 | ♄ | ☉ | ☽ | ♂ | ☿ | ♃ | ♀ |

**Figure 18: Planetary hours from sunrise**

---

[47] That is, Sunday.

[48] *Sui consilii*. Some Latin translators (such as Hermann and Adelard) translate the Arabic "management" as "counsel," as described in *ITA* III.18.

| | Sunday | Monday | Tuesday | Wednesday | Thursday | Friday | Saturday |
|---|---|---|---|---|---|---|---|
| 1 | ♃ | ♀ | ♄ | ☉ | ☽ | ♂ | ☿ |
| 2 | ♂ | ☿ | ♃ | ♀ | ♄ | ☉ | ☽ |
| 3 | ☉ | ☽ | ♂ | ☿ | ♃ | ♀ | ♄ |
| 4 | ♀ | ♄ | ☉ | ☽ | ♂ | ☿ | ♃ |
| 5 | ☿ | ♃ | ♀ | ♄ | ☉ | ☽ | ♂ |
| 6 | ☽ | ♂ | ☿ | ♃ | ♀ | ♄ | ☉ |
| 7 | ♄ | ☉ | ☽ | ♂ | ☿ | ♃ | ♀ |
| 8 | ♃ | ♀ | ♄ | ☉ | ☽ | ♂ | ☿ |
| 9 | ♂ | ☿ | ♃ | ♀ | ♄ | ☉ | ☽ |
| 10 | ☉ | ☽ | ♂ | ☿ | ♃ | ♀ | ♄ |
| 11 | ♀ | ♄ | ☉ | ☽ | ♂ | ☿ | ♃ |
| 12 | ☿ | ♃ | ♀ | ♄ | ☉ | ☽ | ♂ |

**Figure 19: Planetary hours from sunset**

§31. On the other hand, these 24 [hours] enter upon a four-fold division, the first part of which (namely the first six hours of the day) is called "arising, sanguine, hot and moist, spring-like, child-like." But the following six (namely the latter part of the day) [are] "youthful, adolescent, hot and dry, choleric, summery." Likewise they name the six after these (which make the beginning of the night) "manly, retreating, cold and dry, melancholic, autumnal." But the remaining six which impose the end of night are said to be "old people, defective, cold and moist, phlegmatic, wintry."[49]

---

[49] This is virtually identical to the attributions to the quarters of the zodiac in Ch. 1.1.12 above, and the quarters of heaven in Ch. 1.2.1 below. Thus three divisions of time and space are made parallel in meaning: the Sun's time in the seasons (related to the zodiac), semi-diurnal arcs, and hours of the day (related to the quarters defined by the celestial equator).

## Chapter 1.2: Quarters *&* houses

§32. No less also did it please each hour that the [equatorial] circle should be divided into four, with the beginning being made from the Ascendant. The first part of these, from the Midheaven to the Ascendant, is called "arising, sanguine, spring-like, and male." From the west to the Midheaven it is entitled "adolescent, fiery, summery, choleric, womanly." That which is from the degree of the fourth to the seventh [is] "retreating,[50] melancholic, autumnal, and male." From the degree of the Ascendant to the fourth it is said to be "failing, aged, wintry, phlegmatic."

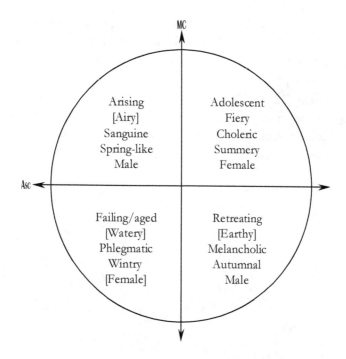

**Figure 20: Quarters of the circle**

---

[50] "Retreating" here is meant to be the opposite of "arising," i.e., when middle age turns into decline. It is not the same as being cadent, which is also described as "retreating" in Ch. 1.2.3 below, as well as in *ITA* I.12 and III.2-3.

## Chapter 1.2.2: Sex and gender

§33. Therefore, the stars are transformed in these quarters: masculine ones into females and females into males. For male ones in female signs and places turn into the contrary sex, and female ones [in those same places] strengthen the indication of their [feminine] signification by two-fold—whence [on the other hand] they take on a manly nature in the male quarters and male signs.

§34. In this manner the signs are even described by the names of the sexes. For all fiery and airy [signs] are described as masculine on account of the virtue of heat; the earthy and watery ones [are described] with the name of the other sex on account of the effect of cold. From which it seems that since Aries is fiery, it retains a masculine title; Taurus, because [it is] earthy, [has] that of the female sex. Also, Gemini (being airy and hot) takes on the title of a man; Cancer (being watery and cold), the title of the female sex. The rest are described in this order, the one with the designation of male, the next female, up to the end.

§35. Again, the designation of each sex discloses both the diurnal and nocturnal hours. For the first hour is called male, the second female, the third manly, the fourth womanly, [and so on]. By this method all odd [hours] borrow the name of "male," and the even [hours] "female."

§36. Likewise, in this ordering, the odd degrees of the whole circle (namely from the first of Aries up to the end of Pisces) are described with the title of "manly," but the equal ones "womanly."[51]

## Chapter 1.2.3: House division and angularity[52]

§37. Moreover, the signs of the circle receive a three-fold division at all hours. For those which take the beginning from the degree of the Ascendant and the seventh, and likewise the tenth and fourth, are called "pivotal and perfect and of complete virtue." But those which follow these, namely [after] their beginning (I say, of the Ascendant, the tenth, seventh and fourth), with 30° being bequeathed,[53] are described as advancing and [having] half-virtue.

---

51 This system does not match the usual ones: see *ITA* VII.8.
52 See also §106 below.
53 See my discussion of al-Kindī's house system in the Introduction, §4.

But those which follow after these take the name "cadent,"[54] from [their] retreating and weak virtue and obscurity. Likewise, the light of the pivots is complete, but [the light] of those which follow after the pivots is mediocre; but [the light] of those which retreat from the pivot is falling, obscure, and deficient.[55]

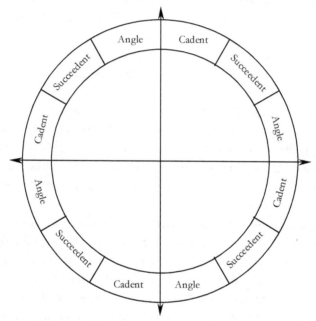

**Figure 21: Angularity of houses**

§38. Likewise, the pivots are disclosing and open. Those which follow the pivots are between disclosing and what is hidden, and obtain the middle between what is covered up and what is public. Those remote from the pivots [signify] hidden things: whence the stars which dwell in those same

---

[54] Lit., "falling."
[55] The diagram below is taken from *ITA* I.12, and retains *ITA*'s vocabulary. The "angle" is Hugo's "pivot"; the "succeedent" is Hugo's "advancing"; the "cadent" is Hugo's "cadent," "remote," "retreating." But note that both angular/pivotal and succeedent houses are considered "advancing" in other traditional authors, so Hugo's decision to call the succeedent places the "advancing" ones, is unfortunate. For more on this, see *ITA* I.12 and III.3-4, and §106 below.

places are falling and obscure, so that [if it] is in the second, the sixth, and eighth, and twelfth, they look at the Ascendant with no regard.[56]

§39. Moreover, the regard of those which occupy pivots is strong and prominent. Those which follow the pivots, portending the steadiness of matters, guide it to an effect[57]—with the exception of those [questions] which designate motion and travel and what is like that, for only the cadents and stars which were in them settle that category.[58] In just that way, those which are cadent do not promise the steadiness of matters, because they are retreating; but the advancing ones (just as one may judge from the name) bring things forward.

### Chapter 1.2.4: Concrete significations of signs and rulerships

§40. In every affair, all of the signs convey the shape of animals of their own proper quality, as well as the nature of their element (fire, I say, earth and air and water): just as Aries means flock-animals [and] sheep, Taurus herds, the sign of Gemini men. But no less does the form of all the rest lay bare the affair of a question that is brought up. Moreover, they likewise represent the will of the mind and appetites [of the animal] whose shape they bear.[59] However, without a doubt you will find whatever [there is] of the proper qualities of the signs [in what] we have reported above: namely heat and coldness, or the moist and the dry, the long or short, hastening [or] straight, or the slow or crooked, the time or place or if they are of this type, or other properties of the signs—all of these things, I say, in which the indication or significance[60] of the signs portends.

§41. Likewise, the faces of the signs named above, and the lords of their matters which they signify, determine faces and figures. Likewise the lords of

---

[56] Unless both Robert and Hugo are confused, al-Kindī has confused being cadent from the *angles/pivots* versus being cadent from the *Ascendant*: (1) places cadent from the angles are the 3rd, 6th, 9th, and 12th, whereas (2) those cadent from (i.e., in aversion to) the Ascendant are the 2nd, 6th, 8th and 12th. By invoking the places in aversion to the Ascendant alongside his quadrant-based houses, he is conflating sign-based aspects with ascension-based houses.

[57] Or rather, "guide it into being" (*effectum*).

[58] That is, if travel (which is associated with the cadent places) is desired, then the cadents *do* produce what is desired. See Ch. 8.

[59] Probably a reference to the humane signs, the bestial signs, lascivious signs, etc. See for example *ITA* I.10.6.

[60] Reading *significantia* for *significantiam*.

the hours and the form of their proper quality declare the manner of their signification of matters. But the bounds lay out the advancement, loftiness, scarcity of value and quantity of profit, in the order of things.

### Chapter 1.2.5: Bounds

§42-43. But for our part there is no definite reason why the order of this kind of signification is ascribed to [the bounds] in directions[61] and in distributions,[62] except that the good judgment of the Babylonians has everywhere recognized, with definite experience, that the indications of the bounds (stated by us above) happen thusly.[63] Likewise, in common [with them] we follow the distributions[64] even in the days, following the successive numbering of the stars.[65] The bounds of the Egyptians:[66]

| ♈ | ♃ 0°-5°59' | ♀ 6°-11°59' | ☿ 12°-19°59' | ♂ 20°-24°59' | ♄ 25°-29°59' |
|---|---|---|---|---|---|
| ♉ | ♀ 0°-7°59' | ☿ 8°-13°59' | ♃ 14°-21°59' | ♄ 22°-26°59' | ♂ 27°-29°59' |
| ♊ | ☿ 0°-5°59' | ♃ 6°-11°59' | ♀ 12°-16°59' | ♂ 17°-23°59' | ♄ 24°-29°59' |
| ♋ | ♂ 0°-6°59' | ♀ 7°-12°59' | ☿ 13°-18°59' | ♃ 19°-25°59' | ♄ 26°-29°59' |
| ♌ | ♃ 0°-5°59' | ♀ 6°-10°59' | ♄ 11°-17°59' | ☿ 18°-23°59' | ♂ 24°-29°59' |
| ♍ | ☿ 0°-6°59' | ♀ 7°-16°59' | ♃ 17°-20°59' | ♂ 21°-27°59' | ♄ 28°-29°59' |
| ♎ | ♄ 0°-5°59' | ☿ 6°-13°59' | ♃ 14°-20°59' | ♀ 21°-27°59' | ♂ 28°-29°59' |
| ♏ | ♂ 0°-6°59' | ♀ 7°-10°59' | ☿ 11°-18°59' | ♃ 19°-23°59' | ♄ 24°-29°59' |
| ♐ | ♃ 0°-11°59' | ♀ 12°-16°59' | ☿ 17°-20°59' | ♄ 21°-25°59' | ♂ 26°-29°59' |
| ♑ | ☿ 0°-6°59' | ♃ 7°-13°59' | ♀ 14°-21°59' | ♄ 22°-25°59' | ♂ 26°-29°59' |
| ♒ | ☿ 0°-6°59' | ♀ 7°-12°59' | ♃ 13°-19°59' | ♂ 20°-24°59' | ♄ 25°-29°59' |
| ♓ | ♀ 0°-11°59' | ♃ 12°-15°59' | ☿ 16°-18°59' | ♂ 19°-27°59' | ♄ 28°-29°59' |

**Figure 22: Egyptian bounds**

[61] Reading for the common Arabic transliteration *ataẓir*.

[62] Reading with Robert for *atartib*. The method of distributions is discussed at length in *PN3* and very briefly in *ITA* VIII.2.2f.

[63] Al-Kindī means both that he doesn't know why the bounds indicate these things at all, and that he doesn't know why the Egyptian bounds are arranged as they are (indeed, I do not believe anyone has explained why they are arranged as they are).

[64] Reading for *altawacim*.

[65] This seems to be a clear reference to distributing the Ascendant of the solar revolution (also known as the "east of the year") around the whole chart over the course of one year. See 'Umar's *TBN* II.5-6 (in *PN II*), al-Qabīsī at the end of *ITA* VIII.2.2, and Abū Ma'shar in *PN3*, II.1 and III.1.

[66] From Robert. I have omitted the last sentence of this paragraph, as it really forms Robert's title for the next section of the book.

## Chapter 1.3: Planetary significations & configurations

*Chapter 1.3.1: Planetary significations*[67]

# ♄

§44. This is a description of the signification of the seven planets. And so, Saturn, being western, indicates old men and affairs of antiquity, even abject matters and those of no value, low-class duties, odors with no scent, tricks and frauds and those duties which are practiced in something moist, and an anxious life. Western, he even means a slowness in those things which are said to be proper to his nature.[68]

§45. But eastern, he indicates new and recent things, but shapeless[69] and off-color, and those duties which come to be in waters, even the more dignified things in agriculture (and its prosperity and abundance), even quick outcomes in matters. [And] eastern, he signifies advancement and the care and repair of cities, long deliberation, respectable counsel, even parents.

# ♃

§46. [Western], Jupiter denotes the manly age, social customs,[70] lovers of divine worship, the religious, hermit worshippers, likewise offices of the law, money, a thrifty life, the underofficials of kings or official attendants, controversies, and it means those things which pertain to the laws (such as secretaries[71] writing decrees of social customs and laws, likewise judges and that type).

§47. Also, being eastern, [he signifies] the beginnings of the manly age and the completion of matters, respectable and appropriate associations,[72] moderation in words and the offices of the law (namely the highest judges), great [and] famous people calling the common people to mutual concord,

---

[67] For lengthier lists, see *ITA* V.1-7.

[68] Reconfiguring this sentence somewhat with Robert. This sentence originally appeared in the following section.

[69] Or, "ugly, deformed" (*informes*).

[70] *Consuetudines*. This can also mean sexual intercourse, which is also a signification of Jupiter: see *ITA* V.2.

[71] Or possibly, "notaries" (*notarios*) or similar government functionaries.

[72] Reading *conversationem* for *conversionem*.

and this in the greatest things and general affairs; he adorns the glory of one's name with a reputation in an analogy to such people;[73] he even signifies children.

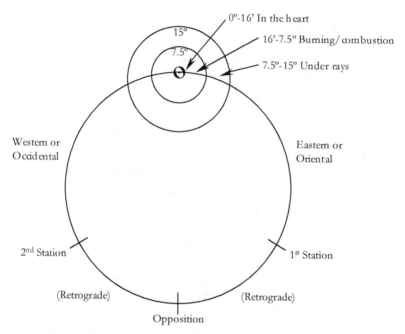

**Figure 23: Generic synodic cycle with Sun (superiors)[74]**

§48a. And so Mars, being western, bears the significance of princes, low-class and insignificant [Martial] business (such as the army)[75] and the arrogance of soldiers of more elegant status,[76] war dances, and it portends what disappears by means of theft, and that type [of thing].

§48b. If however he would become eastern, [he indicates] boldness, the sternness of giving orders and the steadiness of precepts, the counselors of

---

[73] Robert reads this as conferring great wealth.
[74] For more on these cycles, see *ITA* II.10.
[75] Being in the military is not insignificant, but perhaps al-Kindī is simply saying that Mars signifies both high military leaders and the lowest grunts.
[76] Robert reads: "the arrogance of youth." But I can see how both descriptions would fit.

wars, armies, generals, even how all of these things are able to be contrived. He will apply hastening, victory [and] violence to all of these. Also, being eastern, those duties which are practiced by means of fire and iron (such as butchers, craftsmen, dyers, cooks, bakers); but besides these he designates brothers and journeys.

§49. The signification of the Sun particularly concerns the lofty and most powerful of kings, and their glory and value, [and] strength; even the hunt, medicines and whatever seems to pertain particularly to nobles; even bows but especially archers; divinations, he teaches augury, reveals secrets, and brings forth into the common [realm] counsels that are secret. He exhibits sternness of speech and quick results in [his] commands.

♀

§50. But Venus[77] [being western] denotes the wives of kings, adds perfection [in looks], chooses ornamentation, heaps on the heat of love, multiplies joys, conveys happiness, celebrates both exultation and dancing, introduces gifts, stirs up games, renews the appetites, resorts to illicit sex, seeks paintings and whatever is best in clothing. Being eastern, she greatly increases all of these; western, she subtracts. Also, with respect to jobs [she indicates] guitarists,[78] painters of walls, even those who put together silken clothes and ornaments of this kind, whether by looms or needles.

---

[77] Here Hugo begins to be impatient with the lists of significations, and embellishes the lists with his own verbs.
[78] *Citaristas.* Really, players of any musical instrument.

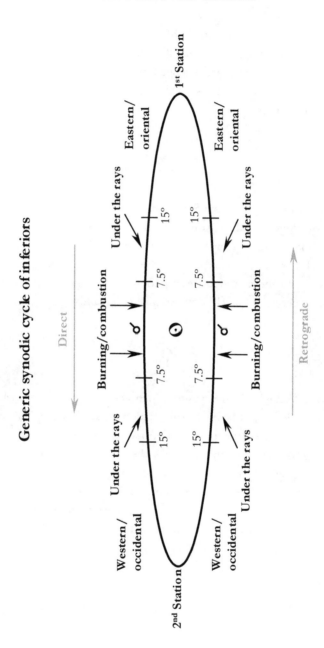

**Figure 24: Generic synodic cycle of inferiors[79]**

---

[79] In the assignment of stations, I follow Abū Ma'shar (*ITA* II.10.2). Burnett, in his edition of al-Qabīsī (II.34), notes that the assignment of stations is reversed in at least some texts.

☿

§51. But Mercury adds prudence, supplies eloquence, commends long deliberation, comes to the sciences, writes books, composes verses, is vigorous in preaching, is in charge of the children of kings. But he oversees those jobs which have influence through prudence and the understanding of discernment, namely those which follow the derivation of the *trivium* or *quadrivium* (such as physics and astronomy); but besides these, commerce and secretaries of tax revenues, and jobs which are like these, namely whose practice demands measurement and weights and caution. Eastern, he completes all of these; western, he bears it away.

However, the westernness of [Mercury] and Venus seems to be less adverse than that of the rest of the planets.

*Mercury cycle related to ages of life[80]*

§52a. Also, from the middle of [his] retrogradation up to his first station, he preserves the boyish years; but from [the first] stay up to [his] assembly with the Sun (namely [when] direct), [he indicates] adolescence; moreover, from assembly and direct motion to the other stay, he commends the manly age. Likewise from that second station to the middle of [his] retrogradation, he flings down the setting of old age.

*Mercury stations and midpoints related to mind and action*

§52b. Again, in the middle of retrogradation [he indicates] adverse things; in his assembly (namely when direct), [he indicates] the benevolence of love, and the performance and partnerships of that.

§53. In the first stay (while he moves quickly to [his] assembly [with the Sun], he presents friendships and opportunities, and the favor of benignness which is sought, and affability. Moreover, in the second station and tending towards retrogradation, he scrutinizes improsperous things, presents discords, generates a period of delay, exerts himself with little cleverness,[81]

---

[80] See footnote to the diagram above.
[81] Reading the Arabic of al-Qabīsī II.34 here and below, for Hugo's "frauds" and "deceits."

and is involved in many affairs—but in the middle of retrogradation, he hastens modestly [and] it weakens the causes of cleverness.

§54. Likewise, turning towards the first stay, he inserts cleverness and introduces delay ([but] after this he confers freedom [and] opens up to cleverness). Moreover, toward the assembly of the Sun (and in direct motion) it hastens more distinctly [and] spreads[82] ingenuity.

Moreover, it is the same with respect to Venus and the five wandering [stars], but it always seems to happen in the centers and places of this kind.[83]

$$\mathbb{D}$$

§55. The Moon designates the slave-girls of kings and of prominent people and of all powerful people, business matters, messengers and those who relate rumors, even the common people. But apart from these, she will indicate the childhood years, particularly from the beginning of the [lunar] month. But from the seventh day[84] to the fourteenth day she portends the time of adolescence. She even extends a signification of the manly age from the fourteenth day up to the twenty-first day. Likewise she indicates senile defects from the twenty-first day up to the assembly of the Sun.

Also, she being scorched and under the rays (or any concealed and hidden star) covers up affairs.

§56. But apart from these, the Moon indicates whatever undergoes the changes of generation and corruption, in terms of the analogy of being born and old age. For, beginning from [her] slightest [shape at the beginning of the lunar month][85] up to where she reflects the fullness of light, it is increased; decreasing after that incurs a defect of her light, until she is seen to be undergoing [her] arising [out of the rays] once more.

---

[82] Again, reading with al-Qabīsī for Hugo's "devises."
[83] Reading the last part of this sentence more with Robert.
[84] Each quarter lasts for roughly seven days, so the seventh day indicates the first quarter, and so on (see diagram below).
[85] Reading *minimo* with Robert for *modico*. This refers to her first emergence from out of the Sun's rays, normally taken to be at 12°. Likewise, 12° on either side of the opposition is supposed to be significant, but note that al-Kindī uses 5° in §59.

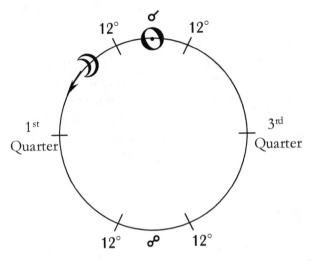

**Figure 25: Synodic cycle of Moon (from Abū Ma'shar)**[86]

§57. Moreover, she signifies the agents of controversies in the beginning of the [lunar] month, [but] at the end those who it is said are going to respond in the case. The Sun [is] to the contrary: in the beginning of the month he defends the accused, at the end the accusers.

§58. Likewise, at the beginning of the month the Moon enhances the full and complete supply of acquisitions and profit; but at the end she makes expenses, disperses what has been built up, [and] scatters what has been acquired.

§59a. In the opposition [of the Sun] she means adversaries; but from the first [approach] to the beginning of the opposition (namely if she were distant from the opposition by 5°), the undertaking of adversity and a wicked lot; also, receding from the opposition [by that same amount], she looks for the causes of expelling adversity.

§59a-60. In [her] exit from scorching or being under the rays, she reveals hidden things. In the assembly of the Sun, she will cover up hidden things, concealed things, and that type. But while she prepares [her] entrance into scorching, she conveys hiddenness. But when she strives towards going out, she likewise begins to preach the revealing of concealed things. Also, in

---

86 These 12° intervals on either side of the conjunction and opposition are also used in weather prediction (Ch. 38).

preparing her exit from scorching, she indicates manifestation and as though returning from a foreign journey.

§61. Moreover, in the [first] tetragon[87] of the Sun she will indicate the deposing of lofty men and the pursuit of the hunt, [and] no less also in the second tetragon—except that in the first tetragon she divulges both things and profits in the signification of the aforesaid things, and greatly increases what is acquired; but in the second one she promises the contrary of these.

§62. Moreover, when the Moon hastens her step, it introduces quickness [and] discloses frauds; but the slowness of this course [introduces] delay.

*Chapter 1.3.2: Planetary effectiveness: easternness, dignities, and sect*

§63. And so, of these stars, individual ones sometimes exhibit a strong effectiveness, sometimes a weak one. But strength is divided into two: one natural, one accidental. Also, weakness receives the same division, for now it seems to be discovered as being properly their own, otherwise not their own.[88]

*Easternness*

§64. The first type of the two-fold virtue of the stars, is if they were eastern of the Sun and, with scorching being left behind, they would traverse in the morning before the east, so that their ascent would precede the Sun.[89] Likewise, one easternness is strong, the other weak. [1] The strong one is if they would leave scorching behind, up until they are separated from the Sun by 30°. But this means adolescence, a respectable and adequate course of matters, and the acceleration of affairs, [and] apart from this, boldness. [2] After that, being remote from the Sun's rays by 60°[90] is called the more infirm easternness. For while any planet bore itself thusly, it maintains a lesser effectiveness than in the [first kind of] easternness.

---

[87] *Atarbe* (a transliteration from Ar.).

[88] *Propria...impropria.* The text is not absolutely clear on how it distinguishes these categories in what follows.

[89] See the diagrams in Ch. 1.3.1 above.

[90] Or rather, being 60° from the Sun, not 60° from the edge of his rays. This condition applies only to the superior planets.

*Dignity (and triplicity lords)*

§65. Likewise, a star being situated in its own proper quality or rather in a place of dignity (house or sovereignty or bound, even the triplicity or face, and that type), will obtain [flourishing].[91]

§66. (And so, the Sun administers the fiery triplicities by day, Jupiter too by night, with Saturn as a lesser partner. Likewise the Moon takes up the earthy signs by night, Venus by day, Mars is a partner to each—but Mercury is associated in Virgo.[92] By day the airy [signs] yield to Saturn, but by night to Mercury, with Jupiter as an associate. But Venus is in charge of the watery signs in a diurnal [hour], Mars by night, with the Moon accompanying.)

|  | Primary | Secondary | Partnering |
|---|---|---|---|
| Fire | ☉ | ♃ | ♄ |
| Air | ♄ | ☿ | ♃ |
| Water | ♀ | ♂ | ☽ |
| Earth | ♀ | ☽ | ♂ |

Figure 26: "Dorothean" triplicity lords

§67. In the same way the houses and sovereignties, bounds and faces bear themselves in the way we described a little bit before.[93]

*Ḥalb and domain[94]*

§68. On the other hand, *ḥalb* (namely the proper quality or bearing of a star) also comprises a dignity of the stars. And so, the bearing of a star is said to be a place agreeing with it in some share. In fact a certain portion of the stars is ascribed to the day, but another is said to belong to the night. If therefore a diurnal star by day would be borne along above the earth, and by night below the earth, this [star] will be said to remain "in its bearing." Which if it happened the other way, we would put it as being "remote from [its] bearing." Likewise, should a nocturnal one by day be staying under the earth,

---

[91] Supplying the object from Robert.

[92] Al-Kindī assumes that the triplicities are closely related to dignities: Mercury is the domicile *and* exalted lord of Virgo, an earthy sign.

[93] Al-Kindī simply means that he has listed these other dignities before.

[94] See *ITA* III.2.

and by night above the earth, it too possesses and occupies its own bearing. Which if it would happen in the other way, it is deprived of its bearing. And[95] in addition,[96] that it would likewise hold onto a sign and quarter proportionate to its [gender].

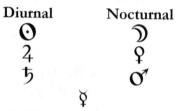

**Figure 27: Diurnal and nocturnal planets[97]**

*Chapter 1.3.3: Analogies of the planetary strengths and weaknesses*[98]

*Dignity*

§69-70a. However,[99] a star flourishing in its own house and its own strength, is compared to a man in his own home and persisting like a man in his own profession.[100] Moreover, in its own sovereignty it is likened to someone reigning supreme. Likewise, being in its own bound is like a man who dwells in his fatherland and with relatives. Also, in the triplicity it retains the form of one who stays among guards and defenders and co-helpers: for the triplicity is said to observe and defend and be supportive of that. But

---

[95] Adding this last sentence from Robert: it describes the situation of "domain" (see *ITA* III.2).

[96] Note that this phrase "in addition" is exactly that found in al-Qabīsī, who is known to borrow from al-Kindī. It is possible that people after al-Kindī (such as al-Qabīsī and al-Bīrūnī) made domain (*ḥayyiz*) a gendered heightening of *ḥalb* precisely because of this sentence, when al-Kindī might have meant *ḥayyiz* to be a separate condition, namely simply being in a sign of the same gender.

[97] Typically, Mercury is considered diurnal if in a position to rise before the Sun, and nocturnal if in a position to rise after the Sun. See also *ITA* V.11.

[98] I have divided the first two sections of this chapter so they match the three topics of the previous one: easternness, dignities, and sect. I have also segregated a few sentences that pertain to such things as detriment and besieging. See similar analogies in §§107-08 below.

[99] For this and the next paragraph, cf. the analogies of the dignities in *ITA* I.8.

[100] Or perhaps, his own business (*professionis*).

appearing in its face, it is reputed to be practically like a craftsman while he carves forms and the figures of images.[101]

### Ḥalb and domain

§70b. Which if it obtains its *ḥalb* (namely the place of its bearing), [it is] virtually like someone who becomes bright with profit and a share of prosperity. Moreover, in the Midheaven like a man in his own work; also, in the Ascendant like a prince settling down in the retinue of an army.[102]

### Other dignity conditions, besieging, speed

§70c. Moreover, being an exile or foreign,[103] like one who is detained in a foreign journey. No less in the hostile house,[104] like someone in the lodging-place of enemies. Moreover in its own fall, like one who is entrenched in prison, incarcerated, like a sick person. Likewise, between two infortunes[105] it is compared to a man besieged. Again, a star accelerating is like a speedy man.

### Easternness and solar phases

§71. Moreover, being eastern [is] practically like a boy; western, an old man. Again, under the rays, like a hidden man; again, in the assembly of the Sun, like an infant while it is being held in the mother's womb; after assembly, like one who is appearing, having already arisen [out of the womb]. Moreover, with [the Sun's] whole body[106] being crossed, like one who has already been removed from the mother's breast, [and] requires other

---

[101] The sense seems to be that he must labor on his own and unaided, even though he is producing something good.
[102] I take this to pertain either to a planet in its *ḥalb* in such places, or else to a planet in any one of its own dignities while being in these places.
[103] That is, "peregrine."
[104] That is, in the sign of detriment.
[105] That is, being besieged: see *ITA* IV.4.2.
[106] That is, his "orb." The Arabic word used for "orb" means "body." See *ITA* II.6.

nourishment.[107] In the opposition of the Sun, like one who has reached the years of manly age.

## Chapter 1.3.4: Some accidental planetary strengths and weaknesses

§72. And so, after laying out the accidents of [such] places, the accidental virtue of the stars [in those places] follows. But these accidents [are] when one of them claims a place in a pivot, another after the pivot, but another the third [place] after a pivot. But another [way] is that it is arranged in a place which designates heat or cold, which we have called male or female above.[108]

## Chapter 1.3.5: Al-Kindī's house system and brief house meanings[109]

§73.[110] We, however,[111] are about to show [you] the disposition of the domiciles, and after that [their] signification. Beginning from the arising degree of the eastern horizon, we fill up the first domicile with a space of 30° according to the ascensions of our clime or region, down under the earth. Next, we also establish the [other] individual domiciles after taking 30° according to the ascensions of the clime or region (as was said before), always with the beginning of the first [domicile] being taken from the degree of the horizon designated above.

§74. The Ascendant is from that number, namely [starting] from the degree of the east, with 30° of ascensions brought down under the earth. But this is called the house of life and the body, because it signifies them.

§75. Another 30° of ascensions follow these, for which the name is the house of money and allies. After these, another 30 is called the house of brothers. Likewise, another 30 exhibit the house of fathers, lands and the end of affairs. Another 30 which follow is called the house of children, joy and gifts.[112] No less do the next 30 make the house of slaves and infirmity and

---

[107] This suggests a kind of independence.
[108] See especially §§32-33 above.
[109] See my Introduction §4, on al-Kindī's house system.
[110] This paragraph is only in Robert.
[111] Omitting Robert's *hoc admonente loco* as a flourish that is hard to make real sense of.
[112] Or, "benefits" (*munerum*). Robert reads, "promise" (*promissionis*). We should remember that the fifth was called "good fortune" by the Hellenistic astrologers, which indicates conventional benefits such as these.

heads of cattle, and short imprisonment, and that type [of thing]. Likewise, another 30 compose the house of the marital bond and adversaries.

§76. But after these, another 30 constitute the house of death and inheritance. Another 30, that of travel and messengers and law and dreams. And another 30 present the house for kings, dignity and glory, and loftiness, and professions and mothers. Another 30, that of friends, hope and prosperity. But the next ascending 30° which remain, comprise the house of enemies, punishment, labor, loss of hope, and long-lasting captivity.

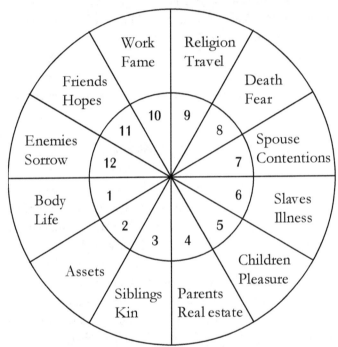

**Figure 28: Basic list of house meanings**

*Chapter 1.3.6: More on accidental planetary conditions*[113]

§77. These things having been carried out, let us pass over to the accidents of the stars. For they are these: whenever a star happens to fall into a pivot or after a pivot; its course being direct and not retrograde; even while

---

[113] Cf. especially *ITA* IV.2.

it ascends in the north;[114] even when it is situated in the regard of the lord of its house or that the Sun and the Moon (or at least of that one which obtains the shift).[115]

§78. [Also], whenever it accelerates in course (namely whenever one seeks with respect to the quickness and increase of matters);[116] even whenever it grows in computation (but apart from these when it is decreased, namely if the question arises with respect to the corruption of things). I say that all of these seem to befall it from its accidental being. Moreover, if it were in its own suitability and place of appropriateness—such as (I say) if a star which designates heat (like the Sun and Mars) would be in hot (and even dry) places of the quarters; but those which portend cold (like Saturn and the Moon, which have a cold complexion) would obtain cold places of the quarters and signs. Moreover, [that] the temperate ones [would be] in temperate places, male ones in male ones, but female ones would not forsake female ones.


*Chapter 1.3.7: Natural significators of topics, and Lots*


§79. In the same way, the significator of the quaesited matter should retain the likeness of its nature.[117] For example, Jupiter shows money, children, law, the evenness of justice, concord, and what is like these. But Venus [shows] women, illicit sex, games, ornamentation, joys, and that sort. Also, Mars indicates wars, victory, brothers, anger, dissent, discord, and jobs which come to be through fire, and things of this kind. Moreover the Saturnian significations are fathers, land, agriculture, and affairs of great age, and so on.

§80. Likewise, belonging to the Sun are honor, dignity, a kingdom, the power of commanding, the revelation of hidden things, and so on. To

---

[114] That is, northern ecliptical latitude (not the same as being in a sign of northern declination).

[115] *Nobam*, a transliteration of Ar. *nawbah*. The Sun is the lord of the shift in diurnal charts, the Moon in nocturnal charts. See Robert's version below.

[116] That is, speed is good for matters which one wants to happen quickly; but it would not be advantageous for matters one wants to proceed slowly.

[117] Robert: "And the nature of the significator and leader should be conferred upon the nature of the matter." This might simply mean that we should assign the appropriate general significator. But in *Search* Chs. I.6.1 and III.1.1, Hermann suggests that the nature of a planet which is in or ruling a house, will more narrowly identify the matter involved: for example, Mars in the seventh identifies the theme of conflict there, Venus that of marriage, Jupiter that of commerce.

Mercury are ascribed knowledge, moderation,[118] writing, trickery, fraud, treachery, eloquence, and that sort. Likewise the Moon takes messengers and the legations of messengers, wares, and such things.

§81.[119] On the other hand, the conjunction of the planet with the Lot analogous to itself (or a regard to [the Lot]) increases its powers for that effect: such as if Jupiter would be united with the Lot of money,[120] or would regard it.[121]

---

[118] Reading with Robert (*castigatui*) for Hugo's "corruption" (*corruptio*), which might itself be a misreading of *correptio*, which classically meant "brevity."

[119] This section is only in Robert.

[120] The Lot of money (or assets or substance or resources) is taken by day and night from the lord of the second to the degree of the second, and projected from the Ascendant. For more information, see *ITA* VI.2.4.

[121] See also §141, which has similar information. My sense is that only an aspect by sign is needed, and not necessarily by degree; but surely an aspect by degree would be more helpful.

# CHAPTER 2: ON THE FAILURE OF MATTERS & THEIR FULFILLMENT[1]

## Chapter 2.1: Planetary significations & configurations

### Chapter 2.1.1: Assembly and whole-sign aspects (with benefics)

§82.[2] Also, the assembly by body [within the same sign][3] or by regard with the fortunes, applies the vigor of the planet. And the bodily assembly is the greatest fortune. Of the regards, the trigon is the most fortunate, for it denotes fortune without difficulty. The sextile is more fortunate than the rest, just as the opposite is worse than the tetragon. For these [latter] regards are partners in difficulty and misfortune.

§83. And so, there is a regard from a hexagon when a star is appearing in the third sign from the [star] which it regards, for then they look at each other in turn. Likewise, a regard from a tetragon comes to be when one will occupy the fourth place from another. It will be called a trigonal regard provided that it will possess the fifth [place] from the other; but the opposition if it will possess the seventh place from the other.

### Chapter 2.1.2: Connection by degree

§84. A regard is the most effective of all if it were with an application.[4] But an application is whenever a quicker star would be crossing fewer degrees in its own sign than the one which it regards does, in *its* own [sign]. The number of degrees will be 6° or less.[5]

§85. Likewise, the strongest [version] of the regard by application is if each [star] would be made equal to the other in degrees.[6]

---

[1] For more complete discussions of these planetary relationships, see *ITA* III.
[2] Reading this paragraph with Robert (but using "assembly" for his "conjunction").
[3] An assembly in the same sign is supposed to be more powerful or intense if within 15°.
[4] In the diagram above, the Sun-Saturn trine is not applying, but the Moon-Jupiter assembly is (or will be, depending upon the effective orbs one uses).
[5] See *ITA* II.6. and III.7 for other theories of degree-based connections or orbs.
[6] Then the application would be considered "perfected" or "completed."

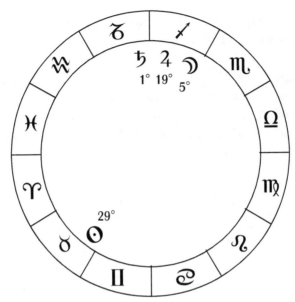

**Figure 29: A Sun-Saturn regard & a Moon-Jupiter assembly[7]**

*Chapter 2.1.3: Reflection of light, transfer of light*

§86. And there is another kind of application, namely when another [star] would appear as a mediator to each: I say, that a light one applies to a heavier one, and the heavier one to a [yet heavier][8] one. But it should be distant from the heavy one by the number of the aforesaid degrees, and [also] from the light one by that many, provided that the heavy and light one would obtain no place of a stellar regard.[9]

---

[7] In this figure, Saturn and the Sun regard each other by sign from a trine. The Moon is in an assembly with Jupiter within 15°. Neither the Sun nor Saturn have any aspectual relationship with the Moon or Jupiter, but are rather in aversion to them.

[8] Reading for "lighter." This relation of heavy and light planets is what Abū Ma'shar and al-Qabīsī call the second type of transfer (*ITA* III.11), but their transfers of light take place between planets which do aspect each other by sign. See the following footnote.

[9] That is, provided that the two planets being connected cannot aspect each other by sign. Al-Kindī's definition of "transfer" is what Abū Ma'shar and al-Qabīsī call "reflection" (*ITA* III.13.1); likewise his definition of collection in the next subchapter. Here, al-Kindī's transfer (but Abū Ma'shar's reflection) enables indirect connections between planets which *are not* configured with each other by sign. The reflecting planet acts like a mirror, such as when we use the reflection in a mirror to view something we cannot see directly: in the example here, the Sun and Saturn do not regard each other by sign, but Mars is in a

§87. For example, let one of them (the Sun) be put in the Ascendant, let Saturn possess the eighth, [and] Mars the fifth from the Sun. But Saturn is placed in the fourth sign from Mars. Likewise the Sun is being borne along in the fifth degree of his sign, but Mars in the tenth, [and Saturn in the fifteenth]:[10] and so, the Sun is applying to Mars, because the distance of the [mutual] regard of each is less than 6°. And so, no less does Mars seem to transfer the efficacy of the Sun to Saturn. But this manner of application is called the greatest motion of transfer.

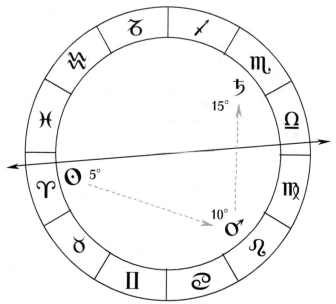

**Figure 30: Reflection of light #1 (transfer from aversion)**

§88. Another application of the stars takes place from a sign whence no aspect proceeds. It is if there is a star between each, applying one to the other, but quicker than each, so that[11] the Sun and Saturn (as we put the first example), holding onto the aforesaid signs, would be conjoined by some mediating star lighter than each. And so, let the Moon be wandering around in the tenth[12] degree of the fifth [sign], receding from the Sun, and applying

---

position to act as a mirror that reflects the light from the Sun to Saturn. For more, see §4 of my Introduction, above.

[10] Adding with Robert.

[11] Reading the rest of this sentence with Robert.

[12] Reading *decimo* for *decimi*.

to Saturn: and she [is] the mediator between each. But this is called the lesser shifting.[13]

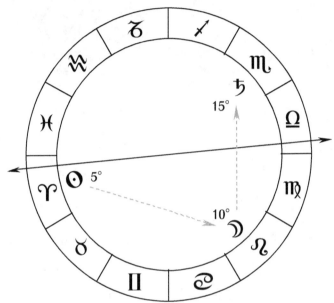

**Figure 31: Another reflection of light #1 (transfer from aversion)**

*Chapter 2.1.4: Reflection of light, collection of light*

§89. And there is another manner of application, namely if two stars apply to the same one: such as if the Moon is within the thirteenth degree of the Ascendant, Venus in the eighth [sign] within the thirteenth of it, but let Saturn be put in the thirteenth degree of the fifth [sign]: an application made by each is finally distinguished. Likewise, the one conjoining the light of each, ties together a common application of the others. And so this kind of application is called "attachment."[14]

---

[13] *Transmutatio*, the term Adelard uses for reflection. This relation of heavy and light planets is what Abū Ma'shar and al-Qabīsī call the first type of transfer of light (*ITA* III.11), but again, their transfers are between planets which do aspect each other by sign. Al-Kindī's collection is the same as Abū Ma'shar's other version of "reflection." See §4 of my Introduction, above.

[14] See the footnote about transfer of light and reflection of light, above. Again, for Abū Ma'shar and al-Qabīsī, a collection of light (*ITA* III.12) is used for planets which are

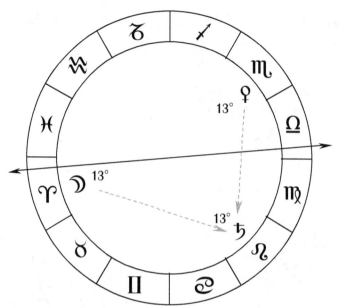

**Figure 32: Reflection of light #2 (collection from aversion)**

*Chapter 2.1.5: Connection by body*

§90. And there is another application besides these: namely when a star would be bodily in the same degree as another star, or would be advancing towards being with it bodily, but the heavier would be separated from the lighter one by less than 6°. And this is called "incorporation" by the ancients.

---

configured by sign alone, but are unable to make the proper application by degree; just so, their second kind of reflection (*ITA* III.13.2) is the scenario described here by al-Kindī, collection from aversion: when two planets are not able to see each other by sign, but are in the proper degree-relation to a planet which can see both of them. Here, the Moon and Venus do not regard each other by sign, but both are completing a connection with Saturn, who sees them both. Al-Kindī may have thought that collection would be unnecessary if the Moon and Venus could already regard each other by sign. The extra step taken by Abū Ma'shar and al-Qabīsī is that the reflecting planet by definition must reflect the light elsewhere, which to me suggests that collection from aversion or the second type of reflection has some uncertainty and unpredictability to it, because the influence might be reflected to some place unhelpful. For example, we would want the collecting planet—which by definition ends up managing the matter—to aspect the Ascendant by sign. But if it were unable to, then it would be as though events and energy and activity gets diverted elsewhere, which could harm the matter.

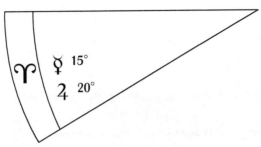

**Figure 33: Mercury connecting bodily with Jupiter, within 6°**

*Chapter 2.1.6: Receptions: four types*

§91. Moreover, every application becomes stronger with reception.


*Reception #1: Pushing nature, mutual reception*[15]

§92. And so, reception is asserted to happen in four ways. First, when one [star] would occupy the house of another in turn, and in a friendly way. But I say that if each takes up [the other's],[16] it especially loves [it], and it especially rejoices with it as though with family and children, and it tenders money to the other.

§93. No less too can this same type happen in the sovereignty of each or in any place of dignity. However, it is more effective in the house or sovereignty—and secondarily in the bound, triplicity or face.[17]

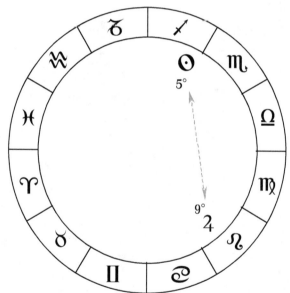

**Figure 34: The Sun pushing nature to Jupiter; mutual reception**

---

[15] See *ITA* III.15 and II.25, where I call pushing nature "classical reception."

[16] Reading more with Robert and his example for Hugo's *Dico autem utramque assumpto*.

[17] Al-Kindī probably derived this from Sahl's *On Quest.* §5.8.

*Reception #2: Mutual largesse with pushing nature[18]*

§94. Likewise, another kind of reception [is] if each[19] would be inhabiting the well of the other: each would be practically leaning on the other and figuring out how they would be able to support each other, and thus they would seem to play the role of friends to one another.[20]

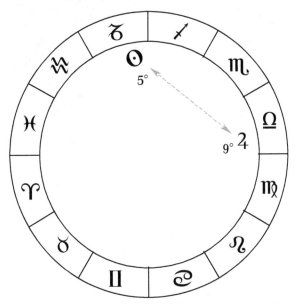

**Figure 35: Al-Kindī's reception #2: In each other's fall**

*Comment by Dykes.* This example of al-Kindī's is problematic. On the surface, it seems to be his own version of what became "largesse and recompense" (*ITA* III.24). In largesse, one planet is in its *own* fall, and is configured by sign or degree with the domicile lord or exalted lord of that sign: in that case, the planet *in fall* is helped by *the lord*. Recompense happens during a later transit, when the planets switch roles: the first planet is now the domicile lord and the second is the one in fall. Here is an example based on Abū Ma'shar, from *ITA* III.24:

---

[18] I have titled this section according to my proposed correction below.
[19] Reading for *altera.*
[20] The figure below is based on Robert's description (but the assignment of degrees is my own).

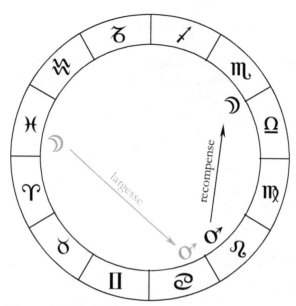

**Figure 36: Abū Ma'shar's largesse & recompense**

Here, Mars starts out in fall in Cancer, but has largesse bestowed upon him by his domicile lord, the Moon. Some days later, the Moon is in her own fall in Scorpio, and is aspected by her domicile lord Mars (who is no longer in fall). Thus Mars pays her back for the help she showed him before. The logic of the situation is clear, because the planet in need is in its own fall and is helped by one of the owners of the sign. But in al-Kindī's description, neither of the planets is in any special trouble since neither is in its own fall: in fact, the Sun is merely peregrine and Jupiter is at least a partnering triplicity lord of its sign (because it is an airy sign).

The other problem with al-Kindī's definition is that it actually describes a situation which Sahl (and later al-Rijāl) *warns* of, and is actually described by al-Kindī below: "not-reception."[21] This happens when one planet is applying to another *from out of the latter's fall*, and Sahl says "it is as if it came to it from the house of its greatest enemy, and it does not receive it and does not come near it." Since the sign of fall represents downfall, depression, and obscurity, the latter planet does not want to recognize or receive or get near, any other planet coming from the sign of its fall—note that Sahl explicitly says this is *not* a case of reception. So in al-Kindī's example, the Sun is in the fall of

---

[21] See Sahl's *Introduct.* §5.9, and al-Rijāl I.10.

Jupiter (i.e., in Capricorn): thus Jupiter *does not want* this unfavorable application of the Sun.

My own sense is that al-Kindī really meant the following: that *each* planet is in its *own* fall, so that the two troubled planets are able to help each other. But since this section in al-Kindī is about matters being completed and strengthened, I would recommend that each planet still have some rulership in the other's sign: that way each one has some inherent authority and resources to help the other. My proposed version below is based on Māshā'allāh's example in his *OR*: both the Sun and Saturn are in their own falls, but each is also the exalted lord of the other's sign: thus there is mutual largesse and a mutual reception from exaltation (i.e., pushing nature).

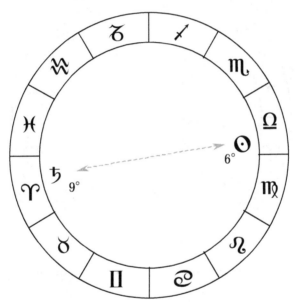

**Figure 37: Proposed correction to al-Kindī:
mutual largesse with pushing nature**

*Reception #3: Pushing power to a dignified planet[22]*

§95. Moreover, a third kind of reception: namely, when the conveying (that is, the applying) star [is] in its own house, but the one to which it conveys [its power] likewise obtains its own. Therefore they will be virtually like those who devise a way to reinforce each other and support each other with *their own*[23] glory and aid. And so the significators of these[24] (namely of the applying one and the one to which it applies) reinforce each other and convey mutual solace.

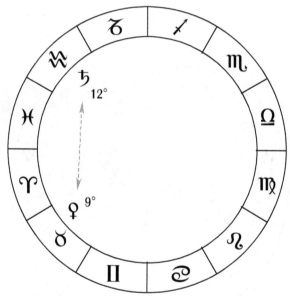

**Figure 38: Reception #3: Pushing power to a dignified planet**

---

[22] For pushing power, see *ITA* III.16.
[23] Emphasis mine.
[24] That is the people represented by such planets.

*Reception #4: Pushing two natures #1*[25]

§96. Likewise, [the fourth reception]: an application when each one agrees in the dignity of the applying one. For these bear the likeness of those who generously support a partner through their own hand by lightening [the burden]. And so in this manner, he whom the applying significator designates,[26] will be said to reinforce the other.[27]

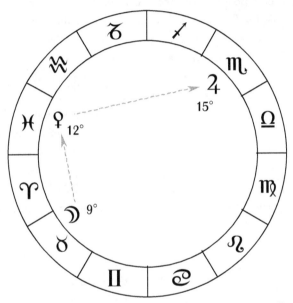

**Figure 39: Reception #4: Pushing two natures #1**

---

[25] For pushing two natures, see *ITA* III.17.1.
[26] That is, the person indicated by the applying planet.
[27] In my example below, the Moon is in her own exaltation (Taurus), and applies to Venus (the domicile lord of Taurus). Also, Venus is in her own exaltation (Pisces), and applies to Jupiter (the domicile lord of Pisces). Similar examples would be the Moon in Cancer applying to Jupiter, Venus in Libra applying to Saturn, Mars in Capricorn applying to Saturn, and the Sun in Aries applying to Mars.

*Chapter 2.1.7: Better and worse aspects and receptions*

§97a. But the best reception of all [is] from the trigon. Tetragonal [reception] is slow and defers prosperity. Also the hexagonal [reception] is like the trigonal, but somewhat weaker. But the regard of the opposition introduces distinct adversity.

§97b-98. Also, assembly cannot[28] happen in one kind of reception named above,[29] for it is impossible for each star to possess the same degree [in the same sign] while [each] one possesses the house of the other. But they can subsist in the same degree, and each one will be able to possess some dignity of the other.[30] Let us take such an example of this matter: if the Moon and Jupiter would assemble in Cancer, Jupiter will possess the house of the Moon, [and] the Moon the sovereignty of Jupiter.

§99. Moreover, the more vigorous regard and application of the fortunate ones proceeds from the assembly and trigon and hexagon, [while] the tetragon and opposition bestow the least gifts of happiness. On the other hand, the stronger regard and application of the infortunes is from the assembly and opposition and tetragon: they especially heap on corruption from these regards. Likewise the corruption is made less from the trigon and hexagon.

*Chapter 2.1.8: Problematic applications*

§100. Moreover, the infortunes are especially strengthened[31] when their regard and application are deprived of reception, namely while an infortune should apply to some star from a place in which it obtains no dignity— especially whenever the complexion of the place where the infortune is staying, is adverse to the [other] star.[32]

---

[28] Adding *non* with the logic of the sentence; Robert and Hugo may have misunderstood the Arabic.

[29] Namely the first kind (mutual reception with pushing nature). One and the same degree cannot be the domicile of two planets.

[30] This would be a case of the fourth kind above (pushing two natures #1), since the domicile of one could be the exaltation of the other.

[31] That is, they are strengthened in their ability to signify misfortune.

[32] In my example below, a peregrine Mars is applying by square to Jupiter: Jupiter is already in detriment, has no rulerships in Mars's place in Virgo, and the cold-dry nature of Virgo conflicts with that of Jupiter.

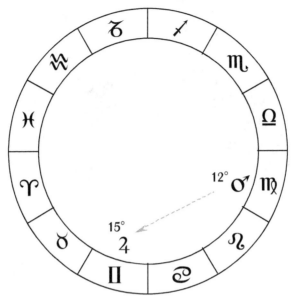

**Figure 40: Hostile aspect from a peregrine Mars (Dykes)**

*Pushing power from another planet's detriment*

§101. For example,[33] let Mars be said to be regarding the Moon from Scorpio, and let the Moon be in Taurus. And because Taurus is opposed to Scorpio, what belongs to that house is said to be opposite in such a way.

§102. Since therefore the Moon applies to Mars, and does so from his unhealthiness,[34] it is like one who presents to his own enemy what [the enemy] abhors and neglects: for it offers a gift of punishment and labor and adversity. Again, it seems to take on the role of one who conveys the worst, unfriendly and fearful gift to some man, and what is contrary to his nature. And so, with the misfortune being taken up, it is to that extent important that he should try to busy himself with expelling the adversity he has taken up, with his own family and money aiding him.[35]

---

[33] This example of applying from another planet's detriment is similar to what Sahl calls "not-reception" (*Introduct.* §5.9): applying from the fall of the other planet (for example, if the Moon in Aries applied to Saturn). In §107 below, Hugo seems to call either al-Kindī's or Sahl's example "refusal."

[34] That is, from his detriment. Hugo has a Latin transliteration of the Arabic (*alwabil*).

[35] Reading somewhat uncertainly: *oportet quatenus propria familia et pecunia iuvante in susceptae adversitatis expulsione satagere conetur.*

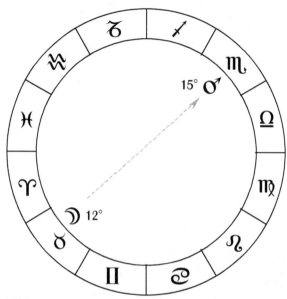

**Figure 41: Hostile pushing power (perhaps with not-reception)**

*An ambiguous combination of detriment and pushing nature*

§103. Likewise, Mars in Libra, and with the Moon applying to him from Aries (which is the house of Mars) or from Capricorn (which is his sovereignty), it happens practically like one who strains to transfer evil to a perverse man, but in such a way that even though it is made fraudulently and in an unfriendly manner, it is pleasing. But on account of the opposition [from Aries], he abhors the perversity [and] yet has esteem on account of the application [being from reception.][36] (But I say that she [must] regard him from the house or sovereignty of Mars.)[37]

---

[36] That is, from pushing nature (adding from Robert).
[37] The idea here seems to be that even if the aspect is hostile (an opposition from Aries or a square from Capricorn), since the Moon is in a dignity of Mars, and so pushes nature to him, Mars still benefits: a planet getting its nature or dignity pushed to it, benefits from it.

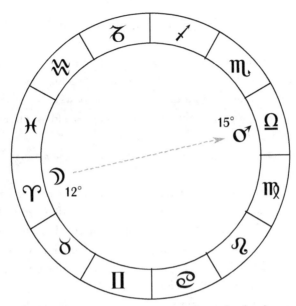

**Figure 42: Pushing nature to a planet in detriment**

§104. Therefore, the rest of the things in every application will have to be pursued by this appraisal of the analogy. For if you knew how to relate individual [features] to individual [features], appropriately and distinctly, the truth of the judgment will be manifestly uncovered. These things, which seemed necessary for the order of [this] work (according to the size of [the material which] follows), have been stated diligently and appropriately enough before: the types of individual ways [the planets may be combined] will display a signification in those things which belong to their kind and likeness.

## Chapter 2.2: Other considerations, significations, & analogies

§105. The signification of the superiors is found to be similar to these things which the inferiors designate. Wherefore, the power and effectiveness of the superiors signifies and greatly increases the powers of the inferiors; in the same way, the weakness of the superiors seems to add to the frailty of the subordinate [planets].

§106. Also, advancement signifies the arrival of stronger things, but retreat means remoteness and falling.[38]

§107. Also,[39] easternness [signifies] the best manifestation and familiarity; westernness, hiddenness and contempt and being deposed.[40] Reception [signifies] accepting, refusal[41] [signifies] neglect. Fortune introduces prosperity, unluckiness adversity. Likewise diminution [of course and light signifies][42] loss, adding [signifies] increase. Treading in direct motion [means] evenness,[43] retrogradation [means] indirectness.[44]

§108. The sideways character of signs[45] [signifies] unevenness, [straightness of signs signifies rectitude. Speedy stars indicate quickness],[46] stationing or staying [indicates] delay. Exaltation [indicates] promotion, fall being deposed.[47]

§109. Moreover, a multitude of assisting [stars] greatly increases [assistance]; in fact, a regard from a place of dignity and friendship brings about assistance more strongly. An abundance of inimical [stars] multiplies enemies (a regard of refusal and adversity seems to confer this).

---

[38] For this section, see also §§37-9 above, and *ITA* III.3-4.

[39] See similar analogies in Ch. 1.3.3 above.

[40] Robert reads, "invalidations" or "refutations" (*infirmationes*). My sense is that this pair of terms refers more to being outside versus under the Sun's rays, rather than being on one or another side of the Sun. In both Arabic and Latin, the "east" also means "rising," and "west" means "setting," and many texts are ambiguous as to whether "eastern/western" or "oriental/occidental" means being visible or hidden, or at what part of the day a planet might be visible outside of the Sun.

[41] See my comments on not-reception above, and Hugo's mention of "neglect" in the above example of pushing nature to a planet in detriment (§102).

[42] Adding with Robert.

[43] Or, "regularity, smoothness" (*aequalitatem*).

[44] Or perhaps, "being sideways" (*obliquitatem*).

[45] This sentence refers to the signs of crooked and straight ascensions. See §22 above.

[46] Adding based on Robert.

[47] Robert reads this in terms of ecliptical latitude: "raising up into the north, being made lofty; being thrown down into the south, descent."

§110. Hot ones will indicate heat, cold ones cold, male ones masculine habits, female ones female ones. Nocturnal ones will divulge nocturnal customs, diurnal ones diurnal ones. But those which are manifold [indicate] many things; but those [which are] few, very little, according to what pertains to them, in terms of nature and ascensions.[48] Moreover, their joy conveys happiness.[49]

### Joys by sign

§111a. And so, the joy and happiness of the stars happens in their own proper houses, and also in signs agreeing with their nature. But [their] misfortune [is] in signs unequal to their nature, according to [their] effective quality.[50] If Mercury were eastern, he is glad in Gemini; western, he rejoices in Virgo.[51] ([He acts] in this manner even under the rays.)

### Joys by house

§111b. Moreover, their status is discerned in this manner, just as the order of the twelve houses demands.

§112. And so,[52] Mercury rejoices in the Ascendant, the Moon exults in the third, Venus is glad in the fifth, Mars does a war dance[53] in the sixth, Saturn reverberates in the twelfth, Jupiter claps in the eleventh; in the same way, the

---

[48] I believe this refers to signs of many children (the watery signs) and of many (straight) ascensions. Robert: "And those which are rulers over many things [indicate] many, just as those ruling over few things [indicate] few benefits, from the nature of the things which came out according to the Ascendant."

[49] See the following sections.

[50] Al-Kindī seems to have omitted the list of joys by sign. Diurnal planets rejoice in their diurnal domiciles (Saturn in Aquarius, Jupiter in Sagittarius; the Sun in Leo is taken for granted), while nocturnal planets rejoice in their nocturnal domiciles (Mars in Scorpio, Venus in Taurus; the Moon in Cancer is taken for granted).

[51] Normally Mercury is simply taken to rejoice in Virgo, but this sect-based consideration makes sense.

[52] The diurnal planets rejoice in certain houses above the horizon, nocturnal ones in certain houses below the horizon. By definition the rising sign is partly above, partly below the horizon, which is appropriate for a flexible planet like Mercury. My thanks to Robert Schmidt for pointing this out.

[53] *Tripudiat*, though Hugo sometimes uses this as a generic verb for any kind of dancing.

Sun renders thanks in the ninth. But the places of the circle opposite what
was said above, seem to be adverse to that arrangement.[54]

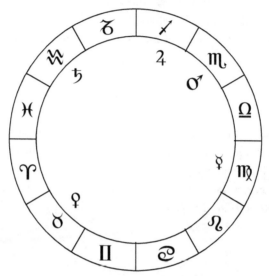

**Figure 43: Planetary joys by sign**

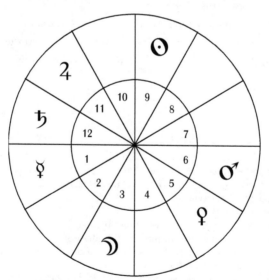

**Figure 44: Planetary joys by house**

---

[54] That is, the planets should be considered "saddened" (Robert) in the opposite of their
joy. This is an extremely rare statement, and offhand I cannot think of another instance of
it.

## Chapter 2.3: Lords of houses in other houses

*Lords of houses in other houses*

§113.[55] [Since] the natures and significations of the stars and signs have already been explained for the most part, next let the sequence of our labors add the effect of the pivots and succeedents of the signs, and the cadents, and of the planets in them.

§114. The pivots and those stars which are staying in the pivots, untie the knot of this question, for they designate noted, famous, and public things. But those which are remote from the pivots (or those which are called "cadent") are to the contrary. In fact the ninth and third [indicate] what is obscure and unknown.[56] Also, recognition of the abject, low-class and hidden things, even misfortune and the whole affair of being sunken down[57] depends on the twelfth and the sixth.

*Lords of the angles in the angles and the eleventh*

§115. Moreover, the pivots and their lords (provided that they were in pivots) magnify prosperity, greatly increase luckiness, [and] put off ruin. But those same [lords] in the remote and cadent [places] take away from fortune, and threaten abjectness and blunders. But if [they were] after the pivots (and first of all after the tenth), if they bore themselves in the manner stated above,[58] they mean a state of middling fortune, they fulfill hope and a favorable opinion, [and] bring friends to bear.

*Lords of the angles in the fifth, second, and eighth*

§116. But those which will be placed after the fourth watch over the steadiness of middling fortune, and they introduce gifts with every [type of] exultation, but because of children. But those which follow the Ascendant bestow the steadiness of the aforewritten luckiness, by means of money and

---

[55] This paragraph is only in Robert.
[56] This should also be taken in the spiritual sense (since these are places of religion): namely, dealing with the unseen, what is mental, conceptual, non-sensible.
[57] *Demissionis negotii*, which could include morale in addition to objective states of affairs.
[58] Probably, being in one of their dignities, regarded by a fortunate planet, *etc.*

family that is not absent.[59] Also, after the seventh, because of inheritance and ancient things. All of these advance according to their own rank [in the houses].

### The lord of the Ascendant in the angles

§117. Finally, the highest and greatest prosperity of all is that which the lord of the Ascendant signifies. Which if it were in the Ascendant, it indicates things will be acquired through his own labor and vigor. But if it were in the Midheaven, he will possess it because of some king and grand duties. Which if it dwelled in the seventh, because of borrowing[60] and adversaries and a betrothal. In the fourth, they especially make the reason for luckiness to be lands, fathers, waterways and the tilling of lands, and the building of cities,[61] even things which are ancient and original.[62]

### The lord of the tenth in the angles

§118. Moreover, if the lord of the Midheaven would indicate this [good fortune] and it [were] in the Midheaven, it confers a command, [such that] some king and the highest duties seem to present the reason for it. Also, the same [planet] in the seventh will give a command and make him calm because of adversaries and a betrothal. But if in the fourth, he is raised to being a king since he abounds in taxation, occupies lands, constructs cities, breaks up riverbeds, guards cities, and excels in this kind of ancient thing. If this [planet] would possess the Ascendant, he is enriched with the benefit of a command through his own effort, and closeness to the king, and the assent of the common people.

### The lord of the seventh in the angles

§119. But the lord of the seventh, being in the seventh: he whom it signifies will benefit in wares and borrowing because of taxes, women,

---

[59] That is, immediate family that is nearby and ready to hand (as opposed to long-lost relatives or those on long journeys).

[60] *Mutuationis.* Or rather, business partnerships generally.

[61] Reading the parts about tilling and building more with al-Qabīsī's Arabic (see *ITA* I.15 and al-Qabīsī I.73), for Hugo's "and the tilling of their leasing."

[62] Or, "deep-rooted" (*ITA* I.15).

adversaries. But with it appearing in the fourth, it blesses with borrowing, women and wares, with the assisting cause of fathers and lands and agriculture. Meanwhile, it being placed in the Ascendant, physics and astronomy and those things which are jobs of his own training and effort, and that type [of thing], greatly bestow the rulership of borrowing and commerce. But if it occupied the tenth, he will redound in commerce, be blessed with a wife, satisfying the king and [his] duties.[63]

### The lord of the fourth in the angles

§120. Which if the lord of the fourth [were] in the fourth, it grants the gift of the aforewritten luckiness and presents the highest borrowing of commerce, is replete with fruits, multiplies agriculture, but it happens [because of] fathers and a gift of some antiquity. But if it were in the Ascendant, he will shine with fruits and agriculture through his own effort, and no moderate deliberation. And in the tenth, he will rejoice in the fertility of fields [and] the resources of fruits, with the king or his own profession conferring it. Which if it would promise it from the seventh, he will redound in the resources of fruits and agriculture, but women and adversaries [and] even commerce will be credited with its cause.

### The lords of pivots in pivots, applying to other planets

§121. On the other hand, whenever the lords of the pivots, appearing in the pivots, apply to other stars also in the pivots, they promise the form of the aforewritten luckiness, and the greatness of its rank, and watch over its steadiness in that same category—[and] in any [matter] they promise that no ruin or harm will come to be for the whole life of its possessor.

Moreover, provided that the lords of the pivots appear in the pivots, if their application should come to be with some stars in what follows the pivots, they transform that height of prosperity into what is lesser.

§122-24. But the same [lords of the pivots] being in pivots, [and] applying to stars cadent from the pivots, threaten that the ruin of the height of luckiness will happen, just as the nature of the one to which the application happens, will teach it.

---

[63] *Regis et officiorum gratia faciente* (Robert reads, "from actions and ruling").

If therefore they applied to Saturn, we believe men of lower rank, fathers, ancient things, and what is like these will enter into the cause.

Which if their application would come to be with Jupiter, it conveys ruin because of some judge, the law, children, money, and fairness, and what is like these.

But if to Mars, brothers, murder or some army, a general and prince of wars, even discords or thieves, drive him away from honor.

But if their application is made with the Sun, a king and those aristocrats who are in charge of ruling under him, sometimes divination or medicine, fathers, hunting and the more promoted people from among the commoners, and an immoderate reputation for excessive consumption and expenses, and the consumption of money, will strip him of luckiness.

Also, applying to Venus, women or being prone to and [having] an irrevocable appetite for games and illicit sex, lack of self-control, immodest love, and that sort of thing, drive him away from honor.

But if to Mercury, they deprive him of luckiness because of the corruption[64] of knowledge, writing, and speech.

Moreover an application of these [lords of the pivots in the pivots] being made to the Moon, they create the loss of downfall because of a royal slave-girl, or messengers, and some change of place or foreign business.

§125-26. But often the same thing tends to happen according to the nature of that house which that [planet] (to which the application happens) is holding onto. If it would make its stay in the Ascendant, he undergoes that harm for the guilt of his own crime. Which if in the second, money shows the reason for ruin. And if in the third, [good fortune] is expelled by the offenses of brothers. Which if [it is] in the fourth, he tumbles down because of the father, lands and some ancient thing. In the fifth, children. In the

[64] Reading *corruptionis* for *correptionis*.

sixth, disease or animals. In the seventh, he will slip by means of the deeds of women and adversaries. Which if it dwelled in the eighth, inheritances enter into the cause. But in the ninth, law or some journey. Likewise in the tenth, duties. In the eleventh, friends and money and the search for money. In the twelfth, he merits being deposed because of enemies [and] captivity.

§127a. Moreover, the sum and principal beginning of the outcomes of this whole occasion [for trouble], is believed to flow from out of the house of the one to which the application of the rest comes to be: namely the nature of [the house] which it supports by its own aspect, just in that way it was said before about the house in which it is [actually] situated.

*Lords of the pivots in the succeedent places and applying to other planets*

§127b-128. Moreover, if the lords of the pivots would appear after the pivots, and their application would happen to [stars] appearing in the same places,[65] the moderate favor of the prosperity which is had, does not forsake [him] for the whole space of life. Which if they, appearing in that same place, would apply to another [star] in a pivot, the present luckiness is converted into something greater. But the arising and cause of this blessedness demands to be noted in the way which was stated above with respect to the cadents.[66]

*Lords of the pivots in the cadent places and applying to other planets*

§129. Again, if the lords of the pivots would be tumbling down from the pivots, they will present no favor of good fortune for the whole life of a man, but rather they will make it flow from something bad to something worse. But those same [lords of the pivots] being cadent, while they apply to those placed after the pivots, [after] the anxiety and the absence of prosperity (by which he will be sad in the beginning of life), he will [later] rejoice in middling luckiness. Likewise, if the lords of the pivots (being cadent) applied to others in the pivots, [after being] free of the prior starvation he will attain the highest honor; and once the cloud of prior difficulty is dissolved, he will have this [good fortune] for longer.

---

65 That is, in the succeedents.
66 In other words, according to the meaning of (1) the planet to which they apply, (2) the house it occupies, and (3) the house of its own which it regards most strongly or best.

## Chapter 2.4: The planet in charge[67]

§130. No less too, does the minister which the Arabs call the "the one in charge"[68] mean the highest fortune, if it crossed the Sun and would appear eastern, so that it would be separated from the Sun by 12° or a little more, and would appear in the east in the morning. Which if it would be arising distant from the Sun by double the number of degrees of the first [distance], it is a sign of middling luckiness. But if it is remote from him by the tripled prior distance, it introduces lesser fortune.

§131. Also, with that same [distance] being quadrupled and it being foreign to[69] the Sun, it signifies a lesser punishment. But fivefold, it designates middling anguish. After that, it harms with greater misfortune until it undergoes scorching.

## Chapter 2.5: Bringing about or corrupting matters

§132. Significators declare the bringing about of the quaesited matter, [if they are] in the pivots or after the pivots, and regarded by [their] partners and the Sun and Moon (or by one of [the luminaries], if that one would obtain a signification, but especially by the one which claimed the shift[70] for itself, if neither obtained a signification).

§133. But if it were asked about the reversal or alteration or corruption of matters, the cadents signify that. Again, an application of the significator with the significator of the quaesited matter shows the same thing. And if there should come to be a regard from the lords of the significators to them ([and]

---

[67] This subchapter seems to give criteria for judging the favorability of the victors to be determined below in Ch. 3—it does not identify a wholly separate victor or ruler. If so, then it should be considered *in addition to* the determinations of strength by dignity (Chs. 3.1-2), just as Ptolemy (*Tet.* III.3 and III.5), and Dorotheus (*Carmen* III.1.1-6) and ibn Ezra (*Nativities* p. 14) stress the importance of solar phase in their versions of victors and chief significators. See especially *ITA* II.10.

[68] Or, "ruler, administrator": Ar. *al-mustawli* (Lat. *almuzeth, almustaul*), from *waliya* (forms I and V), "to be in charge, manage, assume responsibility for." Thanks to Charles Burnett for pointing this out.

[69] I believe this means that it is in a trine from the Sun by sign, so it is "cadent" from the whole-sign angles of the Sun. This would place the planet near the beginning of its retrogradation. But it might also mean that it is in aversion to the Sun (i.e., in the eighth sign from the Sun).

[70] That is, the luminary ruling the sect.

even the Sun and the Moon, or the lord of the shift), they show the same thing.

## Chapter 2.6: Methods of timing

§134. But the degrees of application will indicate the end-point of this effect, to which we sometimes grant days, months, or years, just as the nature or time of the matter itself demands. For there are certain things whose time cannot be ended in anything other than days, [and] others whose time indicates only months (such as those who are enclosed in the uterus of the mother before birth). But certain ones get years, like if someone posed a question about when a palm tree which he planted would bear fruit. In all of these, the nature of the quaesited matter must be considered.

§135. Now, however, we will have to write down which matters' time would be ended in days, months, and years. And so, the degrees of the application frequently take days if their signs were convertible, particularly if [such signs] arise in less than two hours, or in [exactly] two full [hours]. Also, the double-bodied signs take months, especially if their arising had less than two. But a signification of years comes to be if they were fixed signs, especially if their ascension demands more than two hours.

§136a. Again, the quickness of a significator signifies an outcome that is near, slowness [signifies it] after a delay, but the middle [speed] of each indicates in the middle. Wherefore the status of the significator with the signs themselves will have to be discussed, according to the manner and nature of the quaesited matter. From a consideration of these things, the endpoint and hour will be clear.

# CHAPTER 3: ON THE CLASSIFICATION OF RELEASERS

## Chapter 3.1: Victor for a topic[1]

§136b.[2] But whichever one had more powers in the domicile of the matter, and its Lot, and its significating star[3] and the lord of its hour,[4] will be considered to be the manager and administrator of that matter.

## Chapter 3.2: Weighted victor for the querent, taken from all releasing places[5]

§137. Moreover, the significator of the querent is distinguished according to the majority of the stars participating in the five places of releasing. For [the releasers] are the Sun, Moon, Ascendant, Lot of Fortune,[6] [and] the degree of the assembly or opposition which preceded the matter. However, the lord of the house obtains 5 portions or dignities, the lord of the sovereignty 4, the lord of the bound 3,[7] the lord of the triplicity 2, but only 1 is bequeathed to the lord of the face.

## Chapter 3.3: The releaser *& kadukhudhāh*[8]

§138. If one were eager to find the releaser (that is, the significator of life), one will consult the Sun in a diurnal nativity; which if one found him being

---

[1] Cf. al-Qabīsī's version of victors for topics in *ITA* I.18. The subject of victors for topics, charts, and thoughts (with methods and examples) is dealt with completely in *Search*.
[2] This part of §136 is only in Robert.
[3] I take this to be the natural significator (such as Jupiter for wealth, Venus for love, and so on).
[4] This seems to mean the "lord of the hour." See Ch. 1.15 above.
[5] Cf. al-Qabīsī's victor for the chart in *ITA* VIII.1.4.
[6] The Lot of Fortune is taken in the day from the Sun to the Moon, and projected from the Ascendant; by night, from the Moon to the Sun and projected from the Ascendant.
[7] Note that al-Kindī follows the earlier practice found in *Search* and its sources, which assigns 3 points to the bound and 2 to the primary triplicity lord, rather than the other way around. Already in al-Qabīsī they are reversed.
[8] This chapter is only in Robert. For more on releasers, see *ITA* VIII.1.3 and the list of *PN* sources in its Appendix F.

received in a sign or quarter of the masculine sex, and viewed by[9] a [planet] ruling with any power over his place, it would establish him as the releaser, and the viewing one as the *kadukhudhāh* (that is, the giver of the years of life). But if the Sun did not bear himself thusly, then the Moon should be considered: and if she were received in a sign or quarter of the female sex, and regarded by a lord with any power in that place, she should be taken as the releaser, and the one regarding her as the *kadukhudhāh*. But if the Sun and Moon were forsaken of such a condition, [then] if he is born after an assembly [of the luminaries], the degree of the east—being regarded by any of its lords—should be taken as the releaser, and the aspecting one as the *kadukhudhāh*. Moreover, if one has allotted the stated condition to none of these three, then if the Lot of Fortune bore itself thusly, let it be assigned as the releaser, and the one looking at it as the *kadukhudhāh*.

§139. But with the aforesaid four lacking the manner [of bearing] indicated above, finally the degree of the assembly should be judged as the releaser [if it is] allotting that condition, and the one aspecting as the *kadukhudhāh*. But if none of the aforesaid five bore themselves thusly, the native will lack a releaser and *kadukhudhāh*. But in a nocturnal nativity, the Moon should be considered in the aforesaid way;[10] and, being found thus, she is appointed as the releaser and the one seeing her as the *kadukhudhāh*. But if not, after [her] the Sun; and with these [conditions] being lacking, if he were born after the opposition, [look at] the Lot of Fortune (if it were fit); but if not, the degree of the east is allotted the aforesaid dignity; [but] if not, finally the degree of the opposition[11] should be taken as the releaser, and the one regarding it as the *kadukhudhāh*. [But if none of the five bore themselves thusly, the nativity will lack a releaser and *kadukhudhāh*.][12] And so, with these things being found, the force and power of the *kadukhudhāh* should be noted: for, being strong grants the greatest gifts, being weak the least. But its strength is that it would be advancing,[13] eastern, direct, and in its own *ḥalb*, and in one of its own dignities.[14]

---

[9] That is, "aspected" by. I believe this requires only an aspect by sign, not necessarily by degree.

[10] In feminine places, however.

[11] Reading for "assembly."

[12] Adding with the logic of the method, as above.

[13] That is, in an angle or a succeedent.

[14] For more on strength, see *ITA* IV.1-2.

§140. Moreover, the releaser should be directed to the rays and bodies of the fortunes and the bad ones with the greatest accuracy. For whenever and wherever it applied itself to a good one, it bestows good fortune from out of its manner and nature; and conjoined to a bad one, it shows misfortune according to its quality—but especially if it were the conjunction, tetragon, or opposite.

## Chapter 3.4: The use of Lots & natural significators

§141.[15] Also, every Lot which is a significator of any matter, and every sign, should be directed[16] to a thing analogous to itself,[17] so that from this, the time of good and evil ([and] even its greatness and manner) may be perceived. But the power and effect of every sign and every significating Lot is agreed to arise out of and be strengthened by the regards of its own lord and each or one or the other of the luminaries (namely the one whose shift it was),[18] and by comparison of the star similar to it: for example, Jupiter and the Lot of money [are attributed to] the second domicile, and Venus and the Lot of nuptials to the seventh.[19]

This heading must especially be noted as being appropriate to a native, but by it a similar judgment can also come to be with respect to the rest of matters and their beginnings.[20]

---

[15] This subchapter is only in Robert.
[16] This probably refers to profections.
[17] See also §81 above.
[18] That is, the luminary of the sect.
[19] This is probably the Lot of marriage according to Hermes: for a diurnal male or nocturnal female, measure from Saturn to Venus; for a nocturnal male or a diurnal female, measure from Venus to Saturn. The degrees are projected from the Ascendant. But it could also be the Lot of delight and pleasure, taken by night and day from Venus to the degree of the Descendant, and project from the Ascendant.
[20] Or perhaps, "and initiating them" (*initiis*), which in al-Kindī's mind probably includes both horary questions and elections proper.

# CHAPTER 4: ON BEGINNING AFFAIRS

§142. Before everything [else], the Ascendant and its lord must be established, with a certain [1] likeness[1] and [2] prosperity[2] being observed.

[1] Likeness is observed when the Ascendant itself preserves the nature of the quaesited matter, or a likeness of its nature, in quality and manner. But then [1a] the quality of the nature is noted when someone does not neglect to arrange the fiery signs if an inquirer is concerned about the quick and certain outcome of matters, or about some dignity or kingdom; again, the [1b] manner must be brought to bear, just as we look at the signs of Mars when asking about war.

§143. Besides that,[3] [3] the place of the question (or rather, of the quaesited matter) and its lord must be noted. For the place of the question suggests the beginning of the matter and the affair. Also, its lord regulates the middle. But the lord of its lord resolves the end of the whole matter. Likewise, the Ascendant too maintains the querent's affairs, in the aforesaid order. Even the Lot of the quaesited matter and its lord,[4] and the lord of its house, testify to the same thing and in the same order.

§144. Once these things have been established in the order written above, [2] the prosperity or benevolence is increased by the stars' being situated in their own places or in their regard or friendly application, with the unfortunate ones being expelled from these same places. One will even have be beware lest the lord of the Ascendant or of the quaesited matter appear retrograde: for even though all things may be promised as being able to come about, the effecting of the matter will follow after very much labor and long desperation, with many adverse obstacles.

§145. I reckon one must even avoid having the Tail accompany the Sun or Moon (with them being in the assembly or opposition), or just one of them

---

[1] *Similitudo*. Robert reads, "suitability of form."

[2] Robert reads, "good fortune" (*fortuna*).

[3] This section presents a third category to observe, besides [1] the likeness and [2] the prosperity: namely, [3] the appropriate arrangement and choosing of the places, Lots, and their lords.

[4] For example, the Lot of money for financial matters, or the Lot of children for children: see *ITA* VI for these formulas and instructions. Robert adds the Lot of Fortune as well, which makes sense. According to Robert, the Lot of Fortune pertains to the inceptor (or the one who undertakes the matter), and the Lot of the particular matter to the thing asked about.

(with none of them being in an assembly or opposition),[5] and also lest [the sign] it possesses be in the Ascendant or the place of the matter or the Lot of the matter. For [the Tail] corrupts affairs with the causes of low-class people, namely it being wrested away by ignoble people.[6]

§146. On the other hand, one should rejoice if the fortunate ones should appear in the Ascendant or in the place of the question, or [in] the pivots. For the greater fortunate one[7] reinforces everything whose perfection you are inquiring about; also, the lesser fortune[8] establishes and stimulates jokes and women, appetite, even the ornamentation of clothing, gold and gems, even loves and what is like these.

§147. Moreover, we warn you to beware in every question lest the Moon ever occupy the Ascendant, because from that very place she always turns against affairs generally. But the Sun never does so from there: rather, he brings about the matter and removes delay.

§148. Again, it seems one should take the greatest care lest the infortunes hold onto the Ascendant and the pivots, particularly [those infortunes] ruling over the unlucky [places]: namely, the sixth and twelfth and eighth. For if an infortune rules over the eighth, the danger of death, the helpers of his enemies, and hard captivity threaten [him]. Also, the lord of the sixth encourages that one will have to beware the same thing from enemies and slaves and a long-term illness, and from a brief captivity, and sometimes even from four-footed animals. Again, if the same [infortune] has rulership over the twelfth, it signifies punishments, being afflicted by loss of hope and labor, even enemies [and] a captivity of moderate length. Again, with it claiming the rulership of the second, he will undergo loss because of money and friends, even a marriage [or] drinking.[9]

§149. We even order you to take diligent care that a diurnal Ascendant and straight sign be ascending in a diurnal [chart], but a nocturnal and

---

[5] Reading for the transliteration of the Arabic, *alestime vel iztichel.*
[6] Although the Tail can indicate things and people of low status, Hugo is probably adding a bit too much into the delineation. Robert puts it more generally: "it makes the matter unfortunate, subtracts, weakens, impedes, and, drawing it out, aggravates it.
[7] That is, Jupiter.
[8] That is, Venus.
[9] This list of indications for the second house can be viewed in terms of its whole-sign angles: money (the second itself), friends (eleventh), and the financial aspects of a marriage (eighth, the second from the seventh). drinking or partying (fifth),

straight one in the night.[10] Likewise the Sun and Moon as well.[11] Remember to make sure that the lords which we stated before, be strengthened in all things we wrote before. Also, none doubts but that the counsel of the stars and the benefit of the signs happens according to their status and the signification of [their] nature.

---

[10] Reading with Robert for Hugo's choppy sentence. This assumes one wants a long process or result, since signs of straight ascension make things last longer.
[11] This probably means that the sect light should be in a sign of the appropriate gender/sect, and in a sign of straight ascensions.

# CHAPTER 5: ON RELATIONS BETWEEN PEOPLE

## Chapter 5.1: Significators & overview

§150. Those things which are confirmed to happen most frequently between two people, are: controversies, any causes of action,[1] dissensions, wars, friendships, [and] betrothals.[2] Therefore, once a question has arisen concerning these and what is like these, one must note that the Ascendant itself signifies the agent of the whole affair (namely of the cause of action). But the seventh [signifies] him with whom the matter is done.[3]

§151. But the Midheaven suggests the mediator between each. But if a back-and-forth matter of controversy is being undertaken, it claims the judge; if a negotiation, a helper in the matter. If about nuptials, the bridesman;[4] if the action is about war, victory and success; if partnership and friendship, it regulates the cause of their benevolence and esteem. Also, the fourth sign determines the end of the question.[5]

§152. Likewise, the Moon assumes the mediator of the two. But the star from which she recedes, [indicates] the chief of the cause;[6] but the one to which she applies, the adversary. Also, the lord of the Moon decides the end of the matter.

---

[1] Especially in the sense of legal causes.
[2] For more on these, see Chs. 10-12 for wars, Ch. 22 for friendships, and Ch. 20 for betrothals.
[3] This description assumes that the querent is the one undertaking the action (or thinking about undertaking it).
[4] Traditionally, this is a man who arranges (and often pays for) the wedding, usually on behalf of the groom; sometimes this is the one who walks the bride down the aisle and presents her.
[5] See §§165-72 below.
[6] That is, the querent (assumed to be the one initiating the action).

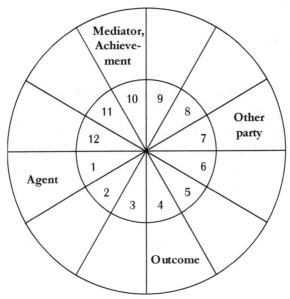

**Figure 45: Angles of the chart & parties in relationships**

## Chapter 5.2: The agent of the action

§153. Therefore, the force of the Ascendant and the one from who the Moon recedes (in the way it was described above with respect to strength),[7] provided that the Ascendant obtains some likeness with the nature of the quaesited matter,[8] and if it acquires the comfort of the fortunate ones (namely their presence or regard) or some shared bearing,[9] [and] even [if] the strength and prosperity of the Moon [is present],[10] they convey victory in the cause, and success to its agent—particularly if the weakness and misfortune of the seventh and the one with whom the Moon's application comes to be, is discovered.

§154. Even the lord of the Midheaven and the Midheaven itself seems to confirm this if the prosperity and robustness of each is made clear. And let there be a regard between these and the Ascendant and its lord, or some

---

[7] See the end of §139, §§63-72, §§77-78, and *ITA* IV.2.
[8] See §142 above.
[9] See §144 above.
[10] See esp. *ITA* IV.5.

bearing of this kind. Also, the Moon manages the same thing as the Midheaven does, if sustained by her witnesses.

### Chapter 5.3: The judge or mediator

§155. Again, the robustness and luckiness of the lord of the Midheaven [indicates] the kindness of the mediator in those things which pertain to him. But his regard (or some bearing) proves the truth of the judgment. Moreover, with the lord of the Midheaven being corrupted, the judge's fraud is diagnosed.

§156. But [if the lord of the Midheaven is] fortunate and weak, it bequeaths trustworthiness to the judge, but removes the effect and power of the judgment. Moreover, it being unlucky and strong testifies to the power of frauds and trickery. The same [lord] being retrograde [indicates] he is uncertain, and wavering [in] what he should do about the judgment, nor does he allow what is suitable to have the power of coming to pass.

§157. Moreover, if Mars is the lord of the Midheaven[11] [and] regarded by Venus, it corrupts the judge with a bribe. Being regarded by Saturn adds that he is underhanded, with one thing in his heart, but another in his mouth. Being in the regard of Jupiter, he wants a just judgment but it shows that he is powerless. In the regard of Mercury,[12] [it signifies] astute orators and those of great counsel, but with no perseverance in it. Regarded by the Sun, it introduces a royal judge.

§158. Again, with the Moon obtaining the rulership of the Midheaven, [and estranged from the fortunes],[13] although she introduces many changes and wrongfully [introduces] various little annoyances, still she suggests it is brought together [even though] with public bribes—unless the regard of the fortunate ones reinforces [her]. In this way one will even have to judge the mediator according to its counsel.

---

[11] Adding with *Judges* §7.50; Burnett's version omits "if…is the lord of the Midheaven."
[12] Reading the rest of this sentence with Robert.
[13] Adding with Robert.

## Chapter 5.4: The other party

§159. Also, the lord of the seventh gets a judgment similar to the lord of the Ascendant, in those things which belong to its own signification.

## Chapter 5.5: The origin of a war[14]

§160. Again, with a question being made about war, should the lord of the Midheaven or the Moon be seen to rejoice in (or rather support) the lord of the Ascendant or of the west, or the star from which the Moon recedes, or the one with whom her application comes to be (I say, whichever one of these two [it was])—without a doubt it enriches [that side] with the triumph of victory. Even the friendly support of Mars means the same thing. But the equality of each [significator] introduces the hope of peace, if their lords enjoy the regard (and a friendly one) of the other.[15] But the degree of the mutual application makes manifest the time of making the peace firm (likewise the Moon assumes [the role of] the mediator between the two).

§161. Moreover, if Mars could corrupt either of [these places] or their lord, particularly from an adverse aspect, it threatens death in the present war, but [the degrees of] their mutual application asserts the terminal point of death. Again, Mars in a pivot indicates a public death in the war. Again, Mars corrupting either one from the eighth, frequently teaches he is going to die while sleeping at night.[16] But if the corruption by Mars were made from the second, it introduces the death of the masters [of the war] and their co-helpers, with fraudulence—especially with Mars [not][17] holding onto a share or possession[18] in the second.

§162. Also, the figure of the sign which Mars possesses, describes the murderer. But with Mars corrupting [a significator] from the sixth, provided that the sign represents a wild animal, he incurs death from a beast of that kind. But corruption made from the twelfth threatens destruction after

---

[14] This section really seems to pertain to feuding and violent conflicts in general, not a national war complete with standing armies.

[15] For more on peacemaking, see Ch. 10.2.

[16] Robert adds: "and the time of it will be perceived from the quantity of the degrees of their conjunction."

[17] Adding with Robert.

[18] *Faciem* (drawing on Niermeyer's medieval usage). That is, if Mars is peregrine in the second.

difficulties from enemies. Again, [corruption] from [the four] signs which
naturally make a regard to others ([that is], from the pivots), [he will in no
way escape the danger of destruction].[19] Should the corruption by Mars
proceed from the ninth, it testifies he achieves death by a public judgment of
the law, or some journey or foreign travel, sometimes a hunt or some
plundering[20] or what is like these.

§163. But if [Mars were] in the ninth [and] the house of the Moon would
be exhibited [there], law and social custom give a capital sentence. And so,
the same house being that of Venus, the law indicates death because of [his]
libido or joking, and sexual immorality carried out with women. If the same
[place] would be found to be a house of Mars, it confers destruction on some
journey. If however [it is] a house of Saturn, he incurs death by fraud and
flattery. Again, if the house of Mercury comes to be in the same [place], he
will lay down [and die] because of words and books.

§164a. Mars corrupting [a significator] from the fifth: he meets death
because of children [or a change of affection].[21] Also, from the eleventh[22] it
signifies that he dies from the king's underofficials or his own friends, [and
this apart from what was hoped for].[23] Again, the misfortune of Mars being
recognized from the third, brothers or some journey or a common judgment
of the law introduces the cause of death.

§164b.[24] Even the lord of the seventh (with the attacking stated above),
being unlucky in all things which belong to its signification, gets a similar
judgment.

§164c. The retrogradation of either one of them teaches that the man
whom that significator indicates, is going to be conquered.

---

[19] Adding missing parts from Robert.
[20] *Depraedatione.* Or, "devastation." The sense is of marauding soldiers traveling from place
to place.
[21] Reading with Robert for Hugo's "or his own will." Hugo repeats *propriae voluntatis* in the
eleventh house as well, which leads me to believe there has been a manuscript error.
[22] Reading with Robert for *decimo.*
[23] Again, reading with Robert for Hugo's "an attack of his own will, [or] because of some
expected thing."
[24] So far, al-Kindī has described Mars's effect on the lord of the Ascendant (namely, the
querent); here he simply means that the same rules apply to harming the lord of the
seventh (the opponent).

## Chapter 5.6: The end of the matter

§165. Also, the status of the fourth and its lord, even the lord of the Moon, will not be silent about the end of the affair. For, they being made fortunate, and forceful, grant a glorious end for the victor. Moreover, their unluckiness and lack of forcefulness [signifies] the contrary. Also, the corruption of the fourth, even a corrupted lord of the Moon (namely so that they would be cadent), signify he is deposed from [his] honor. Moreover, being corrupted by an assembly,[25] they promise death or deposing, [or] poverty, and because of this he will flee from his fatherland.

§166. But corruption made from another place leads harm into the body according to the nature and place and [bodily] part belonging to the one making it unfortunate. Also, the lord of the fourth and of the Moon being affected by these evils, leads these evils into the soul, while they present the fear and anxiety of these things. Likewise, the forcefulness[26] of the lord[27] of the fourth [and] even [the lord] of the Moon being strong (namely that they would be eastern), declares his promotion and long deliberation.

§167. Likewise, Saturn as the lord of the fourth, being eastern, robust and strong, even the lord of the sign which the Moon is holding onto being likewise eastern and strong, promises to render long premeditation, slaves, steadiness, tolerance, the building of cities, the inhabitants of wilderness.[28] Also, Jupiter signifies his justice, piety, firm counsel, introducing respectable ceremonies, [and] enriching the people when he survives. Likewise, Mars retaining the power of the fourth and the rulership of the Moon,[29] [indicates] he is bold, a leading person in society, an effecter of affairs. Also, the strength of Mars conveys fear [of him] to his enemies, and their flight.

§168. Again, the Sun being in full control (and not Mars), establishes many people subject to him, glory, power, being feared, a prominent position, and steadiness of [his] command. However, Venus obtaining this place instead of the Sun ([and] being strengthened by the aforesaid supports) shows that he reigns over the benevolence of strong people,[30] dramatic

---

[25] Probably with a malefic planet (especially Mars), but possibly with the Sun, too.

[26] *Valetudo*, which has connotations of being robust and healthy.

[27] Reading *domini* with Robert's meaning, for *dominus*.

[28] Or, "deserts."

[29] This probably should not read that he rules both, but that he rules the fourth and *in addition* that the lord of the Moon is strong.

[30] *Fortium benevolentiam.*

roles,[31] gifts, drinking parties. Moreover, should Mercury be considered strong (instead of Venus) as was stated before, it makes him excel over [legal] cases, studies, ingenuity, handling tools,[32] writings, and better yet incentives for learning.

§169. Also, the [if] the Moon assumes this [role] instead of Mercury, she manages power, legations, the discourse[33] of messengers, the transmitting of services,[34] even the gratitude of the whole people.

§170. Also, the weakness of one [or another] of these lessens the causes of the aforesaid as well as the quantity of the matter.

§171. Again, the quickness of the one who corrupts the fourth and the lord of the Moon, asserts that [the end] is near, but [its] slowness that it will happen late. But if it is direct, it means [the directness] of it or of the matter; but retrograde, it signifies disagreement in matters and that one of them is in conflict.[35] Also,[36] if fortunate ones would perform in the role of the unfortunate ones, you will judge the promised things in terms of luckiness just as was stated above about the unfortunate ones.

§172. If however it happens otherwise than as was said above with respect to what the fortunate or unfortunate ones carry out, and the strength [of the significators] is diminished—namely so that it would sometimes happen to be more, sometimes less—in whatever way these [planets'] difference bore itself, remember to judge it in the way their admixture (shown above) has taught.

---

[31] Reading *operibus ludicris* with Robert for Hugo's *officia* ("jobs, duties").

[32] *Exercitium* (following a medieval meaning). But this could also refer to various spiritual or intellectual exercises and disciplines. Both tools and these other things are equally Mercurial.

[33] Or perhaps, "traversals."

[34] Or perhaps, "gifts, duties, benefits" (*munerum*). Robert reads, "generosity."

[35] This might also mean "diversity in the things, and that one of them is conflicted" (*rerum diversitatem et alternum earum conflictum*).

[36] Reading this sentence with *Judges* §7.168 for Burnett's version.

# CHAPTER 6: ON THEFT[1]

## Chapter 6.1: General significators; significator of the thief[2]

§173. Whenever you are eager to investigate something about a theft, you must note that the Ascendant signifies the owner of the thing taken by theft; but the seventh [signifies] the thief, also the tenth the king, but the fourth the place where the hidden thing is being held. Concerning all of these, we think one must handle it according to the nature [and status][3] of their lords.

§174. But if a peregrine star (namely, one appearing remote from[4] its own house) were found to be in the Ascendant, particularly [if it were] the lord of the seventh, it signifies the robber. If however it were not in the Ascendant but in the tetragon of the Ascendant (namely, it held onto the Midheaven or the fourth, or even the seventh), if, I say, it were in some tetragon of the Ascendant, it will always designate the robber.[5]

## Chapter 6.2: The physical appearance of the thief:
## Saturn as an example[6]

§175a. The form of the thief is described [according to][7] the figure of stars appearing in these places (namely the pivots), even [the figure] of the sign which holds onto [the pivot].

§175b-176a. So, Saturn in a masculine sign ([that is], of his own sect),[8] and western, indicates a thief that is an old man, pallid or red or black, whose speech is sparing, a wide forehead, large head, foul face, and cunning. Also, in a female sign and female quarter, it portends a castrated man or poor old woman according to the aforesaid form.

---

[1] For this chapter, cf. al-Rijāl II.34. Lilly draws liberally from al-Kindī's rules (but probably as presented in al-Rijāl), in *CA* pp. 330ff.

[2] See also §203b below.

[3] Adding with al-Rijāl.

[4] That is, "peregrine."

[5] I.e., a peregrine planet in one of the angles will show the thief more immediately than the lord of the seventh does, even though the latter is still important.

[6] For more on planetary physiognomy, see *ITA* V.1-7.

[7] Reading *describitur* and *secundum* with Robert for *describit*.

[8] Robert: *ḥalb*.

§176b. Being eastern and in the beginning of his easternness conveys an adolescent [in body but] an old man in his mind, and a sweet look. But in the middle of easternness, a young man imitating old people in sense. But at the end [of his easternness], it shows a man of already completed age, and instructed by old men.

§177. Apart from the aforewritten signification, Saturn in Aries bestows a discordant voice, pale and large eyes, eyebrows that stand out, a thick face, a straight nose, sometimes even cheeks bearded in a youthful way, thin hair on the head, large buttocks, slender shins, [and foolish].[9]

§178. In Taurus, apart from his own proper signification, a broad forehead, thick voice and top of the nose, ugly lips, thinness of hair on the head, a curved stature, large eyes, loose skin on the throat, fullness of the hips and sides, and even the feet, an anxious life, making a living with labor—is [all] designated by Saturn, whose unluckiness [in the chart][10] will seem to have added the most extreme misfortunes.

§179. But with Saturn appearing in Gemini: a good mind is designated,[11] [and] a loud voice, respectable counsel, eloquence, broadness of the shoulders, beautiful lips, beautiful hair on the head—unless baldness impedes that (which if this happened, he remains beautiful in the remaining things)— long deliberation, even fraud.

§180. The same Saturn in Cancer connects black pupils to his own proper signification, [as well as] little dark spots on the face,[12] a broad forehead, dry limbs, large and foul feet and hands, unsteadiness of the mind.

§181. Moreover, in Leo an anxious life[13] is designated, [and] sunkenness of the eyes, an even and large nose, broad nostrils, ugliness of the lips, a short and swollen neck, a fat chest and arms, appropriate buttocks, thin ankles, sometimes a swollen belly, hairy shoulders and neck, boldness, authority, steady speech, even gluttony.

§182. Moreover, Saturn in Virgo assigns benevolence, a large head,[14] a hairy body (especially the arms and feet), long deliberation, fawning, evenness of speech.

---

[9] Adding with al-Rijāl.

[10] That is, in a poor condition.

[11] Al-Rijāl: "with morals mixed of crookedness and those who are shifty."

[12] Al-Rijāl: "a small face," assigning marks on the face to Saturn in Leo.

[13] Robert: "a grim face" (*vultu trucem*); al-Rijāl: "marks on the face."

[14] Reading with Robert and al-Rijāl for Hugo's "neck" (possibly a mistaken transposition of *cervix* and *vertex*).

§183. Also, in Libra it shows a narrow head, length of the nose and neck, black hair on the head, thin shins, narrow sides, high buttocks, long fingers, [long] nails coming from the hands, and nobility on top of that.

§184. Also, in Scorpio Saturn designates straight eyebrows, much thick hair on the head and divided on the forehead, large and foul hands and feet, a saffron color,[15] small eyes, short sides, long feet; besides these, malice.

§185. But in Sagittarius, ample eyebrows that stand out are designated, [and] a long face, a broad mouth and nose, fatness of the shins, flowing hair and much of it, a hairy nape of the neck, a somewhat curved neck, large buttocks; and besides this, arrogance [and very lazy].[16]

§186. In Capricorn, a drawn-out face is denoted by Saturn, [and] seriousness of the eyes,[17] a thin voice, narrowness of the eyebrows, foul extremities of the feet and hands, sexual impurity, rare or nonexistent chastity, a black or red color, stiffness of the hair, a hairy body.

§187. However, in Aquarius: a large head, long face [which is] broad above and narrow below. His profession has to do with water and moist things, like sailing and what pertains to ships and the sea (such as being a fisherman or cook or bearer of water, and what is like these).

§188. Also, with the same Saturn occupying Pisces (provided that he is strong and made fortunate by the lucky ones, and received [by them]),[18] it indicates nobleness of the blood, no matter how low and unremarkable [he seems]. [But] being unsound[19] or namely being struck[20] or corrupted somehow by an infortune, it proves his parents have come from nobility,[21] but he is bad; and [it signifies] the beauty of his eyes, a wide mouth, uneven teeth, a rough body,[22] self-control in his speech, but [also] gluttony.

---

15 Al-Rijāl: "green-saffronish," possibly a kind of light olive or citrine.

16 Adding with al-Rijāl.

17 Robert reads, "soft eyes" (*mollibus oculis*).

18 Reading with Robert for Hugo's "namely, ascending or regarded." Al-Rijāl reads, "in the prosperity of good aspects."

19 Robert reads, "unfavorable" (*aversus*).

20 Reading *azukt* as a transliteration based on *ṣakkata*. Robert reads simply, "harmed."

21 Al-Rijāl adds that they have lost their noble standing.

22 Robert says he has an evenly balanced body, al-Rijāl that he has a quick body.

### Chapter 6.3: The Moon showing marks & blemishes

§189. Also, the Moon in the seventh, while she claims many dignities [over] the place of the peregrine or exiled star which appears in the Ascendant or in one of the pivots, and [provided that] she is lucky, [then], should she be in Aries, it shows a beautiful mark on the head, or the head or face itself is handsome. Also, appearing in Taurus and being as was said above, it bequeaths a mark or ornament to the [neck. In Gemini, the shoulders and arms. In Cancer],[23] the chest and breast. In Leo, it seems to concede one to the stomach and the lower belly up to the pubes. But in Virgo it ascribes one to the back and hips.[24]

§190. Also, that same Moon appearing in Libra as we said before, does not remove the mark and ornament from the flanks [and] lower belly up to the male organs. Also in Scorpio, it enriches the male organs and genitalia with this gift. In Sagittarius, the buttocks. In Capricorn, the knees and lower part of the thighs. Also in Aquarius, she is accustomed to bless the shins with a mark or ornament. In Pisces, she does not remove it from the feet.

§191.[25] But on the contrary, the Moon being corrupted or unlucky in the aforesaid places, portends that there is a blemish or deformity in the places enumerated above. Moreover, if the star making this misfortune worse[26] were adding in course, it causes this increase to overflow in that blemish. But if this unluckiness was being broadened by a star which is increasing in computation,[27] the increase descends into the proper limbs.

On the other hand, if a star diminished in course had supplied this misfortune, it does not repel the harm of this ugliness, [or] the diminution of the limbs.[28] [And if it were diminished in number, the foulness will be diminished in the limb.][29]

---

[23] Adding with Robert.

[24] Higher up, near the waist (*costis*).

[25] This paragraph is a bit unclear to me, because I am not sure whether al-Kindī's vocabulary matches that of Abū Ma'shar and al-Qabīsī in *ITA* II.0-4. Al-Kindī is opposing variations in *course* versus those in *computation/number*. I suggest that changes in course refer to speed, whereas changes in computation/number refer *either* to a planet is direct or retrograde, *or* to a planet's relation to its apogee (if the latter, then probably being close to its apogee makes the marks raised above the skin, while being close to its perigee makes them sink down).

[26] Reading *demutat* with *Judges* for Burnett's *demittat*.

[27] Al-Rijāl: "number."

[28] *Search* Ch. II.1.8 actually has a clearer reading, based on Robert's version of this section: "But she bears this beauty provided that she is fortunate. For, corrupted, [she signifies]

But if it would be going forward in its average course, it manages the beauty mark or defects, and the limbs, without increase or diminution. [If it were equal in number, the mark will be flat, on the surface of the skin of the member, neither high nor deep.][30]

§192a. This above-written understanding of the form can be observed not only for a thief, but even for other people.

§192b. In fact, the Moon being found in the Ascendant permits the [same] or something just like what was in Aries; also, if she appears in the second, she reveals the kind of indication such as that in Taurus. And so, one will have to judge for all places, just as in their opposite signs, up until the judgment comes to an end with respect to the feet, just as was done for Pisces.

§193. But that same Moon in a male sign indicates that the mark is on the right side; in a female sign, the left side.

## Chapter 6.4: Other planets as significators of the thief

§194-196a. Likewise, with some [other] star obtaining the signification of a thief, if Jupiter should have the role of Saturn,[31] it means a white and pale-ish person. But if it were a man, his beard [is] rounded. But the eyes of each sex [would be] black; [in morals], temperate, peaceful, and noble. However, with Mars taking the place of Jupiter, he is portrayed as red-haired, reddishness in the face (no matter what his color is), a round face, small forehead, a sharp look, eyebrows joined together,[32] thin and shiny hair on his head, a quick tread, and a show-off. Again, the Sun taking on Mars's role teaches he is white, a bright face, ready for hunting or augury, or most famous in the medical art, sometimes even a cook or a water-attendant.[33] But if Venus should perform the Sun's role: a white color, lively, ruddy, beauty of the eyes, large pupils, average stature, benevolent; large buttocks and legs are

---

ugliness in those places in terms of the amount and quality of the one corrupting her, [and] in the computation of [her] adding or subtracting [in light]."

[29] Adding with al-Rijāl.

[30] Adding with al-Rijāl.

[31] That is, if he were the significator instead of Saturn (see above).

[32] Al-Rijāl has the eyebrows curving upwards, "like the horns of the Moon."

[33] Al-Rijāl reads, "a singer or diviner, or a physician, or repairer of fabrics."

indicated. But Mercury professes a nimbleness of body, a thin beard, long face, white but reddish, his temples even shorn of hair.[34]

§196b. Also, it is good for the individual things which were said above to be mixed[35] with the signs which [the planets] are holding onto, just as was done above with respect to Saturn.

### Chapter 6.5: Other information on the thief & his location

*Chapter 6.5.1: The thief's future*

§197. A star which was found to be in the Ascendant, corrupted by the lord of the Midheaven:[36] if it was Saturn himself who was corrupting [it], it demonstrates the thief is found to be held in prison. But Saturn being slow and in a fixed and straight sign, asserts the long duration of the captivity; regarded by the lord of the house of death, it threatens death in prison.

§198. Likewise, Mars getting the role of Saturn, and either [Mars] being the lord of the house of death (or [its] partner),[37] or (apart from his own misfortune) [Mars] being regarded by the lord of the house of death, and the lord of the house of the star which obtains the signification of the thief being in a sign cut in parts,[38] it adds death.

§199. But that same significator being corrupted by both Saturn and Mars, permits him to be found and tortured until his blood is shed. Likewise if Saturn bore himself in this way [and were slow in motion],[39] he prolongs the captivity. Likewise, the significators of death being observed in this likeness,

---

[34] Robert adds "subtlety" and "honesty." Al-Rijāl says "talkative" and "vehement."

[35] *Obtemperare*, which normally means "submit" or "obey," but the meaning here is mixture.

[36] Al-Rijāl reads "if you found the planet which was in the Ascendant, or the lord of the Midheaven, to be made unfortunate…" But the parallel statement in §200 does not quite match. Therefore I have retained Robert's and Hugo's formulations.

[37] That is, "having some dignity" there (Robert). Al-Rijāl reads "or a partner of it in the house of death."

[38] Probably the signs sometimes called "defective," such as Aries, Taurus, Scorpio, and Capricorn. Such signs are incomplete, or divided, or show some defect: the neck of Aries is broken, only the first half of Taurus exists, the claws of Scorpio are missing (actually they form the pans of Libra), and Capricorn is composed of two different types of animals.

[39] Adding with al-Rijāl.

and moreover retreating or being remote,[40] signifies death in prison after long tortures, or he is going to die through the severity of the torture, under the blows themselves.

§200. But the exiled[41] star which obtains the Ascendant being fortunate and lucky, [and] particularly being blessed by the lord of the Midheaven, [signifies] liberation. [If] the luckiness is introduced by the lord of the Sun, it is necessary that he be freed by royal decree.[42] But that same [star] taking this prosperity from the lord of the eleventh, introduces liberation by the friends of the owner of the thing taken by theft, or by royal underofficials. Also, with that luckiness being taken from the lord of the twelfth, he is freed by the enemies[43] of the owner. Moreover, with its welfare being taken from the lord of the Ascendant, he will be released by the personal wish of the owner himself. Also, by the lord of the second, he is freed through the helpers of the owner himself, and his money.

§201. Moreover, should the gift of this prosperity come to be from the lord of the third, the brothers and friends of the owner of the missing thing, or the piety[44] of the owner himself,[45] releases him. By the lord of the fourth, he is made free by the parents or compatriots of the owner, in light of an ancient familial tie. But the prosperity being arranged by the lord of the fifth, the children of the one who has lost [the thing], or things which are bestowed, [and] sometimes even a friendship[46] which has been entered into, introduce the cause of the liberation.

§202. If this same thing happens from the lord of the sixth, he will often escape because of slaves or four-footed animals. Also, from the lord of the seventh, he is freed because of a spouse and commerce or adversaries. By the lord of the eighth, he is made free because of someone's death or inheritance

---

[40] Al-Rijāl has them "stable and appearing": I can see stable meaning "in fixed signs," but I am not sure whether "appearing" means "eastern," or what that would even add.
[41] That is, peregrine (al-Rijāl).
[42] Reading for *inventu*, which means "discovery" or "devising." At any rate, the authorities or the king himself will free the thief.
[43] Reading *inimicis* with Robert for *amicis*.
[44] Reading with al-Rijāl for Hugo's uninspired "goodness." The third house is a spiritual house in traditional astrology, and so al-Rijāl's term is better.
[45] Reading with Robert and al-Rijāl for Hugo's "thief." If it were the thief's piety it would probably indicate something like an early parole or reduced sentence due to sincere repentance and good behavior.
[46] Al-Rijāl reads "service" or "servitude" (*servitia*), which sounds like working off a debt.

or the assistants of [the owner's] partner[47] or commerce. Likewise, the good fortune being conveyed by the lord of the ninth releases captives by [flight or][48] some foreign journey or judgment of the law.

### Chapter 6.5.2: Whether it will be made public

§203a.[49] Moreover, the thing will be made public and come out into the open, if the lord of the significator of thief and the luminaries regard each other and the significator, and especially if in addition they regarded each other. But with these aspects being denied, no knowledge of the theft or thief will be given. But if the lord of the significator would regard the lights from any of the pivots, after being hidden and the cloud [of secrecy], it will be uncovered and in the open. And commonly if there were many of these regards from the pivots it will be especially declared [in the open], but from the cadents, not at all.

### Chapter 6.5.3: The significator of the thief[50]

§203b. And so, the significator of the robber is discerned in this art when an exiled star[51] is situated in the Midheaven; if one were peregrine in the eighth, it should be noted; but if not, a peregrine one which is in the fourth should be appointed. Again, if there were none [there], one which traverses in the second should be taken. With none even appearing in that place, [your] intention should be directed to the lord of the seventh.

### Chapter 6.5.4: Whether the thieves are one or many

§204. If therefore it pleased [you] to settle whether it is one [thief] or many, the sign of the above-determined significator should be noted. But [that sign] appearing firm, particularly being straight and of few offspring and a simple form, indicates it was one. Likewise in a double-bodied one or one

---

[47] Reading with al-Rijāl. Robert also includes "the allies of enemies," also a proper signification.
[48] Adding with al-Rijāl.
[49] This part of the section is only in Robert.
[50] Cf. also §173 above, whose list of options is somewhat different.
[51] That is, peregrine.

of much offspring and a manifold form, especially if many peregrine stars would accompany the significator itself, they suggest many thieves.

### Chapter 6.5.5: Where the thief is

§205. Again, if a question is had as to whether he is in that same region or has already fled, the significator of the theft itself [or]⁵² a star in the beginning of some sign (the preceding [sign] already having been left behind), does not deny that his flight has been made very recently. Should the same significator—or any star which enjoys some portion of the signification of the thief—be retreating under the rays, or should any partner of the same duty be separated from the lord of the Ascendant and apply itself to some [star] in the eighth or sixth or twelfth, it suggests the same.

§206. Moreover,⁵³ with the significator of the thief or its lord being found in [some] quarter of the circle, but not in the [same quarter] in which the significator of the one who lost the thing is, it gives notice that his departure has recently been made (or is currently being made) from the region. Being remote or cadent from a pivot, and being wholly estranged from the significator⁵⁴ of the owner of the thing taken in the theft, it asserts the aforesaid flight. Moreover, [if] the companion⁵⁵ of the significator of the one who has lost the thing⁵⁶ [were] put in that same quarter, it no longer allows him to be absent.

[Robert]:⁵⁷ But, withdrawing from its own sign or from the quarter of the significator of the east, [and] likewise it or the lord of the theft departing or being cadent, also [if] it or any planet which is very powerful in its own place would be going out from under the rays or departing from the east, [and it is] an associate of the lord of the eighth

---

⁵² See the next sentence.

⁵³ See a similar treatment in §259.

⁵⁴ Reading *duce* with *Judges* for Burnett's *vice*. I take this to mean that it is both cadent from the pivots and in aversion from (i.e., not configured by sign with) the lord of the Ascendant. But

⁵⁵ This may mean "the domicile lord" of the significator. Compare with al-Rijāl excerpt below.

⁵⁶ That is, if some planet which partners with the lord of the Ascendant (probably by an aspect within orbs) were there.

⁵⁷ Robert adds much more information, but he departs so much from al-Rijāl I am tempted to think he might have added the extra material himself.

or twelfth or second, it announces the departure of the thief from the region. His distance is perceived by the quantity of the departure and exiting of the aforesaid [planets].

[al-Rijāl]: If you even found the significator of the robber or its lord in some quarter of the figure, and the significator of the stolen thing in another quarter, say that he has going out from his house; likewise if you found it cadent from an angle and not aspecting the significator of the stolen thing, you will say that he has gone out from his home. But if the significator of the thief were with the significator of the stolen thing in one quarter, say that he is alone in some house.

§207. Again, the star which shows the signification over his travel (or rather, his flight) manages [the issue of] into what part of the world he is going to take himself, or which has already taken the fleeing man in. Even note the sign in which it traverses, [since] it will not be silent [about this matter]. In a fiery sign, it testifies he is going into parts of the east; in a watery one, the north; in an airy one, the west; in an earthy one too, it suggests the south.

§208. In the same way, discernment of the quarters of the circle is necessary for the same thing. For, if the significator of the fleeing person would appear in the eastern quarter, [it indicates] the east; in the western one, the west; in the northern one, the north; but in the southern one, it decrees the south. Also, the eastern part is bounded by the [space] from the Midheaven to the Ascendant.

§209. The southern one is stretched from the seventh to the Midheaven. Likewise the western one is asserted to be from the pivot of the earth to the seventh. The northern one is left over, [and is] from the Ascendant to the pivot of the earth. And so, with a consideration of the quarter and the nature of the sign being had,[58] we will have to follow through with everything else.

---

[58] See Lilly's treatment in CA pp. 364-65, 391, and 393.

## Chapter 6.5.6: Where the thief's house is[59]

§210. Moreover, the work of the present observation undoubtedly completes the task of what part of the city the house (which the thief inhabits) would be found in, and the specific location of his habitation. For the sign in which the significator of the thief is staying, in its own part of the circle, promises the house is [there].

§211.[60] Which if perhaps you discovered it in the Ascendant, it confirms that the house is in the middle of the east. In the west, it leads it toward the west. In the Midheaven, in the middle of the southern direction.[61] But in the pivot of the earth, we are attracted to the middle of the north. Again, in the second, on the right of the east. In the twelfth shows the left [of the east]. In the eighth, the right side of the west. In the sixth, its left [side] is noted. But in the eleventh, the right [side] of the southern direction. However, in the ninth the left [side] should be sought. Finally, in the fifth it reveals the right side of the north; but in the third, it uncovers the left [side].

### The entrance to the thief's house

§212. Also, by this observation, the entrance of the house—[namely] in what part it showed itself to be—will be laid bare. Commend to [your] memory whether the Moon is in a pivot or after a pivot or remote from a pivot, just as we related above with respect to investigating the location of the house. I say that with her being in the sign which designates the theft, it proclaims the entrance to be in that direction which the Moon designates.[62] But if it were a firm [sign], it reveals just one [door]. But with her in a

---

[59] See also Ch. 7.3 below.

[60] This paragraph offers a rather unusual way of assigning cardinal directions. It seems that the pivots or angles all point to the proper cardinal directions (as they should), while all of the succeedent places indicate the "right" of that, and the cadent places the "left" of that. But this assignment does not make sense to me. One would rather expect, for instance, that the second house would be ENE (east-northeast) and the twelfth to be ESE (east-southeast), as in *CA* pp. 132-33.

[61] Omitting Hugo's "and it is said to be on the right."

[62] But al-Rijāl seems to take this a bit differently: "And judge just as we said before in the judgment about the direction of the door, by taking *eam* from the sign in which the significator of the theft is." *Eam* could mean "her" (the Moon), or the door (*ianuam*). In the latter case, the sign of the significator of the thief/theft shows the direction of the door, but the quadruplicity of the Moon would show where on the house the door is, or what kind of door it is. Lilly (*CA* pp. 347-48) takes al-Rijāl to mean the Moon in both cases.

double-bodied sign, it indicates many or at least two [doors]. Again, in a convertible sign, it confirms [that] it is at a height above the earth, and something is missing from it.

§213. Again, Saturn regarding that same sign indicates it is going to be partly broken or locked up, or black. Likewise, a regard of Mars (and not Saturn) portends it is partly burned or has some evidence of fire. But a friendly regard of Mars confirms there is much iron on the entrance. Again, the friendly regard of each (namely of [both] Saturn and Mars]) reveals it is wholly or for the most part iron. The Moon being corrupted or unlucky[63] means the entrance is worn out with age. But corrupted and defective in light[64] grants that no entrance is prominent.[65]

### *Location of the stolen goods in the thief's house*

§214. Again, you will know the indications which are contained within the home, thusly. The place of the Moon designates watery locations in the home (namely a well and where water tends to be kept in reserve). The place of Venus portends the bedroom and places dedicated to pleasures. The place of Mercury guards treasure, chests and where money is hidden away, even cupboards[66] and books. In the same way, the place of Saturn defends hidden places of the home, namely sewers[67] and stinking places. Also, the place of Mars looks after the kitchen and oven and fireplace, and where blood tends to be shed. The place of the Head holds onto ladders, stairs, and instruments for going upwards. Likewise the Tail defends the bases [of things], porches,[68] pillars, and stables.[69]

§215. Again, Mercury in a double-bodied sign [indicates] a storehouse; in a convertible one, its upper room;[70] finally, in a firm one it wholly refuses the

---

[63] This probably means an aspect from a square or opposition (or even assembly), but perhaps it includes being in detriment or fall.

[64] Robert has the door being inconspicuous only if the Moon is deficient in light, not both deficient and corrupted.

[65] *Imminet.* This must mean that it has no distinguishing features—or perhaps that it is not very visible? Lilly reads this as indicating that the door will be in the back, away from the main road.

[66] Or perhaps, any type of locked cabinet (*armarium*).

[67] Or, "drains" (*cloacas*).

[68] Or perhaps, porticoes (*porticas*), but that word is usually spelled *porticus*.

[69] Or perhaps, any dirty or cheap place on the property, such as a shed (*stabula*).

[70] *Solium.*

house.[71] A corresponding judgment is derived from all the signs [and planets].[72]

[Robert]: The number of these places is perceived from the places of the planets: for example, Mercury in a firm sign says a cupboard [with] one [door]; in a double-bodied one, two connected side-by-side; in a movable one, one above the other. The same goes for the rest of the planets in similar signs.

§216a. Moreover, Jupiter signifies that the house is the palace of the master, and the best [part] of that place.

§216b-217. [On the other hand, in the Midheaven they clarify the interior quality of the place.][73] Again, Jupiter and Venus in the Midheaven show a suitable garden. But Saturn in the Midheaven indicates a well or cistern or some destruction of the flooring in the middle of the home. Also, Mars in that same place testifies that in the middle of the home is a fire vent or where blood tends to be poured out. Likewise Mercury hoards money in the middle of the home, or the beasts of burden belonging to a dependent.[74] But the Sun in the Midheaven means an [elevated][75] well or couch in the middle of the home. Again, the Moon in the Midheaven guards outlets for draining water, even sometimes certain instruments like millstones and that kind of thing, which men tend to have in common use for fulfilling necessary [tasks].[76]

---

[71] Lilly (*CA* p. 353) reads this as "in a house that has no cellar nor other chamber, as many country houses have not."

[72] Reading more with Robert for Hugo's "derived from all houses of the atrium." My sense is that al-Kindī has added to the confusion, and this paragraph is trying to say two things: (1) that Mercury indicates storehouses; (2) that the quadruplicity of any planet (using Mercury as an example) indicates the kind of hiding-place within that type of room.

[73] Adding with Robert.

[74] *Clientelae iumenta*. But Robert reads: "or the place of one's personal property" (*peculii*, which has particular connotations of someone who is a dependent in the home). Perhaps al-Kindī is thinking of a stable boy or someone like that.

[75] Adding with Robert (*elatum*).

[76] *Quae in usus familiaris rei necessitate supplenda solet homines habere.* Robert adds: "a cellar or crypt of underground passages, and instruments of business."

## Chapter 6.6: The kind of stolen goods,
## from the bound lord of the Moon

*Venus as the bound lord*

§218. Further, from what was written above let a judgment be made about the kind of lost thing which is sought. [But the quality of what is stolen is indicated by the lord of the lunar bound, and the one looking at her.][77]

And so, if Venus would rule the lunar bound and is regarded by the Sun, it signifies coins or gold carved in some way, even fine fabrics and costly clothing of the best color, and that type of thing.

Moreover, Venus regarded by the Moon means a silver and sculpted object, or something of the best color, moreover linen or hemp fabrics, and what is of this kind.

§219. But she being regarded by Mercury indicates things of the best craftsmanship, namely clothing for which the wool of animate beings presents the material, such as purple fabric,[78] silk, and what is put together among the Arabs from the wool of sheep or goats with fine skill and calculation.[79]

In the regard of Mars, it declares the works of a goldsmith and that which is formed with the benefit of fire and iron.

She being regarded by Saturn indicates ancient things and those of an old form, and blotted[80] and a pale color—namely earthenware and what is sculpted in stone.

In the regard of Jupiter, it shows what is composed of the pelts[81] of animals, and what is like this.

*Mercury as the bound lord*

§220. Moreover, Mercury as the lord of the lunar bound takes on the signification of books. Regarded by the Sun, it introduces legal books with

---

[77] Adding from Robert.

[78] Tentatively reading *tyrium* for *tiriacium*. Hugo's *tiriacium* resembles *tiriaca* (from the Latin *Gr. Intr.* VII.4), which means "antidote," but does not make sense in this context.

[79] My gloss for *rata cautele…industria*. Al-Rijāl reads, "through geometry." Some exact method of piecing is meant here.

[80] Reading for *pene deletae*.

[81] Probably leaning more towards the use of fur, since Saturn usually indicates leather itself.

precepts written in them, or the manners and customs of kings, moreover golden things or books enclosed in gold.

But in the regard of the Moon, it means written papers of commerce, profit and those things which proceed from just profits in agriculture, recollections, sometimes even silver things.

Likewise, regarded by Venus he guards over books, painted or sculpted things and those of respectable form, often even golden or silver ones, and books enclosed in silver or gold.

§221. Moreover, to the above-stated things the regard of the Sun and Jupiter [together] add costly pearls in the treasures of kings, and things dedicated to the superstitious[82] ornaments of women, moreover good-smelling things (namely musk) and lapis lazuli, lignum aloes and what is just like those.

Likewise, the regard of Mars possesses the silver containers for books, and those same things inscribed with red-colored figures, and that kind of thing.

The regard of Jupiter indicates healing images[83] and books having the praises of the laws and the memorials of ancient forefathers.

Also, a regard from Saturn commends books of black magic inscribed with incantations, talismanic [images], augury, prophecies and what is like these, and those things with no truth;[84] moreover it shows that their container is iron or stone.

§222. Likewise, the regard of Venus and Mars [together] presents musical instruments (namely a lyre, psaltery, drum, symphonia and chorum, even the melodies of the tibia;[85] likewise vessels fit for drinking (namely chalices), and so on; and sometimes even wine itself.

Moreover, the regard of Venus and Jupiter [together] asserts the ornaments of women, namely clothing and things whose odor and color is the best, even healing images, necklaces, ladies' necklaces, earrings, collar-necklaces and ornaments which belong to them, namely clothing and what smells good.

§223. The regard of Mars with the rest divulges bronze vessels which are sculpted very well, which kings and other powerful people tend to import for their own use.

---

[82] This is probably refers to pendants or charms with saints' images and that sort of thing.
[83] *Species medicas.* Robert and al-Rijāl have theological books.
[84] Reading *nulla veritate.*
[85] A kind of reed flute.

Likewise, a regard from Mars and the Sun [together] indicates royal arms and those which nobles tend to use.

§224. But a regard coming forth from the Moon and Mars introduces instruments of agriculture, namely a plowshare, hoes, and that type of thing.[86]

In the same way, if a regard should proceed from Jupiter and Mars, it produces those things which royal dependents[87] tend to use: iron or jagged arms, and whatever borrows its form from the benefit of fire, and what sailors and soldiers take up in their own defense.

And so, in this way it seems the virtue of the regarding [planets] must be imparted according to their nature, whether it is one or more.

### Saturn as the bound lord

§225. Saturn retaining the rulership of the lunar bound [indicates] something earthen or akin to the nature of earth, or sculpted in stone, even put together with lead or iron.

Again, with him in the regard of the Moon, part of the things (taken by theft) which are sought supply maintenance for an attendant of water or a job in agriculture.

With him being regarded by the Sun, a certain part aids kings.

§226. A regard of Jupiter even concedes a certain part to the rest of the nobles.

Moreover, a regard of Mars leaves part for use in the kitchen, baths, furnaces, ovens, even often something necessary for use on a journey.

Likewise, the regard of Venus takes something left for the use of women, like seamstresses and so on.

If Mercury would make a regard with him, it brings about arrows, hunting spears, and the rest suchlike.

### Jupiter as the bound lord

§227. Again, Jupiter in possession of the rulership over the lunar bound, names unsculpted money and beautiful things made of the pelts of animals, [and] what tends to serve the uses of sages or judges.

---

[86] Al-Rijāl has simply, "an instrument adapted for war."
[87] This could mean something like the royal guard or personal retinue.

Also, in the regard of the Sun it particularly demonstrates precious money which customarily enriches the treasures of kings and decorates their ornaments; sometimes even animals of that kind.[88]

§228. Likewise, the regard of the Moon shows money of lesser value which commonly provides for the needs of the common people, even certain instruments made by men for the practice of justice,[89] often even animals (namely sheep and cows and that kind).

Also, the regard of Saturn denotes ancient money and that of no value, even instruments of agriculture, even cheap animals and their pelts, and the limbs of animals (like elephant teeth and everything of the class of ivory, not to mention even rope made of hair).

§229. In the regard of Mars, [it indicates] the defenses particularly of those who, with all hope of returning having been lost, enter into wars, and what is like these. Even those kinds of [instruments] of punishment which avenge certain people's wicked deeds and transgressions of the law or justice.

Also, the regard of Venus introduces the ornaments[90] of women by which they are adorned when entering temples because of lawful observances or prayer.

Likewise, the regard of Mercury does not leave behind divine books [and] instruments of books.

### Mars as the bound lord

§230. In the same way, Mars having full power over the lunar bound assigns iron, arms and what is put together with the help of fire.

Regarded by the Sun, he takes care of the military instruments of kings or the equipment of the royal kitchen.

Also, the regard of the Moon identifies everyday arms and those which pertain to messengers and traveling merchants.[91]

In the regard of Venus, it commends things painted and [what is] beautiful in decor.

§231. [Mars] even in the regard of Mercury confesses instruments for singing, catapults for walls and fortresses, and what is like these.

---

[88] That is, animals that kings tend to have. Perhaps something like peacocks or elephants or stags? Al-Rijāl reads, "noble animals."
[89] Probably instruments of punishment and torture.
[90] Reading for *ditamenta*.
[91] Or itinerant officials (*discursores*).

Likewise the regard of Saturn claims bows and clubs with which wicked deeds are punished, and what is like these.

The regard of Jupiter brings forth everyday arms, hard and harsh—namely breastplates and shields, and suchlike.

### Chapter 6.7: The quality of the object,
### from the bound lord of the Moon & the lord of the hour

§232. Finally, every star obtaining supremacy over the lunar bound, if the bound is being regarded by that lord,[92] it is believed to confirm the best nature of that same thing. Being eastern, a new thing; but western claims an old one. Near retrogradation or in its second station,[93] affirms [it is] in the middle, neither new nor old. Also, being direct conveys evenness of form and a good condition; retrograde, it will confess an uneven and distorted shape, and its breaking or corruption and blemish, and already being in conflict with its proper condition.

§233. Again, in a pivot [it indicates] the strength of its nature and good craftsmanship; [if] remote from a pivot, the unsoundness and ugliness of [its] nature is designated. But after a pivot settles it as being in the middle of strength and unsoundness, good composition and being ugly.

But being lucky, good, useful, proper; unlucky, the contrary.

Moreover, dwelling in a place proportionate to itself,[94] it renders a thing appropriate and agreeable in its category; but being foreign [to such a place], the contrary—or it renders it harmed[95] because of some accident.

§234. If therefore the aforesaid bound seems to be situated otherwise than with a regard from its own lord, the judgment must be changed according to the variation of the regard.

The lord of the hour seems to confirm this same thing as well, from its own direct motion or retrogradation, [just as] the lord of the lunar bound

---

[92] Reading with Robert, and also Hugo's reiteration below.
[93] Reading with al-Rijāl for Hugo's *longe post a retrogradatione remota*.
[94] Robert says "*ḥalb*," which is undoubtedly correct, but we should also consider its dignities.
[95] Reading with al-Rijāl for Hugo's *praeditam*.

does. For everything which it introduces into this judgment, imitates the manner of the lord of the bound of the Moon.[96]


## Chapter 6.8: Whether the object can be found[97]

§235-36. Moreover, the lord of the Ascendant with the lord of the lunar bound, or [with the lord] of the second, or with an application of [either] of them to it, seems to agree [that the object will be found]. For if its application comes to be with either or each of them, or[98] if the Moon would apply with them or with the lord of her own house, or if an application of the Sun would happen with the lord of his own house (while the Moon is being deprived of light)—or, the other way around, [namely] an application of the solar lord or the lunar bound or even the lord of the house, with the Sun—I say with an observation being had of all of the things above, the recovery of the missing things is confirmed—especially if the stellar significator appears in a pivot or after the pivots.

§237. Moreover, if the lord of the lunar bound or house, or even the lord of the second, would be applying to the lord of the Ascendant, they restore the lost things to the owner without the expense of labor[ing for it]. Moreover, an application of the Moon and of the lord of the Ascendant (or either of them) with the lord of the second, ([or] even, in imitation of these, the lords of the lunar bound and house), they grant that he will rejoice in finding the lost things he lamented over, after labor and the difficulties of worrying.[99]


## Chapter 6.9: When the goods would be returned[100]

§238.[101] Moreover, the degrees between the applying one and the one to which it applies itself suggest at what hour it leads back all or part of what

---

[96] Rewriting Hugo's awkward *Omnia quoque quae in aliquid huic iudicio probationis inducunt, praedictam ipsius Lunae terminalis domini modum immitantur.*
[97] See al-Rijāl II.34.
[98] Al-Rijāl reads, "and."
[99] Al-Rijāl nicely says instead, "the owner of the stolen thing will find the stolen goods through investigating and the quickness of [his] ingenuity."
[100] See al-Rijāl II.34.
[101] See also Ch. 2.6 on timing.

they signify to the owner (namely, it brings back the lost things). For the number of their degrees determines hours, days, weeks, [and] months, in turn. But the places of the application lay bare the same thing. For the degrees of the application appearing in convertible signs more frequently reckon hours [or] days for the delay.[102] In a sign of two bodies, weeks and months. In firm signs, they bring years to bear.

§239. Moreover, the significators for recovering this thing being in a pivot or after the pivots or remote from the pivots, determine the aforesaid. For, being cadent from the pivots, they return the lost things under present circumstances;[103] also, in the pivots they imitate [the cadents];[104] after the pivots they involve the thing in no moderate delay. But the judgment of the planets particularly claims this knowledge about the pivots of this question.

§240. Likewise, whenever the Moon or the lord of the Ascendant would reach the significator for finding the thing with its own body,[105] they give assent to the aforesaid things. For when either one of these would reach the significator (or it would [reach] one of them) they restore the lost things. If however it would reach them while retrograde, the lost things will be restored contrary to hope.[106] Direct, it soothes one's hope for the found things.

§241. Again, whenever the lord of the lunar bound would reach its own bound, or the lord of the house of the Moon or the lord of the house of money would reach their own houses, or even the ingress of one of them into the Ascendant, it claims the same.

Likewise,[107] look to see if the Lot of Fortune had some testimony with the lord of the Ascendant or with the Moon: because when it applied to[108] any of them, or one of them to it, or the lord of the house of the Moon to the Moon herself, they are times for recovering the hoped-for things.

Even if the lord of the Lot of Fortune would apply to the Ascendant, or to the second house, or to the place in which the Lot itself was, [or] to the Moon, times of recovery are likewise signified.

---

[102] That is, the time between the question and the objects' recovery.
[103] That is, quickly.
[104] Al-Rijāl says that the pivots indicate something between quickness (cadents) and delay (succeedents).
[105] That is, by transit.
[106] That is, unexpectedly (al-Rijāl).
[107] For the rest of this section, reading directly from al-Rijāl. Both Robert's and Hugo's versions of these conditions are rather mangled.
[108] This probably means "is directed to."

Likewise, look to see how many degrees are from the planet which signified recovery, up to the angle to which it goes first, and that number of degrees is a time of recovery.

## Chapter 6.10: On finding the goods[109]

§242. Likewise, the mutual regard of the Sun and the Moon from the pivots restores the things taken by theft, but signify that it can be found slowly, after labor and difficulty, [and] it confesses many thieves. But if their regard would happen from a trigon, it restores the lost things very soon.[110] Again, no less does the Moon (being in the Ascendant with either of the fortunate ones) bring back the things which were lost. But she being burned up promises what was stolen is either unrecoverable, or permits it to be restored at some time after difficulties and the harshness of labor.[111]

§243. Moreover, the Sun and the Moon being placed below the earth deny the lost things [to the owner].[112] But they accelerate the return of them [if] in the tenth and in the regard of Jupiter. Likewise, the Moon alone being in the tenth or regarding it, [returns the things] with difficulty but introduces labor and impediment. But with her in the Ascendant it does not postpone the finding of the lost thing or stolen goods. Moreover, the Moon being burned up, nor yet with [her] light being renewed, denies [their recovery]. Likewise, if the Sun and the Moon regard the Ascendant from the pivots,[113] they do not curtail the ability to finding [it, but only] after the work of disagreement, wars, and even at some point duress and clashes.

§244. Dorotheus says:[114] the Sun in the Ascendant restores the stolen goods, except [if the Ascendant is] Aquarius and Libra. Likewise the Moon in the Ascendant, relying on the partnership of Venus and Jupiter,[115] brings back the things that are missing or taken by theft.

---

[109] See generally *Carmen* V.35.
[110] See perhaps *Carmen* V.35.42.
[111] *Carmen* V.35.15.
[112] *Carmen* V.35.10.
[113] Al-Rijāl reads: "If both luminaries were nearer to the Ascendant than to another of the other angles….".
[114] Reading with Robert and al-Rijāl for Hugo's *Est etiam haec subscripta super id negotii sententia.* For Dorotheus, see *Carmen* V.35.17.
[115] Al-Rijāl has only Jupiter. But *Carmen* V.35.19 reads rather differently: if we knew the nativity of the owner of the object, and *at the time of the theft* the Moon was in a sign which

## Chapter 6.11: How much ought to be recovered

§245. Moreover, the lord of the lunar house and[116] of the second, and the lord of the bound of the Moon, all of them (I say) decreasing in course or computation (or better yet both), and being regarded by the unfortunate ones, shows that the majority of the lost things will be unrecoverable. Fewer of them being corrupted decrees that less will be missing. Wherefore, we recommend that it be judged—with art and industry being brought to bear—according to the noted consideration of lesser or greater corruption.

§246. Moreover, the amount of the lost thing (which the malignancy of the stars prohibits from returning to the owner's possession) is discovered thusly. Therefore, in the first place, the nature of the star which signifies the loss of the things[117] should be noted, and [the nature] of the sign which it obtains, and place of those in the order of signs with which they bear some correspondence.[118] A consideration of all of them having been discussed, the chosen significator will testify to the nature of the lost thing ([as] laid out above), through the manner of its signification. [And if] the lord of the lunar bound and the lord of the house of the Moon and of the second,[119] were adding [in motion and number],[120] and safe from the infortunes, they return [the things] intact—if their signification does restore the lost things.

## Chapter 6.12: Number & gender of the thieves

§247:[121] At the hour of the question, if the east is a double-bodied sign,[122] or the Moon obtains the pivot of the earth (it being a double-bodied sign): there are many thieves. Then, a firm sign as the Ascendant [indicates] one thief. [The Ascendant] being male and the lord of the hour being male,

---

had a benefic in it *at the nativity*, then the owner will get it back. Thus Dorotheus has an event chart in mind.

[116] Reading with Robert and the instructions immediately following, for Hugo's "or."

[117] Al-Rijāl (II.35) reads: "look at the planet which signifies that one part be recovered and the other part lost."

[118] This is probably a fancy way of referring to the domicile of that planet which it aspects most strongly, etc.

[119] Al-Rijāl omits "and of the second."

[120] Adding with al-Rijāl.

[121] This section is only in Robert.

[122] Al-Rijāl omits this point about the Ascendant.

[indicates] a male; of the other sex, a woman. Just as, if one were of one sex, and the other the other, one designates it is a man, the other a woman.[123]

---

[123] That is, there are two thieves, a male and a female.

# CHAPTER 7: ON FUGITIVES & LOST THINGS[1]

## Chapter 7.1: Five questions about missing objects[2]

§248. There are two kinds of lost things: for they are either animate or inanimate. An understanding of these seems [both] manifold and necessary. Namely, he broods about: [1] in what place the hidden thing is being held, [2] whether it would be found or not,[3] [3] whether as a whole or in part,[4] [4] in what place it is to be found, [5] what is the reason for finding it and losing it.

### Chapter 7.1.1: [2] Whether it would be found

§249. The Moon, as the significator of the lost thing,[5] restores what was lost if there would be an application of her with the lord of the Ascendant or [with the lord] of the second[6] from the Ascendant, or with the lord of her own house. But if there is no application of her with these, nor is she in the Ascendant or in the second, it wholly denies it. Moreover, the lord of the lunar house in the trigon or hexagon of the Ascendant[7] makes a sign of finding it, if it applies itself to the degree of the Ascendant [itself].

§250. Again, with her receding from the lord of the twelfth or eighth or sixth, and should there be an application with the degree of the Ascendant or of money (from whatever regard), she brings back the lost things at the hour of the application—if however the lord of the Moon regards her. With her

---

[1] For this chapter and its subchapters, cf. al-Rijāl II.33. Much of this material is also used by Lilly, *CA* pp. 319ff.

[2] From here up to §269, cf. al-Rijāl II.33.

[3] See also above, §§242-44.

[4] See above, §§245-46.

[5] This is an important point. One might suppose that the second and its lord signify the missing item. But if we look at §282 below, I think we can see a rationale for using the Moon. The second and its lord indicate possessions which are actually under one's control—but by definition a missing thing is not directly under one's control. Therefore, the Moon, which indicates changing circumstances, acts as a proxy for the item.

[6] The 1551 al-Rijāl reads "twelfth," which is clearly where Lilly gets his information, and perhaps why he believes this chapter refers to large livestock (*CA* p. 319). But note that the next instructions involve the Moon being in the second, not the twelfth, and the 1485 al-Rijāl correctly reads "second."

[7] Al-Rijāl specifically mentions the third and sixth.

being applied [along with] the regard of [this lord], the judgment is unchangeable.[8]

§251. Moreover, the Moon being corrupted by the lord of the eighth or sixth or twelfth, makes it clear that it can in no way be wrenched from the hands of the [current] possessor.[9] Particularly while the Ascendant is free of the regard of an unfortunate one [and] likewise the Moon being blessed by one of the fortunate ones, it keeps the thing to be returned safe, [and it is] committed to some just and trustworthy man. Moreover, an application or regard of a fortunate one to the Ascendant, [and] in the same way with the Moon applying herself into the Ascendant, they bring the missing things back. Moreover, the Moon in the pivot of the Sun (or better yet, being with him [in the same sign]) will have brought the missing things into royal possession. Likewise, the Sun looking upon the Ascendant by a friendly regard, [and] even an application of the Moon to the degree of the Ascendant, compels the things to be returned.

### Chapter 7.1.2: [3] Whether as a whole or in part[10]

§252. Moreover, an application of the Moon to the Ascendant from a tetragon or the opposition, restores the missing things with difficulty; it being from a trigon or hexagon, peacefully and completely. Again, the Moon in the Ascendant introduces some adversity in finding it.

### Chapter 7.1.3: [4] Where the missing thing will be found

§253. Moreover, the place of the Moon identifies[11] where the missing things can be found, according to the nature of the sign in which she appears. For, [the sign] being eastern indicates the eastern direction from the place where the thing had been taken. But in a western sign, it shows the

---

[8] Robert and al-Rijāl put it more directly: "But if you found the contrary of these combinations, judge the contrary" (al-Rijāl).

[9] That is, the thief or whoever has it now. I have ended the sentence here, because Robert and Hugo and al-Rijāl all continue with the next clause about the Ascendant. But it does not make sense that the Ascendant being free of the infortunes would *prevent* the object returning, especially given the other conditions in the paragraph. So, I have separated the sentences and connected the clause about the Ascendant to the following sentence.

[10] I believe this is the question as to whether it will be returned in whole or in part: see a similar treatment in §§245-46 above.

[11] Reading *agnotescit* for *ignotescit*.

western direction; likewise, a northern sign, the north; a southern sign, look to the southern direction.

§254. Likewise, the Moon's place [in the figure] settles the same thing according to the order of the signs: in this way, the right and left of each pivot are distinguished.[12]

§255. Wherefore, one will have to judge according to the nature of the sign which the Moon is holding onto. The lunar lord in a human sign indicates the missing things will be in a place frequented by men; in a sign with a sheep-like form (as is Aries and Capricorn), it demonstrates that the place is inhabited by sheep and animals of that kind. In Taurus, it designates a place frequented by cows and heifers and camels. But in a four-footed sign (as Sagittarius is), it declares a place of four-footed animals.[13] In Leo, a place of wild animals (namely forests and deserts [and] caverns).[14]

§256. In Scorpio, it shows a place of creeping things (namely locusts, beetles and those which move without wings and are poisonous). In Cancer, it shows ponds[15] and cisterns, springs and aquatic animals. But in Pisces, it teaches sweet waters and places full of fish. But[16] in Aquarius, even though it is reputed as being among the human signs,[17] it indicates mountainous places, rivers and larger streams. At the end of Pisces (namely from the middle onward), it recounts the habitations of birds.

---

[12] That is, use the actual cardinal direction in which the Moon is. Al-Rijāl: "If she were in the Ascendant, the lost thing is in the east; if in the angle of the west, it is in the direction of the west; if in the Midheaven, it is in the direction of the south; if in the angle of the earth, it is in the direction of the north, or northern. Likewise even contemplate it from the right and left of any of these angles, and judge by mixing this signification with the signification of the sign in which the Moon is." See the next sentence and Lilly, *CA* pp. 364-65.

[13] Al-Rijāl has this as a sign and place of large animals.

[14] Reading with Robert for Hugo's "cliffs." Al-Kindī is probably thinking of bear caves or other places near cliffs and mountains.

[15] Or any hollowed out area such as a ditch or den where animals may hide (Hugo: *lacuna*; Robert: *cavea*).

[16] All three authors read the rest of this paragraph differently. Robert reads: "But in Aquarius, even though it is enumerated with the human signs, it [indicates] mountainous places, torrents, everlasting rivers; moreover, at the end of *Capricorn*, it must be noted that it imputes the place of the lost thing to be that of predatory birds." Al-Rijāl reads: "If she were in Aquarius, it denotes the same [as Pisces]. Moreover, if she were in human signs, it signifies that the thing is where precipitous places are, high mountains, high rocks, and great rivers. And if it were in the last half of Capricorn, it signifies that it is in the staying-places of ships." I am inclined to think that Robert and Hugo are right about Aquarius indicating high places and rivers, while al-Rijāl is right about the last half of Capricorn and ships.

[17] Because it is an airy sign.

§257. Moreover, it seems best to consider the sign the Moon is holding onto in this way: she being in a fiery sign determines fiery places or those near fire; in a watery sign, it signifies watery places or those near waters and water-based affairs; in an airy sign, it suggests windy places and those [places] whose substance cannot subsist without the benefit of wind; in an earthy one, it is believed to be earthy places and those in which the earth shows an effect and strength.[18]

§258. Likewise, the Moon in a convertible sign or with the lord of a convertible one,[19] introduces new and recently cultivated earth, neither [wholly] flat nor mountainous. In a firm one, flat and recently inhabited land. But in a double-bodied one, it demonstrates the most ancient earth, already partly desert, here mountainous, there flat, of the nature of one and the other.

### Chapter 7.1.4: [1] Where it is being held[20]

§259. Moreover, the Moon with the lord of the Ascendant and in the same quarter, if she is distant from him by 30° or less, it permits the missing thing and he who has lost it, to be in the same house. But if the difference were more than 30° and up to 60°, it means it will be in the same city. But if the distance is found to be more than 60° and up to 90°, it portends that so far it is being held in that same region. [But] their being removed from the same quarter, asserts that it is far outside the region.

### Chapter 7.1.5: [5] The reason for losing it

§260. But the reason for losing it (which preceded [the question]) is sought thusly. For, the lord of the Ascendant receding from Saturn or dwelling in a house of the same Saturn, testifies that the thing was lost because of forgetfulness or sorrow or a cold infirmity—which [Saturn's] retrogradation especially seems to be a confirmation of. Moreover, if its

---

[18] Robert: "in an earthy one, earthy [places] and also those producing powers and effects from the earth." Al-Rijāl simply says, "earthy places and where there are houses of earth."
[19] Al-Rijāl reads, "If the Moon or the lord of her domicile were in movable signs," which makes more sense to me.
[20] See also §206 above, and Chs. 6.5.5 and 6.5.6 generally.

receding happens from Mars or it dwells in a house of [Mars], it testifies it was because of fear or some sudden impulse[21] or anger, even fire or enemies.

§261. But receding from Jupiter or in [his] house, it confirms that it happened because of prayer or fasting or the observation of some law,[22] even sometimes a child or controversy. Moreover, receding from the Sun or in his house, a king or hunting, or augury, or a friend's sudden and unforeseen arrival, convey the reason for the missing thing. Likewise, that same lord of the Ascendant being in a house of Venus or receding from her, introduces jokes laughed about among the common people, and women delightful to look at, even sexual immorality [or] longing,[23] into the cause.

§262. Moreover, in a house of Mercury or receding from him, it foretells[24] that books, rumors, commerce and the impediment of some affair[25] are in the cause. Likewise, in the house of the Moon or receding from her, it testifies that a messenger or servant was [relevant to] the cause, because the owner wanted to add something to (or subtract from) the thing.[26]

§263. Moreover, if the lord of the Ascendant would be receding from some star, and it would dwell in the house of the other,[27] remember to connect everything, just as their manner of bearing demands.

§264. Likewise, whichever one of the aforesaid significators (namely the one from whom the lord of the ascendant recedes) is direct, makes it clear that the owner—with foresight and free will, namely being deceived by no dream nor drink nor worry nor error, has put the thing in the place where it was left. Retrograde, it confirms that he was deep in a dream or drunk with wine or disturbed by worry or deceived by error, and affected by misfortunes of the soul like these.

§265. Moreover,[28] it seems one must note with the greatest effort when they are situated in the circle of forty-eight figures,[29] [and] with which of

---

[21] Reading *impetus* with Robert and al-Rijāl, but Hugo's "journey" (*discursionis*) is also a signification of Mars.
[22] In many medieval astrological texts, "law" can also refer to one's religious code.
[23] The Latin reads literally "the sexual immorality *of longing*," which doesn't really make sense in English; so I have separated them to make clear that both elements are involved.
[24] Reading the verb *praefor* for *praesum*.
[25] But al-Rijāl reads, "undergoing a legation."
[26] Al-Rijāl: "is missing by reason of an increase of the lost thing, or a decrease of it, or a messenger or slave lost it."
[27] Robert reads: "But with that very star (whence the separation [*discessus*] happens) holding onto the domicile of the other."
[28] This use of the constellations probably comes from a much older source than the rest of this material.

them the Moon then finally connects [her] ascent. Which if she appeared closer to the horizon, it will be useful to determine the place where the missing things are contained, according to the nature of that figure which then possesses the Ascendant with her; [but] if the Moon were in the Midheaven or closer to it, from the property of the one which is then approaching the degree of the Midheaven with her. But if two or more would accompany the Moon, the observation must be made from the shared nature of their shapes.

§266. Moreover, with the missing thing being animate but not human, all places and [their] statuses acquire a signification similar to that of inanimate things.

## Chapter 7.2: Three questions about fugitives

§267. If it should happen that a question about a human is made, it seems that [the following] come into question: [1] whether he has escaped due to himself or slipped away due to the advice of another; [2] even whether he is living or acquitted the laws of death; [3] even the cause of death.

§268. [1] First of all therefore, the lord of the Moon should be consulted: its withdrawal from some star demonstrates he is free of his own devices. But if another star would be withdrawing from it, it promises he was released by another. With the lord of the Moon being deprived of this evidence, let recourse be had to the lord of the second: it withdrawing from none, nor any from him, so far holds back the one whom we believed had fled, [and] in that same place with which he had been associated.

§269. [2-3] Also, the Moon about to apply with the lord of her eighth,[30] testifies to death. Lacking that, should the lunar lord apply itself with its own eighth or the Moon's, it claims that he has either already died, or his death must be feared. Likewise, if the lord of the Moon is deprived of this signification, the solution of this fear should be sought from the lord of the second. Which if it [too] discards testimony of this matter, it teaches he is unharmed.

---

[29] That is, the 48 northern constellations identified by Ptolemy in *Almagest* VII.5-VIII.1.
[30] That is, the eighth place from her own position.

### Chapter 7.3: Examples

*Example #1:*

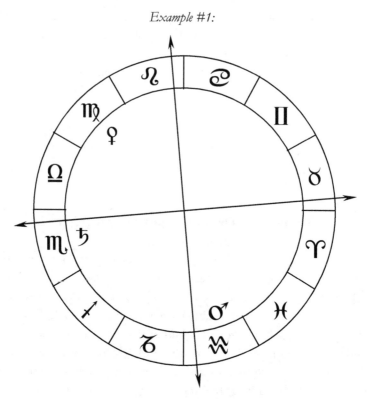

**Figure 46: Example of theft #1 (al-Kindī)**[31]

§270. An example by Abū Yūsuf [al-Kindī]: a question having been made about a theft, Scorpio was the Ascendant, and Saturn in it, obtaining the signification over the robber. The nature of Saturn and of the sign which he was holding onto, determines the form and status of the robber. Mars in the fourth, and being the lord of the Ascendant, conveys to us a certain knowledge of that matter. Therefore, we say that the signified robber frequents the doorway of the [man] whose role Mars takes, with a certain friendship and familiarity; the unluckiness of each [planet] designates that their friendship was false and fraudulent.

---

[31] Based on the information for this chart, it would have been around 8:00 AM and after daybreak, from late September to early October, 867 AD. The client must have come to al-Kindī (or whoever the astrologer really was) right after waking up.

§271. As the lady of the seventh, Venus is consulted: once her status is imparted (along with the nature of Virgo), she is confirmed as [providing] advice for the pilfering of the thing. For she, being the lady of the seventh, always appears adverse to the Ascendant.

*Example #2:*

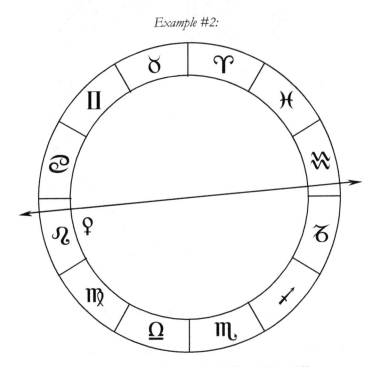

**Figure 47: Example of theft #2 (al-Kindī)[32]**

§272. Moreover, another example by the same astrologer of a missing thing. The Ascendant was Leo, but Venus in the Ascendant. Therefore, this same judge, Abū Yūsuf [al-Kindī], said the missing money was hidden under the bed and under the covers. In the bed, because Leo is counted among the four-footed [signs];[33] he reckoned it was being kept under the blankets for this reason, that Venus in the Ascendant seemed to confirm that. The appraisal must be balanced in this way in the rest of the matters.

---

[32] I take this chart to be from the same year as the first, which would put it at around 8:00 AM, between late June and early July, 867 AD.

[33] Al-Kindī is really saying that a four-footed sign is like a bed because beds have four feet.

*Example #3:*

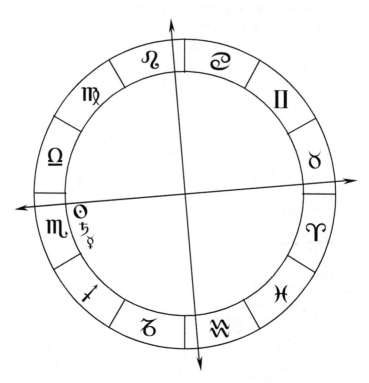

**Figure 48: Example of theft #3 (al-Kindī)**

§273. Moreover [another] example by the same man, in a question about a theft. The Ascendant was Scorpio, but in the Ascendant the Sun, Saturn and Mercury, all of whose signification tends towards the robber.[34] Therefore Saturn in the Ascendant, and being the lord of the fourth, proves that the robber was a relative of the one who lost [the thing], and Mercury [proves that it was] another friend, because he is the lord of the eleventh.

§274. Moreover, another property of them which comes down from the lords of the bounds: for, Saturn in the bound of Mercury shows that he is a common servant (I say, in Saturnian duties). Mercury in his own bound does likewise.

---

[34] Because al-Kindī takes them to be peregrine planets in an angle. Mercury is technically not peregrine because he is in his own bound (see below), but none of them has domicile, exaltation, or triplicity rulership in Scorpio.

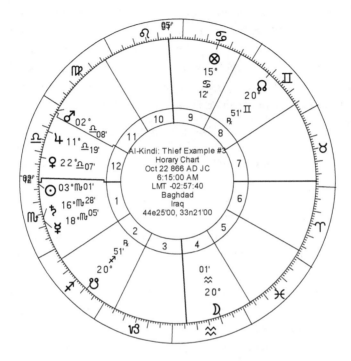

**Figure 49: Likely chart for al-Kindī's example #3[35]**

§275. For what law he belongs to, take Saturn. The lord of the ninth from his own house (namely Aquarius) lays this out thusly: Libra is in the ninth place [from Aquarius], which is a house of Venus. And so Venus signifies the law of the Christians, [because] their places of prayer are entitled to be decorated with figures and images and even paintings and what is like these.[36]

---

[35] There are a couple of problems in dating this chart. Because of the explicit mention of the planets in the Ascendant and the sign of the Moon, I favor 866 AD. However, al-Kindī then mentions the "nearness of the Martial place to Aquarius": if the chart were from 867 as I assume the others were, then Mars would indeed be in Pisces, neighboring on Aquarius: but then Jupiter would be in Scorpio, and the Moon would not be in Aquarius. Is it possible that al-Kindī is speaking of the nearness of the *trine aspect* of Mars to the degree of the IC in Aquarius itself? Unfortunately, al-Rijāl does not discuss these charts at all in II.33.

[36] Al-Kindī does not explain why we should take the ninth from Aquarius—why not from Capricorn? Perhaps because in this chart it is the angular domicile of Saturn. If we had used Capricorn, the thief's religion would have been Mercurial (Virgo). Also, note that most medieval sources attributed Venus to Islam rather than Christianity, perhaps because Venus traditionally indicated rites of purification, a conspicuous feature of Islamic practice (see *ITA* V.5). But Scorpio (and therefore Mars) was also sometimes taken for

§276. The nature of the fourth, and if a star is contained in it, clearly suggests the place where the thing is contained, namely before it would lead [you] out to the home.[37] In the fourth was Aquarius, and it is airy; also the Moon, [who is] moist: it signifies wells and sewers,[38] and that type of thing. But[39] because of the nearness of the Martial place to Aquarius,[40] [it signifies it is] in a related part: the oven or kitchen or a hot bath.

### Chapter 7.4: The home of the thief[41]

§277. Moreover, this same Abū Yūsuf [al-Kindī] designates the home in which the thief is hidden, thusly. Let the place of the Sun be given to the home (just as he instructs), but the Moon claims the door for herself. And so, the Sun in an eastern sign indicates the home is to the east of the home of the one who is missing the thing.

§278. Moreover, he teaches that the place of the thing taken by theft must be investigated in this order: the place of the star[42] established as the significator of the thief should be compared to [that of] the lord of the fourth, and noted whether [its signification] agrees with it. If [the signification] is remote,[43] the place of the thing will be asserted more surely from the place of the [lord of the][44] fourth. For a convertible sign indicates a place that sticks out;[45] a firm one shows one underground; likewise a doubled-bodied sign calls out to the roof.[46]

§279. Moreover, this same recognition proceeds from the nature of the signs. For in a fiery sign it shows places dedicated to fires; but in a watery one, both watery places and those near watery ones; in an earthy one, places

---

Islam, because the Saturn-Jupiter conjunction heralding its establishment took place in Scorpio (see *ITA* VIII.3.2).

[37] In other words, know what you are looking for before you barge into someone's home, in search of your goods. For this paragraph, cf. *Carmen* V.35.25*ff.*

[38] Or, drains (*cloacas*).

[39] Reading this sentence with Robert.

[40] See footnote above on the dating of this chart.

[41] See also Ch. 6.5.6 above.

[42] Reading with al-Rijāl II.34.

[43] That is, if they do not agree.

[44] Adding with al-Rijāl. But Robert and Hugo read that the fourth itself should be used, which also sounds plausible: see *Carmen* V.35.27-37.

[45] Or a "lofty place" (al-Rijāl).

[46] One would expect the roof to be the movable sign, and the common sign to indicate a place in the middle, between an underground spot (fixed) and the roof (movable).

sticking out more from the pavement, near steps and staircases; in an airy one, it portends neither fiery nor airy [places] but mixed of both.

### Chapter 7.5: More on the significator of the thief

§280. Likewise, when the significator of the thief renders its own power[47] to another star, it expels the thing from out of his hand and control. But if not, it concedes that he possesses it yet.

§281. Moreover, the significator[48] of the robber being lucky and in the bound of an unfortunate one, describes that he [was of a good family, but][49] has disfigured the nobility of his parents through his own bad reputation. [But if the significator were an infortune and in the bound of a fortune, he is of low stock, but is now in a good condition.][50]

§282. By the authority written above, the lord of the second designates all money, except for that taken by theft, which [the querent] is complaining about: the lord of the lunar bound principally claims for itself the signification of his missing thing.

---

[47] That is, "pushing power" (see *ITA* III.16). But this could simply mean "pushing management," in which it simply applies to another planet (*ITA* III.18).
[48] Reading with Robert for "lord."
[49] Adding with Robert and following al-Rijāl II.34.
[50] Adding with al-Rijāl II.34.

# CHAPTER 8: ON TRAVEL[1]

## Chapter 8.1: Whether the querent will travel[2]

§283. For a question on travel, as to whether or not counsel of a stellar nature would permit it to happen, the Sun and Moon and lord of the Ascendant and [lord] of the Lot of Fortune, even the lord of the assembly or opposition [of the lights], come especially to be considered.[3] All of them being remote from the pivots confers the effecting of travel, particularly if there would be an application of the lord of the Ascendant with the lord of the ninth or third, or even [with] Mars, and Mars is remote from a pivot.

§284.[4] Moreover, if the lord of the third or ninth, or Mars, would apply themselves with the lord of the Ascendant, [and] moreover should an application of the Moon with her own lord or that of the ninth or third or even with Mars be noted, [and] moreover [if] the lord of the house of travel [would be] in the Ascendant (I say, a little bit drawn back or nearly remote from the Ascendant),[5] or the lord of the Ascendant itself in the ninth or third—all of these, I say (and an observation of them being thus noted), confirm that the travel will undoubtedly come to be. But [if they were] foreign from this arrangement,[6] they wholly deny travel.

§285. Moreover, [if] the five releasers[7] [are] in the pivots or after the pivots, [then] even though the lord of the Ascendant or the Moon may apply with certain ones of the afore-stated (namely those which obtain the

---

[1] For this entire chapter, cf. al-Rijāl III.4-6. Much of this chapter is also echoed in Lilly (*CA* pp. 423ff), though Lilly omits references to the victor from among the releasers (see also below).

[2] For this subchapter, cf. al-Rijāl III.4.

[3] Note that these are all derived from the list of releasing places for the victor over the querent in Ch. 3.2 above.

[4] For this section, al-Rijāl first seems to say that the lords of the third and ninth should be cadent, too (if the lord of the Ascendant should apply to them, as at the end of §283). Then he continues: "And should Mars be cadent from [i.e., in aversion to] the angle of the Ascendant, or as though he is falling from the Ascendant by entering into the twelfth, and the lord of the Ascendant would be in the ninth or third, all of these signify that the travel is completed and happens; but if you found the contrary of this, judge the contrary."

[5] I believe this means he is dynamically cadent: in the rising sign, but more than about 5° earlier than the rising degree itself.

[6] This must mean that *none* of the above conditions are met.

[7] See Chs 3.2-3, but note also the modified list above in §283. The Latin al-Rijāl seems to say that only the primary releaser. See also §311 below.

signification of travel), he will never acquire the effect, even though he seems to be able to complete the travel without any hindrance.[8]

## Chapter 8.2: Timing of travel

§286. Moreover, if the generosity of the celestial circle already confirms the effecting of the travel, the number of the degrees of application determines how long the delay[9] is: namely, the space of their hours or days or months. An application of [1] the Moon in her own course with the lord of travel;[10] or [2] of the star whose signification we follow in travel with the degree of the Ascendant or of the Moon or of the Lot of Fortune; even sometimes [3] the exit of some star[11] from under the rays, or [4] the transit of the lord of the Ascendant from its own sign into another, or [5] the advancement of either of these to the Lot of travel[12]—I say all of these determine the time when the hope of carrying out the travel is had.[13]

## Chapter 8.3: What will happen on the journey[14]

*Planets in the Ascendant (beginning of travel)*

§287. If therefore there is no hesitation about travel left, the stars which hold onto the pivots reveal how it will go, and what will happen to him on the road. Finally, if a lucky star is situated in the Ascendant, it anticipates a journey with much prosperity before he exceeds the border of his home.[15] In the Midheaven, it no less happily hastens the travel. But if in the seventh, the

---

[8] That is, if all of the releasers are angular or succeedent, they will override the usual indications of travel.

[9] *Dilatio.* I read this as the time between the question and the actual date of travel. But Burnett (1993, p. 81) believes it means the length of the whole trip.

[10] Al-Rijāl: "the planet which signified travel: that is, the planet which demonstrated that the journey is completed."

[11] Robert: "one of the aforesaid stars."

[12] The Lot of travel is taken by day and night from the lord of the ninth to the ninth, and is projected from the Ascendant.

[13] It seems to me that we should probably consider the real-time transits of these planets as well, and not just convert their degrees into units of time.

[14] For this subchapter, cf. Al-Rijāl III.5.

[15] That is, before he leaves, or perhaps near the beginning of travel.

land entered by him furnishes him with many riches. But in the fourth, he is entitled to pray for a return with much glory of resources.[16]

### *Planets in the Midheaven (prosperity during travel)*

§288-89. But if a fortunate Jupiter is established here [in the Midheaven],[17] it will bring the generosity of money to bear according to the dignity which its lord obtains in the circle. For, [if Jupiter is] in the house of the Sun, it is promised that he will be ennobled by kings and magnates and those of this kind, or by hunting or augury. In the house of Saturn, it does not deny that he will be enriched by old men or because of some ancient thing, or some land. In the house of Jupiter, the law or a magistrate of the law, [and] sometimes even children or just men increase riches for him. Moreover, in the house of Venus illicit sex, games, exulting, [and] love do not take it away [but rather give it]. In the house of Mercury even, the aforesaid cause attributes [wealth] because of writing or business or eloquence or books. In the same way, in the house of the Moon, it forces clients and servants, sometimes even messengers, to be conveyed to him.[18]

§290. Moreover, if a lucky Venus has control over the tenth, it really brings in joy and exultation and Venusian things and things delightful to practice. Moreover, the Sun as the prince of the Venusian house designates it is from kings and the rest, just as was stated above about the Sun in the judgment of Jupiter. Moreover, [Saturn as] the lord of the Venusian[19] house consents to those things which were stated about Saturn in that same judgment of Jupiter. Therefore, with respect to the [rest of] the individual stars, you should follow the judgment about them written above in the heading [pertaining to] Jupiter.

### *Planets in the seventh and fourth (prosperity at the destination and while returning)*

§291. Moreover, a lucky star in the seventh enacts, what was said before about the causes, and prepares for him [something] of that kind in the region [to which he goes]. In this way, even, if some lucky one would be inhabiting

---

[16] That is, the benefits will come more while on his way back.

[17] Adding with Robert.

[18] Al-Rijāl adds gambling as a source of income, which one would normally expect to come from Venus.

[19] Reading *veneriae* for *saturnalis*, with Robert and the logic of the paragraph.

the fourth, one will have to affirm about it what was laid out for the tenth and seventh. If it should hold onto the Ascendant, a good of the same kind (and by similar things of those causes), is promised to take place, just as was stated in the rest of the pivots.

*Planets in the quarters*

§292. But with no fortunate [star] appearing in the fourth or tenth, while one does traverse between the tenth and the seventh,[20] in the middle of his departure while on the journey, he should be secure in expecting good according to the distance of that star from the seventh—in proportion to the corresponding distance from the region that is sought. And so in this way, [if there is a fortunate one] between the fourth[21] and the Ascendant, it undoubtedly rewards him with the promised goods in the middle of his return, according to the distance of the Ascendant from the fortunate one, and of his home from the region he has left. Likewise, it appearing between the Ascendant and the fourth, you will note[22] the distance of the Ascendant and fourth, according to the nature of the stars and the signs of their places which are allotted in the circle.

*Events according to planetary signification and rulership*

§293. Every place of the circle is entitled to claim a signification for itself according to the place of the sign in the quadrangular[23] disposition of the signs, and [according to] the nature of its place.

§294. For example, let one of the unfortunate ones be the lord of the twelfth, and let it be Saturn; also, let the sign have no likeness to an animal: it signifies a cold and dry illness, according to the claim of the astrologers. But in an animal sign, it testifies that that same cold and dry danger will come upon[24] him because of some animal. In a human sign, it encourages him to beware of murderers and that type of thing.

---

[20] Reading "seventh" with al-Rijāl for "fourth." But generally in this paragraph, the logic has to do with the distance from the Ascendant and the Descendant, not so much with the particular quarter.

[21] Reading "fourth" for "tenth."

[22] Reading *notato* for *notata*.

[23] This reference to square charts seems to be Hugo's own, as Robert and al-Rijāl omit it.

[24] Reading instead of *discedere*.

§295. Moreover, Mars having acquired this role of Saturn (if he took on the rulership of the twelfth), warns him that acute diseases, robbers, fear of his own body, often four-footed animals, and poisonous reptiles are to be avoided. Also, Mercury taking over for Mars, and Saturn being in his regard or being a partner to him in some bearing,[25] teaches worthless men and violent lawsuits and reproaches are to be avoided.

§296. Moreover, Mars being related to [Mercury] by some companionship, claims there are going to be plunderers and those who set traps around roads, [and] the tricks of certain fraudulent men should be feared. In the same way, if a link is had [between] Mercury and some fortunate one, it seems the signification of each must be mixed in their natures.

Moreover, if Venus takes over for Mercury, it makes prosperous things available from women, jokes, drinking, but [also] by those who are enemies to him, or who play the role of enemies.[26]

§297. Jupiter summons profit, money, dignity, from[27] men who present the likeness of enemies, or they are enemies of his sect and his lineage.

Also, the Moon brings profit from the public treasury and one's livelihood, [and] from heralds and couriers."[28]

Finally, the Sun joyfully extols a lofty magnate, also the hunt; or it demonstrates that he acquires many things from those whom we said before, through the gift of prediction.

§298. Finally,[29] should any star corrupt or save the lord of the Ascendant, if this [star] would be situated in the eleventh, it wholly supports the judgment stated before, except that (with an assessment being made [of this]), it confirms this will emanate from friends or the king's servants, or from his own profession[30] or the teachings of his job.

---

[25] One of the standard types of planetary configurations or connections, such as an assembly by body, or a close connection by aspect.

[26] This still assumes that the planet indicating success and wealth is the lord of the twelfth: al-Rijāl appends this statement about enemies to the rest of the planets below, to emphasize the point.

[27] Reading the rest of this sentence with al-Rijāl for Hugo's *a vulgo si inimico vel inimici vice potito.*

[28] Reading with Robert for Hugo's *censum et totius adquisitionis profectum ab eisdem.*

[29] From here through §302, our sources are somewhat vague as to whether we are dealing with the rulerships or locations of the planets. I'm sure both should be considered, but most of the delineations have the planet ruling these houses.

[30] The eleventh is the second (wealth) from the tenth (profession).

§299. But if it would rule the Midheaven, it everywhere resembles the aforesaid, but he would be entitled to get it because of his profession, even his mother or from the king.

In the rulership of the ninth it does not withdraw from the aforesaid, but he is entitled to be enriched by the pretense of law or honor or travel or some change.[31]

But if it enjoys the rulership of the eighth, it does not differ from the prior [statements], but concedes riches because of inheritances, prison or some death, or because of the money of adversaries or the spouse, or some hidden affair.

§300. Moreover, if the aforesaid judgment changes to the rulership of the seventh, it enriches him by adversaries or commerce or that business because of which he applied himself to that region, or by grandfathers or the money of slaves.

Also, the lord of the sixth makes the above statement firm, but slaves or another's anxiety tend to honor him, or a disease or weakness or prison or some hidden affair, and sometimes the paternal money or that of children.

§301. But the lord of the fifth does not flee the aforesaid reasoning, but he will possess the riches of children or gifts or paternal money, or of those who turn against their friends.[32]

Moreover, the lord of the fourth praises the aforesaid highly, but does not neglect to make him be revered by fathers and the money of brothers or sisters, [or] a revived memory of an estate or fief or some ancient thing.

§302. But the lord of the third responds to the same things, nevertheless it adds a benefit belonging to the brothers or travel or some change [of place] or the enemies of the father.

Also, in the second it agrees in every way with what was said above, but greatly bestows money or the benefits of the father's friends.

---

[31] Or "shift" (*transmutationis*), but probably a change in place is meant.
[32] The fifth is the seventh from the eleventh.

## Chapter 8.4: Other considerations

§303. Moreover, the degree of the seventh being in the face of Jupiter[33] shows that he is to be feared[34] by the inhabitants of that region, [but] praised in the attentiveness of his speech. Moreover, if Venus would rule the face of the seventh, it portends that he is loved by the same [people], listened to thankfully, [and] what is sought is procured, particularly while Venus is situated in the aspect of the lord of the Ascendant by a trigon.[35]

§304. But Jupiter regarding the lord of the Ascendant from a pivot of the lord itself,[36] strengthens his own signification. Moreover, [if in addition] Jupiter [is] in a pivot, it professes he will obtain it from those who are powerful among the common people or who are brought forth as being advanced; but after the pivots, from the rank of someone lower; remote from a pivot, from the lowest people. One will have to make a judgment just like it with respect to Venus.

§305. Moreover, the lord of the fourth and even [the lord of] the Moon[37] should be consulted, [and] likewise the star with which the Moon's application comes to be: namely as to whether they are lucky [by nature], made fortunate, whether strong, whether in pivots or after the pivots, whether retrograde or direct, whether eastern or western, whether burned, whether in their *ḥalb*[38] (namely, enhanced)[39] or outside it, whether in their own power or place of proper quality, or peregrine and exiles.

§306. A consideration [which is] had of all of these determines the extent to which [what they signify] is in the end of the journey. Therefore, [1] a fortunate partner in the fourth or with the lord of the fourth in some bearing, or [2] [with the lord of the Moon's house],[40] or [3] should the star to which the Moon's application is coming to be, bear itself in some way with a fortunate one, it claims that good will ensue at the end of the whole affair, in

---

[33] The Latin al-Rijāl only has the Descendant being on *a* or *the* dignity of Jupiter (or Venus, see below); the fact that both Robert and Hugo mention the face leads me to think that they are right. The use of faces for travel is old and may go back to the original Egyptian uses for decans. See *Carmen* V.25 for the use of the Moon in the faces for electing travel by water.

[34] Probably in the sense of awe and respect.

[35] Reading with Robert and al-Rijāl for Hugo's "tetragon."

[36] That is, being in a whole-sign angle of it.

[37] Reading *Lunae* with Robert and al-Rijāl for Hugo's *Luna*.

[38] The Latin al-Rijāl uses "domain" (*ḥayyiz*). See *ITA* III.2.

[39] *Ornatae.*

[40] Adding with Robert and al-Rijāl.

accordance with the nature of that fortunate one, or of the house in the circle which it possesses,[41] just as was said about those things which seem to happen on a journey or [in] a region.

§307. Likewise, an unfortunate one declares evil conclusions to the journey, according to the nature of that infortune and of its house in the circle which it claims, namely in what house of that unlucky one its regard would appear to be more robust.

§308. Moreover, a judgment of those things which resolve the last parts of the travel: a retrograde [significator of the end of travel][42] heaps error and disturbance into the whole matter, wherefore it permits something to be exacted from him at the end of the journey. Direct, it preserves all things to the contrary. All [of them] being direct, they accomplish[43] everything justly, gladly and evenly.

§309. Moreover, the majority being direct [means] you will judge the majority of the whole matter to likewise [move forward], especially that [part] which seems to pertain to the nature of the direct significators;[44] moreover, [judge] more or less with respect to error or disturbance and hindrance, according to the [nature] of the retrograding ones, just as we told [you] about the direct ones.

§310. Likewise, all [of them] being eastern, they accelerate the effecting of the matter without hindrance, according to the signification of that easternness, and according to the nature and kind of the matter itself. Western, the contrary. Moreover, they (or part of them) being in the pivots or after the pivots, they show the advantageous end of the matter without divergence[45] or hindrance. But cadent or remote, they throw into confusion and pervert and block. And so, in this way those which are in their own ḥalb[46] (namely, in their own fortifications) [show] evenness and aid in the matter; remote from that fortification, they rob it of the same.

---

[41] Certainly by its location, but also whichever of its own domiciles it happens to be regarding more strongly (see the next paragraph for this explicit statement).

[42] Adding with Robert and al-Rijāl. That is, either the lord of the fourth, or of the Moon's domicile, or of the planet to which the Moon is applying.

[43] Reading *consummant* for *consumant*.

[44] Again, of the three listed above.

[45] Reading for *divorcio*.

[46] Again, the Latin al-Rijāl reads "domain."

## Chapter 8.5: On returning from travel[47]

§311. But concerning [his] stay or quick return, the significator of travel (namely, the minister of those things which happen on a journey)[48] should be consulted. For, this one being quick of course and western, indicates a quick but hidden and laborious return. Being quick and eastern, it means a fast but public return, and one impeded with minimal labor. But being slow, it throws a delay into the stay.

§312. Moreover, the star which shares some bearing of partnership[49] with the significator of travel should be noted, for no less does it manage the manner of the return. But that star from whose bearing the significator recedes, ascribes corresponding things and significations of this kind to the beginning of the journey.

§313. Likewise, the firmness[50] of the sign[51] of the seventh, and having many ascensions, testify that the stay in the [foreign] region is not middling [but rather long]; but in a double-bodied one, it shows a changed journey; also, a convertible sign signifies a moderate stay on the journey.

§314. Moreover, [1] the retrogradation of the lord of travel,[52] or [2] its application with lord of the seventh (and with [the lord of the seventh][53] being retrograde), even [3] the Moon applying with some retrograding [planet], portend that he returns from the journey before he arrives in the desired place. Moreover, the significator of the return (and the one which snatches away [his] pursuit of travel)[54] being fortunate, shows the return to be useful and healthful. Also, an unlucky one [shows] loss according to the nature of the star which impedes the journey and of the sign which it is holding onto, and according to place of it and its sign in the circle.

§315. Likewise, the lord of the seventh being lucky, and taking in[55] the lord of the Ascendant with a friendly regard, prepares good in the region

---

[47] For this subchapter, cf. al-Rijāl III.6.

[48] The Latin al-Rijāl reminds us: "the one which has the rulership in the causes of it, and makes the matter, and the victor among the five releasers." See the footnote to §285.

[49] That is, if the significator is applying to it.

[50] That is, being in a firm or fixed sign.

[51] Reading with Robert and al-Rijāl for Hugo's "lord."

[52] Probably the victor from among the five releasers as described in §283.

[53] Following Robert and al-Rijāl for Hugo's "it."

[54] That is, one of the retrograde planets just mentioned. Al-Rijāl: "the planet which signified impediment and the destruction of the travel."

[55] That is, "receiving" (al-Rijāl).

which was visited, with exultation and friendliness. Moreover, a bearing being shared between the lord of the seventh and of the Ascendant, [but] with [the lord of the Ascendant] not being received, [but nevertheless] being fortunate and strong, wrenches good from the inhabitants of the region, although they are unwilling.[56] The lord of the seventh being received by the lord of the Ascendant conveys his success with the cities and inhabitants, with generosity and benevolence.

§316. Moreover, the lord of the seventh being unlucky, but associated with the lord of the Ascendant from a friendly regard, greatly bestows good from the inhabitants, but acquired dishonorably. But being unlucky[57] and conjoined to the lord of the Ascendant from a perverse aspect (or in its assembly), conveys harm according to the place and strength and manner of its bearing. Moreover, the lord of the Ascendant corrupting the lord of the seventh, corrupts the inhabitants of the region with its own evil according to its own place and virtue.

§317. Moreover, the lord of the bound[58] of the Ascendant being lucky, makes him be rewarded by powerful and famous men—whose status is determined by the lord of its bound. Also, the lord of the degree of the Ascendant being lucky, promises things will be obtained according to [its] nature, status—and the strength or unsoundness of that status.

§318. Furthermore, the reception[59] of the lords of the triplicity of the seventh denotes steady, faithful friends in the region that is sought,[60] and those blocking many adverse things, particularly [if] the lord of the Ascendant and of the seventh are safe from the infortunes. Also, the lords of the triplicity being cadent and remote show them to be unfaithful and weak, and they deny the hope of all help. The lord of the Ascendant being cadent seems to assent [to this] just like these [triplicity] lords do.

§319. Then, it seems the ninth[61] place should be noted. For if it were in a double-bodied sign, and its lord with some star in a double-bodied sign, or

---

[56] The lack of reception seems to indicate their unwillingness.
[57] Reading with Robert for Hugo's "lucky."
[58] Reading with Robert and al-Rijāl for Hugo's "degree," here and throughout this paragraph.
[59] Al-Rijāl speaks of their being in pivots or succeedents, not reception.
[60] Reading the verb *peto* with Robert for Hugo's *repeto*.
[61] Al-Rijāl reads "eleventh" throughout this paragraph, instead of the ninth; it is probably a mistake.

associated in some bearing with the lord of a double-bodied sign,[62] or [the ninth sign is] regarded by its own lord, the journey will be doubled, or he will have to go on a very similar one next (that is, consequently), especially while the lord of the ninth [is] after the pivots. [But] being in a sign remote from a pivot demonstrates that he has already gone out previously on a journey just like this one.

---

[62] Al-Rijāl has the lord of the ninth applying to a planet *in* a double-bodied sign, which makes more sense than it being the *lord of* a double-bodied sign (which would by definition only include Mercury and Jupiter).

# CHAPTER 9: ON ATTAINING POSITIONS OF HONOR

## Chapter 9.1: Whether & how honor is obtained

§320. With a question made about the obtaining of some dignity, the star which was the victor (namely, the more powerful) for the Ascendant, and the [victor for] the Midheaven, should be consulted. For, their mutual application, or with them being regarded by their own lords—[and] moreover the Sun and the Moon (or at least that one which obtains the shift) being in the regard of their own lords, grant the benefit of the honor. Moreover, with the common regard of the Sun and Moon being taken away, nor [would they be] regarded by their own lords, they deny the hope of honor.[1]

§321. Moreover, with all doubt about obtaining the honor being taken away, the strength and weakness of the lord of the Midheaven should be noted: namely, whether it is direct or retrograde, whether appearing or being hidden, whether eastern or the contrary, whether fortunate or unlucky, even the luckiness or misfortune of the Midheaven itself, would settle the judgment. For, all things which are considered to befall the Midheaven itself or its victor-lord (namely the stronger one), these same things do not abandon the master of that honor.[2]

§322. And so, the Sun being the one to save and bless the Midheaven or its lord more strongly, and being its very powerful supporter, introduces honor from a superior king. But the Moon taking this role of the Sun, [it will be] from the common people. However, Saturn introduces aristocrats and old men, the cultivation of deserts, the spring waters of lands, streams and rivers, and he brings back that kind [of thing which is] in the common use of citizens, into the reason for conferring honor.

§323. Also, Jupiter greatly bestows it from the aristocrats of the people, and those of a more prominent name, and the just. Moreover, Mars brings in the leaders of the army, people powerful in war, [and] masters of booty and plunder into the benefit of the bestowing of this honor. Venus obtains the

---

[1] In this paragraph, the domicile lords of these planets seem to stand for the authority who is granting the dignity or position.

[2] In other words, those qualities will also attach to the quality of the honor itself, or the experience of the person possessing it. It is possible that they also pertain to the authority figure who is granting the honor.

dignity by means of women and the benefits of women, [and] dug-up materials of gold and silver. Also, Mercury gets the honor in turn through writing, advice, commerce, administrating the royal provisions,[3] reason, [and] eloquence.

§324. Moreover, with the Sun being the very lord of the Ascendant,[4] he acquires a kingdom with labor. He being the lord of the house of money, brings it through underofficials and through his own money. But as the lord of the third, he testifies that [the querent] gets it from brothers and much traversing. With him appearing as the lord of the fourth, he climbs up to the honor because of some land or estate, or a city or some hidden and ancient affair. But as the lord of the fifth, children or the friends of brothers or the paternal money revere him with this gift.

§325. Moreover with him as the lord of the sixth, slaves or animals or someone's disease conveys it to him. Likewise, in the rulership of the seventh, he is promoted by the inhabitants of the land, [and] sometimes even because of adversaries or women or commerce. But as the lord of the eighth, it establishes the cause of the honor as being the money of adversaries and women or merchants, sometimes even inheritances or provisions acquired through someone's death, or the besieging of cities or someone's long captivity, or treasure. In the same way, with him as the lord of the ninth he is entitled to obtain it by law, travel, or some change.[5]

§326. Also, as the lord of the tenth advances him to an honor because of the king and the benefit of royal counsel, or his own profession or the mother or a woman who performs the role of a mother. In the rulership of the eleventh, friends or the hope of some matter, and [his] reputation and the prosperity of fortune, even the royal family and its money, are believed to greatly bestow it. Also, as the lord of the twelfth, he is entitled to attain this from enemies and because of someone's departure and remoteness, sometimes even with anxiety.

---

[3] *Census.*

[4] That is, while he is also the best and most powerful planet making the Midheaven fortunate, etc., as above. Al-Kindī is using the Sun here as an example of what to do with all planets.

[5] *Transmutatioe* (Robert: "movement," *motione*). This most likely refers to moving from one place to another.

§327. And so in this way, one will have to consider it by the individual signs, if the fortunate ones[6] would hold onto them or [the signs] would be made prosperous by them.

§328. The eleventh sign denotes the royal money:[7] which if it would be blessed by some fortune, it indicates it will be much and very advantageous, according to the nature of that fortune. Likewise, it signifies the royal underofficials and it releases the accepted luckiness into them according to the proper quality of the one making [it] fortunate. Also, the twelfth sign being lucky, since it means the brothers and friends of kings, shows its luckiness to them. Again, the Ascendant denotes royal parents and their estates, mansions, and treasures. But the second [denotes] children by [the king], whose prosperity brings forth many benefits of the kingdom to him.

§329. The third contains the king's captives and beasts and disease. Therefore, they take on whatever [kinds] of prosperity are in them, according to the nature of the one blessing [it]. Also, the fourth designates the royal wife, but one which he takes [as a wife] *after* accepting rule; it even indicates the king's adversaries and business partners.[8] Likewise, they incur whatever [types] of prosperity or loss [there is], according to its signification. Once more, the fifth claims the king's adversities and loss, disturbance [and] corruption. Which if some luckiness would attain it,[9] it applies what is signified by it, to those [things].

§330. But the luckiness of the sixth[10] watches over royal travel and [the king's] treaties, testimonies, faith, and these [things]. Also, the seventh (namely the tenth from the kingdom or the house of the king) suggests (and defends with its luckiness) the affairs of the king and his counsels, by means of which the stability of the kingdom endures. But the eighth [indicates] the heads of the military and underofficials of the kingdom, and those great men among the leading people of society or lords, who make him [king], commending his acts, [and who] try hard to obtain what is useful for him. And its benignness looks after those things which belong to its signification.

---

[6] Reading *fortunatae* for *fortunata*.
[7] From here through §332, al-Kindī considers the houses as derived from the tenth, so topics relating to the king. If the Sun were the lord of the eleventh it could certainly also denote the friends of the querent.
[8] *Negotiatores.*
[9] That is, if a benefic planet is in it.
[10] Reading *sexti* for *sextum*.

§331. Finally, the ninth place takes the enemies of the kingdom, and the envious, and those who gloat over its confusion; and it mitigates these same things with its good fortune.

§332. If therefore they bear a signification of improsperity, remember to judge in the same way concerning unfortunate [stars] as was stated above with respect to the fortunate ones.


## Chapter 9.2: The timing of prosperity

§333-34. It is well known that whatever good or prosperity, fortune or misfortune he would incur, is plainly understood thusly. And so, one will have to make a direction[11] of the Ascendant and the Moon: and should it arrive at some fortunate degree, without a doubt he will rejoice there (being put in possession of prosperity), according to the degrees of the direction— by taking hours, days, months, [and] years in turn, according to the manner of the signs which are in the direction (namely if they are double-bodied or convertible or fixed), in the way it was stated above with respect to the instruction on times.[12] And so, the type of the prosperity in all modes will be changed according to the very blessedness of the lucky one itself, or [the blessedness] which is taken up from another. In this way, even if the order of the direction reached an improsperous degree, harm will be reported (with, I say, the forcefulness, places, portion, [and] causes of the unlucky one being noted, just as was said before).


## Chapter 9.3: The affairs of kings[13]

§335. Moreover, for royal affairs the degree of the Midheaven should be distributed by direction. Which if it reached a fortunate degree, declaim goods; if an improsperous one, the contrary. Likewise, its application to a fortune [which] blesses, and it is receiving it, portends the increase of the kingdom, the strength of the king, victory. But to an infortune and what is dissimilar [with what we said before], the contrary.

---

[11] Reading for the transliteration *atazir*, here and throughout.
[12] See Ch. 2.6.
[13] This section assumes that the king or an authority is the querent.

§336. If therefore that infortune would enjoy the rulership of the fourth, or some bearing of it, it threatens the king from adversaries. Also, [if it is] the lord of the eleventh, it brings in a sudden attack or assault by his underofficials and their partners. Moreover, as the lord of the twelfth it compels the enemies of those executing [his orders] into the harm of the kingdom.

§337. But the same [infortune being] the lord of the Ascendant, the king or prince himself releases the causes of corruption and the losses into his own kingdom. Performing the rulership of the second, it corrupts the kingdom because of money. With it appearing in the rulership of the third, brothers and those whom he embraces in the role of brothers attack the kingdom, or [it is] because of some law or journey. Again, while it would manage the rulership of the fifth, the kingdom is pressed down by [his] children.

§338. With the rulership of the sixth being occupied, slaves, disease and animals introduce the cause of the corruption. Moreover, while it enjoys the rulership of the seventh, it warns he should beware of adversaries and those whom he incites through the injury of [his] underofficials, and his own business [partners], and women. Moreover, in the rulership of the eighth, because of some death or inheritances; sometimes even the spouses of underofficials and adversaries taint the kingdom. With the rulership of the ninth being attained, it perverts the kingdom because of law or some road or journey.

§339. No less does it seem that the rest of the pivots should be noted, and the leadership or signification of every matter should be chosen by means of their decree.

§340. The[14] direction of the degree of the seventh clarifies what happens to the underofficials of the king or those who are in charge of lands. The direction of the degree of the fourth, what [happens to] the ends [of things]. Wherefore, with it reaching a prosperous [planet], good will be judged; but an unlucky one,[15] the contrary, according to the nature and strength of that fortunate or unlucky one which it claims in the circle (or in the square arrangement of the signs),[16] just as has already been said enough before.

---

[14] Reading the first two sentences with Robert.
[15] Reading *infelicem* for *infelix*.
[16] This must also include the domicile of its own which it aspects most powerfully and favorably, as has been said before.

## Chapter 9.4: On his predecessor *&* successor

§341. Moreover, if a star were found in the ninth, it sufficiently declares him who preceded the minister, powerful man, or king, and his nature and status and manner; but if [there were none in it], the lord of the ninth does so. Again, if there were a star in the eleventh, it accurately suggests what kind of successor he should expect; but if [one were] not [in it], the lord of the eleventh itself does so. Therefore, whatever strength or weakness, fortune or misfortune (and so on) the lord of the eleventh would convey, do not fear: it indicates the same about his successor. Also, with respect to [his] predecessor, remember to affirm [it] according to the nature of the star which holds onto the ninth place, or according to the lord of the ninth itself.

§342. Moreover, you will note the kind and fatherland of the predecessor or even the successor, thusly. For Saturn shows he is going to be an Indian or Arab (or of their lineage) if [Saturn] enjoys some bearing of Venus. Also, Jupiter suggests a Babylonian or Persian or one of their tribes. But Mars grants a Roman or the progeny of Rome. But Venus introduces an Arab, Mercury someone from the western parts or what neighbors these. The Moon, from Thrace.[17] The Sun confirms he is going to be from the east or from a royal family and house.

§343. Therefore, whichever one of these significators appeared in a house of Saturn, advances an ignoble or old man. Moreover, in a house or bound of Jupiter, it claims he is of the sages, or numbered among merchants, or the rank of the law. In a house or bound of Mars, it advances a leader of armies or chief of wars or a victor, even one by whose hand blood is somehow in the habit of being shed, even one whose works frequently demand fire.

§344. In the house of the Sun, it conveys he is an underofficial of the family of the royal house, even an augur or astrologer, or a hunter, or of some excellent profession. Even in a house or bound of Venus, it introduces a singer, a lover of women, or one who, being of this type, greatly delights in jokes. In a house or bound of Mercury, a writer,[18] courier or teacher of children or a man of respectable counsel and appropriate succinctness is introduced. In the house of the Moon, it commends some courier or one given to messengers and legations and that class of the common people.

---

[17] Robert: "a Parthian."
[18] Following Robert and omitting *aut alidbe aliquis videlicet*. *Alidbe* is probably a transliteration of Arabic.

§345. If however it were in a house of some star and the bound of another, it seems the virtue and signification of each must be united in the inquiry of a matter of this kind.[19]

§346. Moreover, at the limit of easternness (or even in its beginning), it testifies he is an adolescent; western, one already of advanced age.

§347a. Moreover, it seems that the manner and nature of all of the stars generally which represent the signification of the past or future leader, must be considered.

## Chapter 9.5: His rule, from event charts or elections

§347b. The hour at which the honor and power of ruling is ascribed to him, describes his strength or weakness in [his] rule. Also, the hour at which he enters the honor, elicits the discretion of ruling, and [his] counsel, and the care of the kingdom. But the hour at which he arranges his official duties, supplies his precepts, [and] begins to rule, undoubtedly lays bare his vigor or how long he is going to rule.[20]

---

[19] Perhaps the domicile indicates things such as origin and personality, while the bound indicates physical appearance.

[20] In the United States, these three moments probably correspond to the moments of: (1) the election results; (2) swearing the oath of office; (3) making the first decisions after the celebrations of Inaugural Day are over.

# CHAPTER 10: ON THE SIEGE OF CITIES[1]

## Chapter 10.1: Overview of sieges

§348. For a question as to whether enemies are going to besiege a city, he[2] consults the Ascendant. For, infortunes or adverse stars in the twelfth and second,[3] claim the besieging is [already] in the present circumstances, but being remote from those places they do not permit it to happen yet. Moreover, the infortunes in the eleventh and[4] third denote that the enemies are nearby, however they do not liberate the city from besieging. The same [planets] in the fourth and tenth they mean it [will be] besieged, but they do not release it from the enemies' entrance.

§349. Moreover, with a question being made as to whether or not it would be occupied, infortunes in the Ascendant testify to it. Being removed from the Ascendant but still in the pivots, the same. If therefore Saturn, [being the lord of the twelfth or sixth],[5] would enter the Ascendant or the pivots, it impairs very many in prison, [but] few by death. Mars in possession of this role of Saturn's, and being the lord of the eighth, the other way around.[6] Moreover, Saturn and Mars doing this in common, bind very many with each misery. Also, the Sun as the ruler of the Midheaven, being a partner of the Ascendant by no bearing, but nevertheless holding onto the Ascendant itself or the pivots with the unfortunate ones, reveals the entrance into the city [by the enemy] to the king or authority.

§350-51. In addition, with all doubt about the besieging being removed, if the truth is sought about the city's assault and the status of the citizens, it will have to be noted that the greater infortune being in [the Ascendant's] first trigon (namely in the fifth) or even in the eleventh or in the Midheaven, [and] moreover Mars being associated with the Ascendant by some proper quality,[7] promise the comfort of friends [and] the expulsion of the enemies by the

---

[1] This chapter assumes that the querent rules a city and is worried about whether or not an enemy will initiate hostilities. In Ch. 11 below, the querent himself wants to initiate hostilities.

[2] This must be Hugo referring to al-Kindī.

[3] Reading "and" for Hugo's "or": namely, a case of besieging by sign (see *ITA* IV.2).

[4] Again, reading for "or."

[5] Adding with Robert.

[6] That is: many dead, a few injured.

[7] This probably includes rulership.

citizens. The [greater] fortune, namely Jupiter, in the Ascendant, removes enemy harm to the citizens, and announces their well-being, especially with the lord of the Ascendant being cleansed of the infortunes and regarding the Ascendant itself. Moreover, the Sun and Moon in the trigon or hexagon of the Ascendant confirm the same. Venus taking the role of Jupiter brings in the same joy to the citizens from the enemies in that campaign, that Jupiter does. Moreover, one of the fortunate ones being under the rays and in the beginning of its exit [from out of them], should it even consider the Ascendant by a friendly aspect, it brings forth the friends of the citizens and the allies from out of traps, pursues the enemies, throws the army into confusion, disperses the assembly [of soldiers], restrains their powers, [and] tramples the arrogance of the proud.

§352. Likewise, either of the fortunate ones in the Ascendant or in a pivot of the Ascendant, and it is the lord of the Ascendant or of its sovereignty, introduces comfort to the citizens from the prince. That fortune being the lord of the bound of the Ascendant—[and] if that were Jupiter—it conveys relief from a teacher of the law. Venus taking up Jupiter's role promises the comforter is of the secular princes. Moreover, if that same fortunate Jupiter would bear the rulership in the face of the Ascendant, it introduces an expert of the law. But Venus in the same position and taking over the place of Jupiter brings in a secular power.

§353. Also, Mercury gaining the role of Jupiter and Venus, and he being fortunate, brings forth a comforter of his signification: namely a writer or merchant or sage, [or] philosopher.

§354. The Moon supporting the Ascendant with a benign aspect, sends messengers or a scout as relief. Moreover, the entrance of the Moon into the Ascendant, if she would be mixed in some relevant way[8] with infortunes which attack the Ascendant, inflicts harm upon the citizens by those same messengers.

§355. Also, Jupiter in the signification of the aforesaid, being weak and exiled, shows the unsoundness of the friends whom he designates, even should they seem to labor at this and exert themselves. [But] strong, he reports no little help from them. It seems [the same thing] must be judged from the strength and weakness of Venus, [and also] with respect to Mercury if he appeared as a supporter of the Ascendant.

---

8 *Proportione.*

§356. Moreover, should the infortune designating the besiegement[9] be at the beginning of a sign, with the Sun appearing at the end of the following sign,[10] and it is burned up by [the Sun] before its exit from the bound which it is holding onto, it destroys the enemies and relegates the captives to the discretion of the greater king.

§357. In addition, *Cor Leonis*[11] and *Cor Scorpionis*[12] in the degree of the Ascendant, shows a vigorous man in partnership with the citizens, bold to enemies and especially feared. In fact, Leo rising affirms he is in the race of kings, Scorpio in the Ascendant shows a most famous general or prince, and their type. Scorpio, I say, in the Ascendant and regarded in a friendly way by the fortunate ones, applies relief and liberation to the citizens once the prince has been accepted. Moreover, Leo ascending and regarded in a friendly way by the unfortunate ones, releases the citizens through that same bold man.

§358. Again, the aforesaid stars: *Cor Leonis* in the Midheaven, [and] likewise the Sun bringing comfort to bear on the Ascendant,[13] presents victory over the enemies to that same king and powerful men. *Cor Scorpionis* in the Midheaven, if Mars would confer aid to the Ascendant, expels the enemies and frees the citizens through the vigor of the prince.

§359. But those same stars in the seventh or the pivot of the earth, submit the citizens to the enemies by a like vigor, if the leadership of the aforesaid signification would deprive the city of victory.[14]

---

[9] Reading more with Robert for Hugo's "the one designating the misfortune of besiegement."

[10] This does not seem right. Perhaps it means that the infortune is at the end of a sign, and the Sun is at the beginning and moving towards it.

[11] Regulus, at 29° 08' Leo in 2000.

[12] Antares, at 9° 04' Sagittarius in 2000.

[13] Robert's version does not specifically state that the Sun and Mars are benefiting the Ascendant, only that they show their aid. So, unless Hugo's version is more faithful to the Arabic, the Sun and Mars might be supporting the Midheaven instead.

[14] The fourth would represent the enemy's king or leader.

## Chapter 10.2: Legations of peace

§360a. In addition, the Moon receding from the lord of the seventh, and an application of her[15] with the lord of the Ascendant, [and] the receding and application being friendly, brings about peace with the consent of the citizens, once messengers have been sent over from the enemies.

Moreover, the Moon's friendly recession [but] perverse application, portends the enemies will demand peace in vain from the reluctant citizens, and especially with the lord of the Ascendant being retrograde.

§360b-361. On the other hand, the Moon's recession from the lord of the Ascendant and application with the lord of the seventh, signifies that the citizens on both sides rejoice in a friendly way, peace having been obtained with the assent of the enemies.

A friendly receding but adverse application, the citizens are disappointed in the peace that is desired through messengers, but particularly with the retrogradation of the one with whom the application is happening.[16]

Again, the [recession] unfriendly and the application safe, [indicates] the citizens fraudulently demand peace from the enemies.

Moreover, perversity in both the application and recession, indicates the trickery of the messengers (on both sides) sent to obtain peace.

§362. Likewise, if the lords of the application and recession were considered,[17] [and] even the Moon (but likewise the infortunes)—if they would be regarding those places into which the application comes to be, and from which the receding comes to be—they testify that a virtually forced peace is made, with those on each side being invited. But the regard of the infortunes into the same [places], breaks off the peace. For the receding and application of [the Moon] bears the signification of legates.

§363. Which if this unfortunate one were Saturn or a Saturnian [fixed] star,[18] it captures the messengers. But Mars or a [fixed] star similar to Mars threatens death.

---

[15] Omitting Hugo's incorrect parenthetical explanation: "([namely], the star from which the Moon is receding, [that is,] the one assuming the rulership of the seventh)." The Moon is doing the separating and applying in this subchapter, not the lord of the seventh.
[16] Namely, the lord of the seventh.
[17] I take this to mean the domicile lords of the planet from which she recedes, and of the one to which she applies.
[18] Robert reads this as though the Moon is on one of these planets or fixed stars.

§364. Furthermore, the nature or moral qualities, and even the form, of the messenger could be discovered by this method. For the lunar lord and its nature demonstrates the moral qualities. Moreover, the sign which the Moon is holding onto describes the form. Also, the lunar lord's place or house in the square arrangement of signs (namely the one which is in its stronger regard), reveals [the messenger's] kind.[19] About all of these, one will have to relate it just as was stated above with respect to corresponding [types of people].

§365. In addition, the Moon settles the faithfulness of the messengers, namely [in terms of] whether they show a stronger assent towards those from which she [recedes], or those to which she goes. For whether the familiar bearing is found to be with the one whom she leaves behind or the one to which she applied herself, the messenger seems to look after the side of the one whose signification that star claimed.

### Chapter 10.3: Attacking the city, and when

§366. Moreover, if an infortune would hold onto the pivots, it will declare when the city does not deny entrance to the enemies. If the application reached the degree of the Ascendant itself, the city will be unlocked for the enemies on that day.

§367. Likewise, by how many degrees the degree of the Ascendant is distant from the rays of an unlucky star, [then] if the significators promise delay, the assault on the city will be set aside for that many days or months or years. Moreover, by how many degrees the Ascendant was distant from an infortune,[20] you will note that many [increments] of 12 1/6 days.[21]

§368. Moreover, the Moon receding from an infortune or from the lord of the seventh, and applying with the degrees of the Ascendant, threatens the most severe attack by the enemies on the citizens. Moreover, the Moon receding from Saturn and applying herself with the degree of the Ascendant,

---

[19] *Genus.* That is, the type of social role (slave, sibling, *etc.*).

[20] Or more likely, including its rays as well.

[21] This is a profection. Here, each degree of the zodiac is equated with 12 1/6 days, which makes each sign (or increment of 30°) almost exactly equivalent to one year.

threatens the undermining of the walls, and hurling mechanisms,[22] and tortures, and even frauds and things of this kind. Also, Mars taking over for Saturn produces fire and arrows and flying missiles. [Mercury being dressed in the nature of Saturn, tricks and frauds.][23]

§369. [Mercury] sharing in the nature of Mars, prepares the fraud of tricks and more prominent tortures for the citizens, the drawing of arrows, and walls being undermined from below.

In addition, the Tail of the Dragon applying itself to the Ascendant, [indicates] a common[24] cohort of foot soldiers and vassals, [and] compels the projecting of scorpions, lizards, poisonous things of this kind or stinking corpses, and that kind within the walls.

§370. Moreover, the sign in which the star (which besieges and attacks the city) was, will denote from what direction the citizens would incur harm. In an eastern [sign], it warns that one must beware of it from the east; in a western one, from the west; but in a southern one, from the south; also, in a northern one, from the north.[25]


## Chapter 10.4: The response of the citizens


§371. Moreover, the lord of the Ascendant will indicate the courage and status of the citizens, and in what frame of mind they are protecting the places devoted to their defense. For, it being direct increases their courage in defending [them], [their] steadiness, even [their] faith and vigor. But retrograde, the contrary. Eastern, it tends to their cunning and powers, and claims they will be young men, for the most part. Western, the contrary.

§372. But in a pivot, it shows steadiness in assaulting the rebellious, and that they are courageous against the assaults. After the pivots, they are for the most part supported. But remote from a pivot, it deprives them of everything which pertains to the defense. In its *halb*[26] and in some place of its own proper quality, it brings the strength of forts, and defenses, and ramparts to

---

[22] *Fundibula*: that is, catapults. The difference between Saturn and Mars here must be that the catapult works by brute force to smash things (Saturn), while Mars's missiles are designed to burn and kill.

[23] Adding with Robert.

[24] That is, of unprofessional soldiers, the general public.

[25] See the diagram and discussion in Ch. 6.5.5.

[26] Following Robert for Hugo's synonym, "shelter."

bear. But remote from these places, it renders them impotent and inexperienced in protection.

§373. Moreover, the fourth place and its lord should be noted. For if the lord of the fourth would make the Ascendant or its lord fortunate in a friendly way, and the lord of his Ascendant would enjoy a manifold analogy[27] with the fourth, it presents an end to the whole war, and the victory of the citizens over the besieging. Contrarily, with the bearing of the lord of the Ascendant being remote from the fourth, and with the companionship of the lord of the seventh being taken up with the [lord of the][28] fourth, victory is granted to the enemies.

## Chapter 10.5: The collapse of the city

§374. In addition, Saturn in an earthy sign (if he would be corrupting the Ascendant) and his lord in an earthy sign, also the Ascendant being earthy and its lord in an earthy sign, provided that the significators promise [the enemies'] entrance into the city, it defeats the city decisively through thirst and a lack of water. But apart from this, the lord of the second being western,[29] and there being no application of him with the Ascendant and its lord, and being in a fiery or earthy sign and in the regard of Mars, makes the citizens surrender to thirst and starvation.[30]

§375. Also, the ascending sign being watery and its lord in a watery sign, and likewise those who participate with his Ascendant, moreover should Saturn corrupt the Ascendant from a watery sign (especially Cancer and Scorpio), they bring about an assault on the city through an onrush of waters and [their] immoderate impact.

§376a. In addition, the slow course or even stationing of the infortunes which attack and are besieging, generate a pause in the besieging and the anxiety of the citizens.

---

[27] Robert reads, "it had manifold power in the fourth."
[28] Adding with Robert.
[29] Omitted by Robert.
[30] The second normally signifies wealth, but in particular it indicated the provisions and sustenance of one's livelihood, one's immediate means of support: *victus, quaestus* (which is

## Chapter 10.6: Allies

§376b. But, [many] stars in the second give over very many allies to the citizens. With the lord of the Ascendant [joined] in a friendly way to these, or [if they had some power in the Ascendant],[31] they testify to their faith and steadiness in attacking the enemies.

§377. [But] just one [star] in the second, and it being a partner of the Ascendant or regarding its lord in a friendly way, promises the help of few [allies] for the citizens, but [it also promises] their faithfulness and steadiness. Finally, with no [star] appearing in the second, if the Ascendant itself and even its lord would be lacking the friendly regard of all, they affirm that the citizens will be altogether destitute of aid.

§378. Conversely, the lord of the eighth being blessed by the friendly regard of many, [and] also the lord of the seventh and the eighth [sign] itself, or if [many planets] would be holding onto the eighth, they console the enemies with the aid of many. But if they bore themselves otherwise, the judgment will have to be changed. Again, those stars being friendly to the seventh or the lord of the seventh, no less too to the eighth or its lord, indicate [the enemy's allies] are strong in war, prudent, even faithful. Also, an alteration of how they bear themselves makes the other judgment.

## Chapter 10.7: The justness of the enemy cause

§379. Moreover, the lord of the seventh being lucky, in some place of his own analogy,[32] in a firm sign, indicates the cause of the enemies is just; but being unlucky and in a convertible sign, they are worthless and unjust and moreover foreign to what is true.

§380. Moreover, if in a double-bodied and fiery sign,[33] and it being lucky, it denotes that the part of the cause which he gives as a pretext, and by which he frees himself from blame, is just; but [his own real motive] is unjust, and that he is hiding that [fact], and that he is a show-off. In a watery [and double-bodied] sign,[34] [it means] the enemy cause is just, but [he has one

---

[31] Reading with Robert for Hugo's line, which seems to refer to the lord of the Ascendant instead.
[32] *Proportione*. Again, Robert reads "powers."
[33] Namely, Sagittarius.
[34] Adding with Robert. By definition this would be Pisces.

motive inside, and another in his speech];[35] he even defends the humble and the religious, it means deep counsel, but covers up minor secrets, [and] he takes no partner or confidant.

§381. Moreover, the lord of the seventh in a double-bodied sign and an airy one,[36] indicates twin enemies, and reveals two men or brothers unanimous in counsel, that they exhibit much foresight in matters, and less popularity or sympathy in [their] subjects, but public ambition for victory. The same [lord] in a double-bodied and earthy sign[37] portends their evenness, justice, piety, advantageous power of discernment, care in administering things, benevolence toward men.

---

[35] Reading with Robert.
[36] That is, Gemini: note the reference to twin enemies.
[37] That is, Virgo.

# CHAPTER 11: ON WAR[1]

## Chapter 11.1: Significators *&* overview

§382.[2] A sound intellect generates more clarity and results, but error the opposite; therefore let your mind inspect the order of this chapter all the more diligently, compared with the rest. And although the previous chapter does not suggest well enough (to those looking diligently) whether there will be a war or not, still, here we decree that it in no way is appropriate to succumb to silence.

§383. Also, concerning the combatants [one may] imitate the above-written judgment. For the ascendant signifies him who is provoking [a fight], and the seventh his adversary.

[Robert]: And so, since the lord of the east signifies him whence it is asked, and the lord of the seventh the one who is resisting, a conjunction of these (and its manner) should be noted with the utmost effort. For, these regarding each other in a hostile way, or joined in any way through an unlucky [planet] in a pivot, with all conditions of favor being removed, war will undoubtedly take place. But with them being joined in a friendly way, and particularly when received, and likewise with them being united together, peace will intervene. And if the Moon, leaving one of these behind, joined herself to the other, here it wholly portends the same thing about a legation that it did in the preceding chapter.[3] The signs, and the places of the circle, and the natures of the significators, clarify both the size of the war's circumstances and its difficulty.

§384. Therefore, the lord of the seventh being mixed together with the lord of the Ascendant by a perverse aspect, but with each being in a double-

---

[1] In the previous chapter, the querent was someone worried about enemies who already planned to attack. Here, the querent is the person who wants to provoke a fight.
[2] This paragraph is only in Robert, and probably originates with him. I have translated this sentence somewhat freely from Robert's truly unusual original.
[3] See Ch. 10.2 above.

bodied sign, it increases his army by the number of each.[4] The lord of the second and of the eighth in a similar bearing suggests the same. But the corruption of one being made toward the other, confounds him whom the corrupted one seems to watch over or signify.

§385. Moreover the one of them which holds onto the pivots, indicates that his army is stronger than the other. But with each one in pivots, the virtue of both is confirmed, and their endurance for wars.

§386. Likewise, the one whose easternness is discovered to be stronger: his vigor, steadiness, [and] eagerness for war is highly praised. But a stronger westernness of either makes him known as being unsound, timid, not wanting to fight. Moreover, the one of them which obtains a peregrine place: it takes away his diligence and counsel for wars.

### Chapter 11.2: Allies & support

§387. In addition, he in whose second [place] Jupiter appeared, shows his money to be much; it multiplies the faith of those assisting, first by love of money [but] then by reason of the law. Moreover, he in whose second place Saturn dwells (or should he become the lord of the second, and regarding it), it indicates less money, mistrusted allies; even the distorted will of its master and his mistrusted mind provokes [the allies] to fraud. Moreover, should the lord of the second corrupt one of them, it warns that his allies might abandon him.

§388. But if the corruption comes to be from Mars and from a perverse aspect, particularly from a pivot of the Ascendant, it threatens destruction from an attack by his own soldiers. But if a regard of some fortunate one would reinforce [it], after the wounds it promises hopes of living: the strength or weakness of the regard of the one making it fortunate will teach a definite experience of that judgment.

---

[4] Hugo is probably trying to say that his army will be twice as big. At any rate, it seems a double-bodied sign will increase the army's size.

## Chapter 11.3: Capture & death for the querent's side

§389-390a. Furthermore, the lord of the Ascendant in the seventh and corrupted by the infortunes, or scorched or retrograde, pursues the chief [person] of the city.[5] Corrupted by Mars, it hands him over to the enemy in captivity, or afflicts him with death. But this corruption proceeding from Saturn, frightens him with long-lasting captivity [among] the enemies.

§390b. Moreover, the lord of the second being with the lord of the Ascendant in the seventh, and corrupted by Mars, taints the chiefs of those who convey aid to the citizens with captivity or death through the hands of the enemies. Mars in particular, as the lord of the eighth and [placed] in the second, multiplies the massacres of the citizens and allies, no less even than with him in the eighth. Moreover, Saturn corrupting the lord of the second [while] he is in the seventh, ushers the city combatants and allies into captivity. The same [planet] as lord of the eighth, or at least being in the eighth or second, explains the killing of citizens.

§391. Moreover, if the lord of the second is being corrupted by Mercury, [and] he is the [lord of][6] the house of death, and in the bearing of Mars, it contaminates the supporters of the citizens with sudden mortality and plague.[7] In the regard and aid of Saturn, that same Mercury disseminates blisters which we say are a type of smallpox, [and] compels many to die because of that disease.

§392a. Moreover, it seems one must conclude that, should the lord of the Ascendant in the seventh be tainted by Mercury, and he is in the eighth or [is] the lord of the eighth, it afflicts the captured citizens with the aforesaid evils. Which if the lord of the Ascendant [were] in the Ascendant, tainted by Mercury—provided that he does not lose the [aforesaid conditions]—it corrupts those presiding over the city and the citizens with the aforesaid infortunes and similar evils within his own city and tents.

---

[5] In other words, the person on the querent's side will be chased and in trouble. (It is not important here that he runs a city.)

[6] Adding with *Judges* §7.155.

[7] Or perhaps simply, "death" or "destruction" (*peste*).

### Chapter 11.4: Capture & death for the enemy's side

§392b. Contrariwise, the lord of the seventh in the seventh, abused by Mercury (and [Mercury being] mixed with Mars and Saturn), weighs down the princes of the enemies and their battle line, with the above-written adversities—provided that Mercury would have possession of the rulership[8] of the second.[9]

§393. Moreover, the lord of the eighth being mournful (by means of the aforesaid improsperity), and it being in the eighth or seventh, destroys the enemy hand and his allies by means of the aforesaid plague—with Mercury, I say, claiming the rulership of the second.

### Chapter 11.5: Victory

§394. Moreover, Mars himself staining the seventh, but being estranged from the lord of the seventh [and] likewise from the Ascendant and the lord of the Ascendant, and he [also] being in a fiery sign, introduces fire into the tents of the enemies. Conversely too, Mars corrupting the Ascendant itself, [and] also estranged from its lord and the seventh and the lord of the seventh, proclaims the burning of the [querent's] city. Which if he would be regarding the lord of the seventh, and from a fiery sign, it threatens that the burning of the city will come to be by the enemies.

§395. Moreover, the lord of the Ascendant being in the seventh, strong, eastern, direct, aided by fortunate [planets], [but] with the seventh and its lord being corrupted by infortunes (particularly with the lord of the seventh being cadent), likewise with the lord of the Ascendant in its own *ḥalb* (that is, its fortification) or triplicity or bound or face, and that same [planet] regarding the Sun or Mars in a friendly way, [indicates] an attack or assault by the princes of the city upon the enemy army; it afflicts some with death, [and] leads others away as captives.

§396. Moreover, if the lord of the seventh is cadent (that is, remote), even scorched or in the pivot of Mars or with his body (namely in [his] assembly), it kills the enemy prince.

---

[8] Reading *dominio* for *domino*.
[9] Or that he would be in it, in order to parallel the opposite conditions above for the lord of the Ascendant.

§397. And so, in this way, the lord of the seventh being strong, while the lord of the Ascendant is turned away from it and from the fortunes,[10] [and], I say, the lord of the seventh being in the Ascendant, aided by the fortunate ones, eastern, free from the infortunes, with the lord of the Ascendant cadent (particularly in its own depression),[11] it opens the city to the enemies, [and] encloses some by death, others by prison. Which if Mars would be situated with the lord of the Ascendant or in its pivot, it kills the prince of the city.

§398. If however the lord of the seventh and of the Ascendant appear to be equal in virtue and power, the one of them which was in possession of the assent[12] of Mars and Mercury is enriched with the triumph. Moreover, he whose partner appeared to be Venus [likewise] has possession of joy and victory: for she signifies joy and exultation, also joy and glory in wars, victory, and exultation.

§399. But he who claimed the testimony of Mercury for himself, will shine with the prudent management of the fighting, and in counsel. For, Mercury being fortunate, strong, cleansed of the infortunes, increases the success of victory, pillaging, spoils and arms, by his own acquired care and counsel—by all of which, the harming and trampling of the enemy is brought about.

## Chapter 11.6: Election: Initiating the war[13]

§400.[14] That one of the warriors who commences the beginnings of the war by night, being stronger than the one who went out by day, is crowned with the victory. And we call the "beginnings of the war" the hour at which he heads to the path against the enemy (once all things are arranged, [there is]

---

[10] Reading *fortuniis* for *infortuniis*: it would be a good thing for the lord of the Ascendant to be in aversion to the infortunes.

[11] That is, "fall" (and omitting "or death").

[12] That is, "is in the best relationship with" them. For example, regarding them from a trine with reception would be more favorable or show more assent than being in a square without reception.

[13] Although I have labeled this chapter as pertaining to elections, the editors of *Judges* used §§403-06a in their horary material, which was probably a correct thing to do. For §§406b-408, see also al-Rijāl Ch. VII.57a.

[14] This paragraph does not seem right to me, and I think it is better read as with Sahl's *On Elect.* §90a and Bonatti's Tr. 7, 7th House Ch. 3 (p. 762): the general who was *born* at night, and in whose nativity Mars played an [important] role, will win—otherwise, every attack at night would be favorable, all other things being equal.

a call with the clamor of trumpet and clarion, [and] the battle lines are arranged). For even though the lord of the seventh and the Ascendant may appear to be equal in virtue, the one who goes out by day is conquered and confused; but he who [does so] by night is confirmed as the victor.

§401. Moreover, the overall equality of the lord of the seventh and of the seventh [itself], generates peace. Likewise, whenever the lord of the seventh would be deprived of the regard of the Ascendant and its lord at the beginning of a war, and Mars in a cadent [place][15] and being estranged from them, it means the delay of the war, scatters the battle lines, sometimes produces peace, [and] reduces all things to quiet. But if they did regard each other, especially from the pivots, [and] likewise Mars in a pivot, and the signs are convertible, it portends a public and immoderate war, [and] declares that aristocrats and the most famous people, and those of a widely-known name, and those eager for a reputation, will get involved.

§402. Again, the lord of the second and of the eighth will declare what side [such people] will follow. For the one of them which was in a pivot or its own house or sovereignty, or being eastern from the Sun, or in a convertible and pivotal sign (or at least its lord), likewise the one of them whom the Sun and Moon support by an appropriate aspect, that one will keep for himself the company of the aforesaid powerful people, the final triumph and glory of the war, [and] the parade and advantage.

§403. Likewise, the Moon comes to be noted to the greatest extent. For, she being made fortunate, is very advantageous to the one who commences the beginnings of the war. But made unfortunate, she presents trouble to him and the harm of the whole affair. In fact, corrupted by Mars and from a pivot, she threatens death and blood, especially if Mars were harmful to the Moon and the Ascendant [at the same time], or he himself were the lord of the eighth or of the eighth[16] from the Moon.

§404. With these bearing themselves thusly, and the lord of the Ascendant being direct, it prepares a death to be feared when hostilities are initiated. Also, being retrograde kills [him while] fleeing. But it warns that he must beware of death in his own bed and tent, [if] the same [planet is] in one of the wells[17] or in an obscure place or in a nocturnal sign. But in a diurnal sign and in a shining degree,[18] it threatens death in the day and among his own

---

[15] Lat. *azucut*, a transliteration of Arabic as in §133.

[16] Reading *octavi* for *octavus*.

[17] That is, one of the welled degrees (see the next sentence). See *ITA* VII.9.1.

[18] See *ITA* VII.7.

battle lines (or not far from them). But if some unfortunate and pivotal [planet] would corrupt it, and it was Saturn, and he in a moist sign, it tramples him with the feet of horses, and humbles him, often in a river or the mud of a river, or it kills him at the seashore and what is like these in terms of causes.

§405. Moreover, an eclipsed Moon introduces an opening in the earth, or the collapse of a bridge, or the falling of some ruin, into the cause of death.[19]

§406a. Likewise, the lord of the fourth or of the Moon being corrupted by Mars and from a pivot, pollutes the end of the affair with death, once victory is had. Moreover, the lord of the end[20] being made fortunate by another, conveys health and prosperity after the business of war is accomplished.

§406b-407a.[21] Furthermore, I warn the king (namely him against whom the other has raised up) to the utmost degree, lest he should ever go into war with the Moon made fortunate. But one must observe that with her being corrupted, he should not flee. But he who begins the encounters of war with the Moon being corrupted, should refuse the war. But he should advance and be about to fight with the Moon being safe, especially with the lord of the Ascendant [also being made fortunate and in the Ascendant].[22] Moreover, with the Ascendant and its lord being corrupted with the Moon, he should never presume to attack.

---

[19] I omit here a garbled sentence which only appears in Hugo, and which appears differently in *Judges* §7.165. It refers to the Moon being free of the infortunes and lucky, and being either of the sect of the significator of the one who is attacked, or perhaps if it is simply at night. I cannot easily determine what Hugo means. In *Forty Chapters* it reads: *Luna quoque ab infortuniis libera et felix, in adaulahu ipsius quem agressus iste est videlicet in fine regiae prosperitatis, illud autem audaulahu solatio forte iuxta terram victoria privat.* But *Judges* reads (underlining indicates differences): *Luna quoque ab infortuniis libera et felix, in admunitione ipsius quam iste aggressus scilicet in fine regiae prosperitatis. Illud autem adaulahu solatio et adminiculo forte iusta terram victoriam privat.* The word *adaulahu* is probably the Ar. *al-dawlahu*, "its state/administration," but *Judges* reads the first instance of this as *admunitione* (prob. *munitione*) or "fortification," which is Hugo's normal synonym for the condition of *ḥalb* or "sect." The passage seems to be saying that if the Moon is unharmed and is somehow more favorable to the one attacked, then it deprives the attacker of victory.
[20] That is, the lord of the fourth.
[21] For this paragraph, remember that the benefit or harm of the Moon's condition belongs to the initiator of the conflict. So, if the rebel has initiated hostilities under a good Moon, it is unwise for the king to respond; but if under a bad Moon, it is right for the king to respond, since the Moon indicates a less effective attack by the rebel. On the other hand, if the king were initiating hostilities, he should do so under a good Moon, but it would be unwise for the rebel to respond, etc.
[22] Adding with al-Rijāl; omitted by Robert.

§407b. Moreover, [if] the first of the aggressors is about to attack in the parts of the east, he should establish the Moon in the west; but going towards the west, he should establish the Moon in the east; but if in the south, in the north; which if [he advances toward] the north, let him consider her in the south.[23]

§408. Likewise, Mars in the eastern part of the circle (namely from the tenth degree of Taurus to the tenth degree of Leo, and from the tenth of Scorpio to the tenth of Aquarius) warns him that it should be fought[24] in the direction of the east. In the western part (namely from the tenth of Leo to the tenth of Scorpio, likewise from the tenth of Aquarius to the tenth degree of Taurus), it encourages him to fight in the parts of the west.

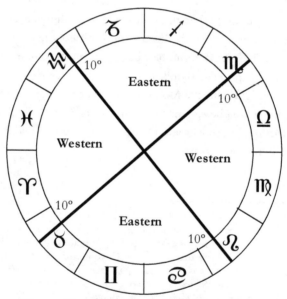

**Figure 50: Al-Kindī's directions for fighting**

---

[23] In other words, the Moon should be at his back.
[24] According to al-Rijāl, the "rebel begins the battle" in that direction (Burnett 1993, p. 91).

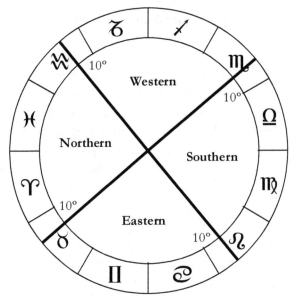

**Figure 51: Al-Rijāl's proposed correction to al-Kindī[25]**

---

25 Al-Rijāl (II.2) points out that al-Kindī's division of the zodiac would only allow the armies to advance from the east or west, rather than from all directions. So, he proposes a different division, apparently also based on the four royal stars and the seasons: the Sun is in Taurus at the middle of spring, which is associated with the east, etc. (see §23 above), and the constellation Taurus (with which the tropical sign Taurus used to correspond) contains the royal star Aldebaran; likewise for the other seasons and royal stars: summer and Regulus (Leo), autumn and Antares (Scorpio), and winter and Fomalhaut (really in Piscis Australis, but close to Aquarius).

## Chapter 11.7: Election: The *bust*[26]

§409. Moreover, let the general or prince of each cohort take care to observe with the greatest diligence not to enter into his own affairs in the wicked and bad hours which they call "scorched": namely, from that [hour] in which the Moon enters the assembly of the Sun on the same spot, until the completion of twelve hours. The principal affairs of the significators and princes of kings wholly abhor the malice and perversity of these hours.

§410. But the subsequent twelve [scorched] hours should also not be put out of one's memory: the beginning of which is drawn out once eighty-four have been crossed after the assembly of the Sun and Moon on the same spot. But the end [of this second group of hours] accompanies ninety-six hours after the assembly: once the eighty-four have been drawn out in sequence, the following twelve hours from the beginning of those whose name is "scorched" begin at[27] ninety-six. Therefore, a discernment of the hours should be observed in this sequence up to the end of the month.

§411. For example, let an assembly of the Sun and Moon, being discovered on Sunday at its first hour, be noted—namely when the Sun arises by half of his body. I say that from the beginning of that hour up to the subsequent setting of half the solar body, the hours which we call "scorched" should be noted. But next, we set apart the subsequent twelve hours of that day (namely, the first day), its nocturnal ones, [and] even the diurnal and nocturnal ones of the second day, [and] in the same way both the diurnal and nocturnal [hours] of the third day, [and] the diurnal [hours] of the fourth day.

§412. Moreover, the beginning of the scorched [hours] is stretched out from the outset of the nocturnal hour of the fourth day, up to the morning (namely the beginning) of Thursday. The rest of the [hours] of Thursday, both diurnal and nocturnal, lead to those of Friday, even to Sunday, in order. Whence likewise the beginning of the scorched [hours] are bounded from the beginning of Sunday to its end. And so it will have to be done in this way until all the hours of the [lunar] month reach the end of the counting.

§413. Once again, let the assembly following the beginning of the subsequent [lunar] month be described: so, the scorched ones take their

---

[26] For this section, cf. al-Rijāl VII.57a. See also *ITA* VIII.4. *Bust* is an Arabic rendering of the Sanskrit *bhukti*, an ecliptical distance covered by the Moon in a certain time.
[27] Omitting "the end of," in order to make the sequence work.

beginning from the first hour of the assembly (namely at which the Sun and the Moon embrace on the same spot), until twelve [hours] are completed. Therefore, whatever prince undertook the beginnings of a fight in these scorched hours, chooses the greatest loss: the death or severe harm of his own body or of those whom he has [in his power]. But the first four[28] prepare death while the beginnings of the war are advanced in that space [of time]. The following four infest the body, the last four [his] money, and they condemn his subordinates when they hold onto the same sign.[29]

| Day | Hours | Scorched/Burnt |
|---|---|---|
| 1 – Sunday | Diurnal 0-12 | **Scorched** |
|  | Nocturnal 12-24 | Unscorched |
| 2 – Monday | Diurnal 24-36 | Unscorched |
|  | Nocturnal 36-48 | Unscorched |
| 3 – Tuesday | Diurnal 48-60 | Unscorched |
|  | Nocturnal 60-72 | Unscorched |
| 4 – Wednesday | Diurnal 72-84 | Unscorched |
|  | Nocturnal 84-96 | **Scorched** |
| 5 – Thursday | Diurnal 96-108 | Unscorched |
|  | Nocturnal 108-120 | Unscorched |
| 6 – Friday | Diurnal 120-132 | Unscorched |
|  | Nocturnal 132-144 | Unscorched |
| 7 – Saturday | Diurnal 144-156 | Unscorched |
|  | Nocturnal 156-168 | Unscorched |
| 8 – Sunday | Diurnal 168-180 | **Scorched** |
|  | Nocturnal 180-192 | Unscorched |

**Figure 52: Time-based scorched period,
from New Moon on Sunday morning**

*Comment by Dykes.* This time-based approach to the scorched (or "combust") period is very close to the method of determining the crisis hours in decumbiture charts, and may in fact be related to them. Since the hours are calculated according to uneven seasonal hours (that is, dividing the period of daylight or nighttime by 12, instead of using a regular 60-minute

---

28 That is, the first four of the scorched hours.
29 This probably means, "if the Sun and the Moon are in the same sign during the last twelve hours."

hour), the actual distance of the Moon from her original position will change according to the season and latitude. So, in al-Kindī's example, if the days were very short and the nights long, then the scorched hours would last for less than 12 of our standardized hours, and the distance traveled by the Moon in that time would be less than at other times of the year.

But if we used an idealized 60-minute hour and her average daily speed (13° 10' 36"), the Moon will be in her idealized Quarters and Semi-Quarters, because she will have traveled approximately 45° between the beginning of each period of scorched hours. For example, if the scorched hours began on Sunday at dawn, they would end at sunset after the Moon had traveled 6° 35' 18". The next period would begin on Thursday at dawn, when the Moon had traveled about 45° from her original position; the next period of scorched hours would take place at about 90° from her original position (i.e., an idealized First Quarter Moon); and so on. *However*, since seasonal hours are uneven, and because the Sun also moves, these scorched hours will not always coincide strictly with the true Quarters and Semi-Quarters: for by the time the Moon reaches, say, 270° from her original position (an idealized Third Quarter), the Sun will already have moved about 21°, and so the Moon's position will fall short of the true Third Quarter. This means that calculating the actual time of the scorched hours a bit complicated, since one cannot simply look at the Moon to tell just when they begin and end: one really needs tables of sunrises and sunsets, or an astrology program which lists the times of the planetary hours.

A distance-based version of the scorched hours is given in Māshā'allāh's *Book of Aristotle* II.4 (in *PN I*). There, the scorched period is defined as 12° of *distance* traveled by the Moon (close to her average every day), instead of 12 seasonal *hours*. This version makes a bit more sense, if we remember that the Moon is often taken to come out of the Sun's rays at a distance of 12°. If we use a non-scorched distance of 84° instead of 84 hours, then the Moon's position at the beginning of the scorched hours will coincide almost exactly with her Quarters: the next scorched period will happen at about 96° from her original position—but since the Sun will have moved about 7° in the meantime, they will be almost exactly 90° apart, i.e., the true First Quarter. The next period will put her at 192° from her original position, but since the Sun will have moved about 14° in the meantime, this also puts her at almost exactly 180° from him: the Full Moon. And so on with the rest.

And so, the time-based scorched period is an idealized division of the zodiac into 8, using the Quarters and Semi-Quarters, and is more complicated to reckon. The distance-based scorched period uses only the actual Quarters, and is relatively easy to reckon (in many cases one may do this from sight alone).

## Chapter 11.8: Making peace[30]

§414. Moreover let the lord of the Ascendant and of the seventh be noted, as to whether they are holding onto the same sign, and if any star would be situated between each. For, that middle one being lucky describes a man who labors to bring about peace on both sides. It being situated in a place of its own authority, indicates a native and noted man.[31]

### *The nature and status of the mediator*

§415a. Also, the nature of the star by which [this mediator] is signified (namely, its advancement or retreat,[32] moreover whether [it is] eastern or the contrary, [direct or retrograde, well-protected[33] or the contrary])[34] will declare his nature and status, lineage and fortune. For, it being in a peregrine and an exile place, indicates he is foreign-born. The same [star] being an exile and foreign [only] from its own house and sovereignty, but [still being] in its own triplicity, bound or face,[35] he is known by all even though he is foreign.

### *Whom the mediator favors more*

§415b-16. Moreover, you will note what side he seems more likely to favor. Therefore, what sign [the star] resembles with a greater commonality of property (namely, the Ascendant or the seventh), he commends that one's

---

[30] For this subchapter, see al-Rijāl VII.57b.

[31] Robert specifies: in its own exaltation or domicile or triplicity, a man native to the area; but in its bound or face, a well-known one.

[32] That is, whether it is in a pivot or succeedent (advancement) or a cadent (retreat): see Ch. 1.2.3 and *ITA* III.4.

[33] That is, in its own *ḥalb*.

[34] Adding material in brackets from *Judges* §7.169 and in accordance with Robert.

[35] Reading with al-Rijāl. Hugo has the star being peregrine from domicile, exaltation and triplicity, but in either its own bound or face. Robert omits this part.

side in a more familiar way, [and] strives to pursue those affairs with greater feeling.

## *The mediator's style and position*

§417a. Moreover, a fortunate star as the mediator [between] the aforesaid [two stars] lays bare his status, nature, and moral qualities. Which if it were Jupiter, it signifies a minister of the law, honest, respectable, [and] venerable. Venus brings forth one liberal, proper, polite,[36] elegant in [his] bearing.

§417b-418. Moreover, it seems the nature of the fortune and its lord[37] must be combined, just as we have already taught above. For, Saturn as the lord of that fortunate one, indicates an old man, and that type. Jupiter: one experienced in law, or a minister, [or] generous judge. Mars: a bold man, a prince of wars. However, the Sun shows he is from a royal house and family, or of royal blood. Venus: pleasant and delightful. Likewise Mercury introduces [someone] skilled, a master of succinctness, modest, a writer or most wealthy businessman. Also, the Moon involves a messenger and underofficial of some legation, and what is like these.

§419. Moreover,[38] you note which one of its houses (which it obtains in the circle) it would be looking at with a familiar aspect. For, combining the nature of that house[39] with the proper quality of that star will be useful.

§420. [Now] it remains to relate such a judgment of this matter. Which if the mediator happened to be the lord of the Ascendant,[40] it denotes a relative or greatest and bosom friend of the one who has claimed the beginnings of the war. Which if the mediator of the aforesaid appeared as the lord of the second, [it indicates] an assistant. The lord of the third, a brother and this type. But the lord of the fourth, from the paternal stock or that of forefathers.

---

[36] Or, "clean" (*mundum*).

[37] In this paragraph, Hugo mixes in the mediating planet's domicile lord; but al-Rijāl mixes in any planet *aspecting* the mediator. I tend to think al-Rijāl is right, but since astrologers do also mix the qualities of planets with those of their domicile lords, I cannot be sure which represents the true al-Kindī.

[38] In this paragraph I follow al-Rijāl's reading. Hugo seems to be confused as to which planet should be aspecting whose domiciles. We should be identifying that domicile of the *mediating* planet, which it aspects best and most strongly.

[39] Reading with al-Rijāl for Hugo's "its lord."

[40] And if it aspected the Ascendant better and more strongly, etc., than its other domicile.

§421. It being even the lord of the fifth, [indicates] a child or one whom he has adopted in place of a child. But the lord of the sixth portends followers of lower rank. Moreover, the lord of the seventh claims he is of the stock of the adversaries. The lord of the eighth, a supporter of the side turned against him. Also, [the lord] of the ninth brings forth a minister of the law or a partner in his own travel and the roads,[41] into view. But the lord of the tenth establishes a friend of the kingdom and of his own profession. Finally, the twelfth testifies to an enemy.

§422. Conversely, with the mediating star being corrupted, it indicates a bad man who personally taints and corrupts each side with the poison of unfaithfulness and poison of fraud, and leads [them] into dissension. Which if this were Saturn, it claims he will be an old man of long-lasting deliberation, a cautious man, fraudulent. Mars, a plunderer, eager for blood just as the nature of Mars and his lord seems to demand. It even seems that [the nature of the planet which the mediator][42] consoled by a friendly aspect (namely in the square arrangement of the signs) should be considered in the same way.

---

41 This seems only to pertain to travel, but it is intriguing to think that "path" could be meant in terms of a spiritual paths, such as belonging to the same religion or sect.

42 Reading with al-Rijāl. Hugo has us mix it with the nature of the lord of the domicile which it had aspected; but by definition, this would be the same planet.

# CHAPTER 12: ON ONE WHOM ONE SUSPECTS OF TREASON[1]

### Chapter 12.1: Significators & overview

§423.[2] Being consulted about someone as to whether he would rise up against his own king: if you found the Moon remote from the east,[3] or the lord of the east retrograde, or a retrograde star in [the east], you should confirm that he is resisting his own king and is rising up against him. But the east and its lord obtain the signification of him whence the question comes. The south and its lord belong to the king, the seventh and its lord to the man sent by the king to fight him.

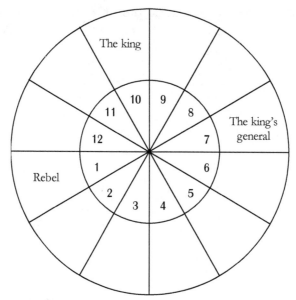

**Figure 53: Al-Kindī's scheme of angles for rebellion**

---

[1] As with other questions, in this chapter the Ascendant signifies the initiator of action (or someone asking about him): namely, the rebel or traitor, who is referred to as "the enemy" throughout.

[2] Reading this paragraph with Robert, as his version is more complete.

[3] This is probably more accurate than Hugo, who has the Moon cadent from an angle. If the Moon is cadent from the Ascendant, then she is in aversion to it: such places are traditional spots of secrecy.

§424. Therefore, with a question as to what end the matter of each is going to have, the lord of the Midheaven [and] even the Sun himself being lucky and fortunate—but the lord of the Ascendant unlucky—convey victory to the king. Moreover, the eclipsing of the Sun or Moon in the Ascendant, or [should this eclipsing happen][4] with the lord of the Ascendant, it ruins the hostile cohort [and] afflicts the [rebel] soldiers with death. The Tail of the Dragon in the Ascendant, [and] likewise Mars as the lord of the second corrupting the lord of the Ascendant from a pivot, promise that the enemy who has risen up will die by iron at the hands of his own family, soldiers and supporters, and even the common people.

§425. Moreover, the Tail in the same place [but] Saturn occupying the role of Mars: he will be overwhelmed by his own soldiers and beset by stones at the hands of the common people, or led as a captive to the king. Moreover, the retrogradation of the lord of the second (and he being in a perverse place, namely lacking the regard of the Ascendant), provided that there is no star in the second, banishes[5] his family, brings his cohort down, and leaves him as though alone.

§426. While they bear themselves in this way, and Mars as the lord of the seventh is corrupting the Ascendant and its lord, the general sent out by the king to fight this kind of enemy rebellion, kills him. Also, With Saturn holding onto [this] role of Mars, and being in the rulership of the seventh, he incurs death (but without iron) from that same general or powerful man.

§427. Furthermore, the lord of the eighth corrupting the Ascendant and its lord explains that the enemy, being deceived by some art, will be killed by the family of the general himself or friends or scouts or the wife of the general. Furthermore, if the Moon and [her] lord would assume the roles of the Ascendant and its lord, namely so that [they] would be corrupted by Mars as the lord of the seventh or eighth (or by Saturn in possession of the same rulership), they will bestow the same misfortunes which the enemy got from the Ascendant and the lord of the Ascendant being corrupted.

§428. Also, if the above-written arrangement of stars taints the enemy side and denies victory to him, the scorching of the lord of the Ascendant kills him by royal decree, as a captive. Likewise the Moon or the lunar lord being peregrine and exiled in the seventh hands the enemy (being captured by the above-stated general) over to the royal authority as someone about to die.

---

[4] Reading the meaning with Robert, for Hugo's puzzling *annuit*.
[5] Reading *amovet* for *amovit*.

§429a. Moreover, the lord of the Midheaven strong, even the strength of the Sun, [and] with the Ascendant and its lord being corrupted from the eleventh, affirms the enemy's death.

§429b. Which if the lord of the seventh were situated as an exile in the Ascendant, or Mars himself would corrupt that same lord of the seventh—or the seventh itself—it leads the general (whom we said had gone out to resist [them]) as a captive to be killed at enemy hands.

§430. Moreover, the lord of the seventh peregrine in the Ascendant, with no corruption of it or of the seventh by Mars having been incurred, if an application of it to the lord of the eleventh or tenth would come to be, [and] meanwhile the lord of the Ascendant is unlucky, it shows the escape of the general (who was already losing hope for his life) and the king's consequent victory. Likewise, the lord of the Ascendant being corrupted by the Sun or by the lord of the Midheaven or the eleventh, after the achieved victory the enemy will meet death.

§431. But next, the lord of the Ascendant being direct, pivotal and eastern, [but] with the Sun and lord of the Midheaven being cadent, particularly Mars tainting the Sun from a square or opposition, makes a confused king submit to an enemy gloating over victory. Moreover,[6] with the lord of the Ascendant not suffering this misfortune of the Sun, but [Mars] attacking the Midheaven and its lord [while the lord is] cadent, it indicates the king is subdued and killed by the enemy.

§432. But the lord of the Ascendant in a pivot, eastern, direct, in the place of its own *ḥalb*[7] or authority, blessed by the fortunate ones with a friendly regard, or in their assembly, moreover with the Sun or the lord of the Midheaven or of the eleventh being corrupted by Mars, it kills the king by an assault of the hostile cohort, [and] leaves victory to the enemy. But Saturn entering the role of Mars captures him or confines him, besieged.[8] But [if] he [is] the lord of the eighth, it kills him [while] besieged.

§433. Moreover, with the lord of the Ascendant being defended by the aforesaid strength, likewise the lord of the eighth being strong, also the lord of the Midheaven being somehow weak (namely retrograde and that kind [of

---

[6] Reading this sentence more with Robert, and emphasizing Mars as the corrupter instead of the Sun. Hugo reads: "Moreover, with the misfortune of the Sun being remote from the lord of the Ascendant, while the Sun himself attacks the lord of the Midheaven and the Ascendant itself…".

[7] Reading with Robert for Hugo's synonym *munitione*.

[8] Omitting *cuilibet*.

thing]), and likewise the lord of the eleventh, while the lord of the Ascendant or of the second would corrupt the lord of the eleventh (they regarding it from a square), they conquer[9] the king in a fight, [and] attack his [people] with much slaughter.

§434. Also, the lord of the second or of the Ascendant corrupting neither the lord of the eleventh nor that of the Midheaven, but with each one retrograde and cadent, they disturb the cohort, stimulate the flight of the king, [and] free the fleeing one from death. Likewise [if] the lord of the Midheaven [is] cadent, retrograde, scorched.

§435. Also, an Aries or Leo Ascendant, likewise the lord of the eleventh being unlucky and cadent, but the Sun being regarded by the lucky ones, and [also] the lord of the second in their regard, [and] the lord of the Midheaven, I say, corrupted from a square after its initial emergence from scorching, it threatens death to the king ([who is] deprived of victory), [and] confounds his [people] with much slaughter.

§436. But besides this, the Midheaven itself being corrupted from a tetragon devastates the kingdom, it is deserted by the inhabitants, the citizens are left abject and despised. Again, the lord of the Midheaven being corrupted in the Midheaven itself,[10] means a most famous and public death, such as cutting off the head, and [the rebel] sets [the king's] head up in public view of the people for them to understand.

§437. Moreover, the lord of the Midheaven corrupted by [the lord of][11] the eleventh, and the lord of the eleventh regarding the lord of the Ascendant in a friendly way, [and] with the lord of the Midheaven, I say, cadent and retrograde and scorched as was said, the princes and powerful men of his own cohort will slaughter the king and offer his head to the enemy as a gift. Again, the lord of the fifth place from the Ascendant being scorched and corrupted from a square, exposes the king's son to be killed.

§438. But if the lord of the Midheaven (being cadent, particularly in the twelfth) would be enclosed[12] between the two infortunes (with one preceding it, the other following behind), [and] should it traverse by sign [with][13] or in the same way apply to the lord of the twelfth, it shuts the king up in prison as

---

[9] *Convincunt.*

[10] But Robert reads: "if one found the one making the [Midheaven] unfortunate to be in the south," which makes somewhat more sense.

[11] Adding from Robert.

[12] That is, "besieged" by degree (*ITA* IV.4.2)

[13] That is, "be in the same sign as," i.e., be in an assembly with.

a captive. If it would reach an infortune (Mars, I say), it warns that death in prison is to be feared. But if it reached Saturn, it especially reveals the same thing if that infortune to which it is said to come, has possession of the rulership of the eighth.

§439. Moreover, the lord of the Midheaven being cadent and remote (or rather, retreating), [and] the lord of the Ascendant being strong, but there being an application of it made with some fortunate one in the Midheaven, and the same [planet] being free of the pivots of the unfortunate ones,[14] after flight and disturbance and conquering, it restores the kingdom to the king, but the enemy perseveres for a long time in the malice of his rebellion. If these are bearing themselves in this way, [and] the lord of the Ascendant is applying to a cadent and corrupted star, it confounds the enemy rebel, and after getting the kingdom from the king and reinforcing [it], it takes away his hope of fighting [more].[15]

§440. Moreover, the lord of the Midheaven in the seventh, or the lord of the seventh itself, or likewise the Sun, and they being strong, pivotal, it signifies the king will enter into a duel [in order to] fight it out with the enemy through his own hand. Wherefore, the lord of the Ascendant being cadent and weak grants victory to the king. Moreover, the lord of the Ascendant being strong produces dissension, and strengthens the enemy's rebellion. Likewise, an application of the lord of the Ascendant with the lord of the eighth harms the enemy [while] persisting in his malice.

§441. Which if Mars appeared as the lord of the eighth, and in a pivot of the lord of the Ascendant,[16] it beheads the one who is thus far rebelling, and pours out his blood. Moreover, Saturn in possession of the rulership of the eighth and in a pivot of the lord of the Ascendant, destroys the enemy with trickery or drowns him in water, or tramples him under horses' hooves, and—so that I might speak more truthfully—he loses his life without iron.

§442. Moreover, while the lord of the Ascendant bears itself thusly, its application with a cadent star means the enemy's flight. Again, if the star to which the application of the lord of the Ascendant comes to be, is applying with the lord of the seventh or the Sun, the enemy demands a truce after fleeing, [and] he greatly desires discussions with the king. Which if the lord of the seventh or the Sun would receive that star to which the application of the

---

[14] That is, not being in their whole-sign angles.
[15] That is, his victory is only temporary.
[16] That is, in his whole-sign angle.

lord of the Ascendant is made, after the truce and with many gifts being accepted by the king, he is made into a friend.

§443. But an unfriendly or perverse application, [and] the Sun not received, even the lord of the Ascendant in possession of a pivot of the infortunes, he is killed after [his] pledge is received by the king.

§444. Moreover, an application of the lord of the Ascendant with the lord of the seventh or with the Sun, or with the Sun in the seventh, or if the lord of the Midheaven or the lord of the seventh [is] in the seventh (this application, I say, being friendly and received), it denies the enemy's flight but he demands a truce and observes things given [to the king]. [But if],[17] in the midst of all of this, the lord of the Ascendant would be retrograding and estranged and absent from[18] the Sun or the lord of the Midheaven,[19] likewise the Moon or the lord of the Ascendant being in a double-bodied sign, he violates the accepted truce, throws peace into confusion, and once again hastens to rebellion.

§445. Moreover, the lord of the Ascendant in possession of a tetragon of the infortunes[20] (particularly of Mars), the end of the enemy's whole affair is ended in death.

## Chapter 12.2: The relation of the rebel to the king

§446. While these bear themselves thusly, the lord of the Ascendant or the Moon in the second from the Sun, or in the second from the Midheaven, or if either of them would rule over those same places, it suggests the enemy is going to be a near to the family of the king. On the other hand, either of them as the lord of the third from the Sun or from the Midheaven, shows he was a brother of the king or one having the role of a brother, and that type [of person]. Moreover, either of them as the lord of the fourth from the Sun or from the Midheaven, or at least dwelling in the fourth from the Sun or

---

17 What follows is a case of revoking (*ITA* III.20), in which a planet preparing to complete a connection goes retrograde. It is stated a bit more clearly by Robert.

18 That is, "in aversion to," i.e., not regarding it by sign.

19 Robert omits this part about being in aversion to the Sun and the lord of the Midheaven, which makes sense because the lord of the Ascendant would have to regard them by sign in order to be in an application with them.

20 Again, being in their whole-sign angles; but probably more intensely if close by degree.

from the Midheaven, it adduces that the enemy is a parent of the king or of
the parents' stock.

§447. Either one as the ruler in the fifth from the Sun or from the
Midheaven, or established in those same places,[21] it admits that the royal
children or those accepted in place of the children are in dissension with the
king. Moreover, while either one would rule over the sixth from the Sun or
the Midheaven, or should it appear in that same place, it brings in royal
slaves and that type. Which if either would rule over the seventh from the
Sun or from the Midheaven, or be found in that same place, it adduces that
the enemy is numbered among the king's adversaries, very often even his
sisters.

§448. Likewise, should either of them be the ruler in the eighth from the
Sun or Midheaven, or with it holding onto that same place, the servants and
followers of the adversaries or sisters come forth, or those who previously
were held in the king's prison. Either of them as lord of the ninth from the
Sun or from the Midheaven, or if it were in that same place, it compels a
doctor or underofficial of the law, or a partner in travel, to dissent with the
king.

§449. Also, either one in the tenth from the Sun or from the Midheaven,
or as the lord of that same place, it picks out the rebel as being a king or
someone of royal stock, or an advisor or counselor of the king, or in the
administration of [royal] affairs, engaged with the royal authority. Also, in the
eleventh from the Sun or from the Midheaven, or either of them being the
lord of that same place, [it indicates] an intimate of the king, and a secretary,
and it especially reserves a friend in the greatest distress of necessity.[22]

§450. But either of them as the lord of the twelfth from the Sun or from
the Midheaven, or dwelling in the twelfth from the Sun or from the
Midheaven, it testifies the rebel will be an ancient enemy of the king, of a
great name.

§451.[23] If however the lord of the east and the Moon held a different
place and [were in] a different[24] regard of the Sun and the lord of the south,
the judgment must be moderated from the nature of each place.

§452. For example, the lord of the Ascendant being in the eleventh from
the Sun (and in the second of the Midheaven),[25] portends the enemy will be

---

[21] Robert simply has them in these places, not ruling them.
[22] That is, the friend feels that (for some reason) he must rebel, but feels anguish about it.
[23] Reading this paragraph with Robert, as it is clearer and more succinct.
[24] Reading *alio* for *alium*.

from the rank of the king's friends and his underofficials. For the second place from the Midheaven denotes the royal family, but the eleventh from the Sun decrees the royal friends. And so, if the lord of the Ascendant would bear himself thusly, but the Moon would occupy the sixth place from the Sun, once the nature of the above-written place has been observed, the lunar place and status and what she signifies in that place, comes to be combined: whence the enemies would be said to have revolted against[26] the king from among [his] friends and the rank of underofficials and the company of slaves.

---

[25] This would put the Sun in the Ascendant.
[26] Reading *decidisse* for *decivisse*.

# CHAPTER 13: ON SEEKING WEALTH[1]

## Chapter 13.1: Significators & overview

§453. Anyone worried about accumulating money, [who] burns avidly [with a desire] to increase his possessions, [but is] uncertain by what means or from whom or where and whence he would be able to acquire it, should consult the lord of the Ascendant. For an application of it with the lord of money,[2] and being received by it, it even being in the regard of the Sun and Moon (particularly if the lord of money would regard the Ascendant itself or][3] the lord of the Ascendant), greatly increases the hope of acquiring it.[4]

§454. On the other hand, an application of the lord of the Ascendant[5] with the lord of the Lot of Fortune, and [the lord of the Lot's] status (or rather its manner of bearing itself) with the Sun and Moon being no other than with the lord of the second, especially with the Moon regarding the Lot of Fortune, indicates the same.

But if an application of the lord of the Ascendant with the [lord of the][6] Lot of Fortune is removed, but an application of the same [is] transferred to the lord of [the Lot of][7] money, while the lords of the Ascendant and of the Lot of money bear themselves with the Sun and Moon as was stated before, they mitigate the hope of acquiring it.[8]

---

[1] For this whole chapter, cf. al-Rijāl I.24-25.
[2] This must be the lord of the second.
[3] Adding with al-Rijāl.
[4] Robert reads: "The lord of the east joined to the lord of assets, and received by it, and seen by the lights (especially if the lights would be aspecting the lord of assets)."
[5] Al-Rijāl reads this as the lord of the second.
[6] Adding with al-Rijāl.
[7] Adding with al-Rijāl. But one might expect this also to work with the lord of the second, as Hugo has it.
[8] That is, they relieve the querent's sense of urgency precisely because his hopes will be fulfilled.

## Chapter 13.2: Jupiter

§455. Jupiter seems to confirm the same thing [when] regarding the Ascendant [or] its lord [or the significator of assets],[9] whichever of these three significators of money it was. Also, Jupiter is asserted to be stronger in the signification or leadership of money when he appears in the second with the lord of the Ascendant and the significator of money, or in the Ascendant,[10] or in the eleventh or in the tenth or in the rest of the pivots, or even after the pivots.

§456. But if he were established in the Ascendant, it multiplies the acquired resources through his own labor. Also, with him appearing in the second as we said before, he gets rich through the actions of those serving and attending him, and through the profit of money. Appearing in the tenth, he is made rich because of the king or a royal affair. Again, in the eleventh, from the underofficials and friends of the king, and even hope, and [his] storehouses will overflow with due ease.

§457. Which if [Jupiter were] in the seventh, he incurs riches from women and trade, controversy and quarrels. The same [planet] even in the eighth introduces inheritances, things deposited for safekeeping, [and] goods acquired through someone's death into his possession. Moreover in the fourth, because of some ancient thing or land or agriculture. Which if he would dwell in the fifth, [his] possession is increased through children and gifts and promises.

§458. On the other hand,[11] Jupiter being situated with the lord of the Ascendant[12] and the significator of money in the twelfth, although [he will suffer] badly from enemies, resources are often gathered together because of charity[13] and the benefits of the dead, and prisons. But with him appearing in the ninth, journeys and certain low-quality and less fitting affairs, even things found on a journey, will show the increase of riches.

---

[9] Probably the lord of the second (adding with al-Rijāl), but see §460, which suggests the significator of money is the victor over the matter as described in Ch. 3.1. Al-Qabīsī, drawing on al-Kindī, describes his own victor of money in *ITA* I.18.

[10] Al-Rijāl reads as though Jupiter is in the second with the lord of the Ascendant, while the significator of assets is in the Ascendant, eleventh, etc.

[11] This paragraph refers to Jupiter in the cadent places, but note that he requires the help of the lord of the Ascendant and the significator of money.

[12] Al-Rijāl reads as though Jupiter *is* the lord of the Ascendant.

[13] Reading *elemosinis* as a transliteration of the Ar. ʾinsāniyyah, "charity, humanity." This also appears in Sahl's *On Quest.* §10.3.

§459. In the sixth, slaves and people of this kind, and humble things (and so on), someone's disease, animals, a short captivity, render him rich. But if in the third, brothers, journeys and his own friends, [and] the father's friends, adorn him most abundantly with riches.

## Chapter 13.3: Other indicators of success

§460. Again, the lords of the Ascendant and of money, even Jupiter and the significators written above, appearing with the significator of money,[14] in the pivots, show manifold and steady money, and of a stronger nature.

§461. But among these, the Ascendant is established as being best, after this the tenth, then the seventh, lastly the fourth. But of those which follow the pivots, we choose the eleventh in first place, then the second, after that the fifth,[15] finally the eighth.

§462. Moreover, the significator of money or Jupiter being eastern and direct in some place of its authority, and being received (as was said above), describes much and the best money. Moreover the significator being received and regarding Venus and being cleansed of the infortunes, hastens the same thing. Likewise, Mercury in the [significator's] regard and receiving[16] it, he being fortunate and strengthened in his own light, indicates the success and enjoyment of money. Which if they would bear themselves otherwise, they bring a different judgment.

## Chapter 13.4: The time of wealth

§463. The degrees of application declare the hour at which acquiring money should undoubtedly be expected, by alternating days or months or years according to the nature of the signs.

---

[14] Again, this is probably the victor of the topic from Ch. 3.1.
[15] Al-Rijāl has the fifth before the second. This list is probably the source for ibn Ezra's house strengths in his victor calculation (p. 14). This particular assignment, which seems to be based on the Nechepso version of advantageous houses (see *ITA* III.2-3) is not used in the methods drawing on "Māshā'allāh" and Dorotheus in *Search* I.3.4 and III.1.1.
[16] Reading *recipiens* for *respiciens*, with Robert.

## Chapter 13.5: Yet more indicators of success

§464. Which if there would be an application of the lord of the Ascendant ([and] no less, even any of the significators of money)[17] to the fortunate ones in a pivot, it promises long-lasting and useful supplies.

§465. Moreover, the significator of money applying to the lord of the Ascendant: he acquires it easily. But the application of the lord of the Ascendant [to the significator of money] does not bring it without labor and training.[18] Which if this application happened from retrogradation, he amasses riches from something unexpected. The retrogradation of all of the significators (once their signification would already incite the hope of inquiring about money), puts dangers and impediments in front of it.[19] Their unluckiness attacks and perverts the same thing according to the nature of the infortune itself and its own house (namely the one it looks at with a familiar aspect).[20]

## Chapter 13.6: Seeking wealth from a particular person or place

§466. If however a question of this kind happened with respect to a [specific][21] man or some land, the Ascendant designates the one seeking it, but the seventh bears the signification of that man from whom he greatly desires to obtain it, or of the region about which he set forth the question.

§467.[22] Wherefore, [1] an application of the lord of the Ascendant with the lord of the money of the seventh;[23] or if [2] the lord of the Lot of

---

[17] Reading *cuiuslibet ducum pecuniae* (following Robert) for Hugo's *cuiuslibet eorum assignant* and *Judges' cuiuslibet eorum qui assignati*. Al-Rijāl has the lord of assets.

[18] *Exercitio.* One might have preferred *nisu* or *studio*, "effort."

[19] That is, their connection shows he will get the money, but he must overcome obstacles first.

[20] Al-Rijāl reads, "and of the house in which the infortune was, and according to the aspect which it had with the significators." Robert seems to agree with al-Rijāl.

[21] Adding on the basis of al-Rijāl. That is, if the querent is not asking just about wealth in general but about getting money from a specific man, or through a journey to a particular place. See also Ch. 22.

[22] This paragraph must have been particularly vexing in the Arabic, as none of the Latin authors agrees on all of the conditions. What makes it complicated is that it requires separate calculations of the Lots of Fortune and assets/money, for both the Ascendant and the querent. So for example, the Lot of assets or money of the seventh would require counting forward from the lord of the eighth to the eighth, and projecting that distance from the degree of the Descendant; in the same way, the Lot of Fortune of the seventh

Fortune of the seventh or the Lot of money of the seventh would apply to
the lord of the Ascendant or of the second; or [3] the lord of the Ascendant
[would apply] to the lord of the Lot of money of the seventh or to the lord
of its Lot of Fortune—if the witnesses which we said before were present—
they confirm the hope of acquiring money.

> [Robert]: And if there were a conjunction of: [1] the ruler of the east
> with the lord of the assets of the seventh, or conversely; or [2] of the
> lord of the assets of the seventh with the lord of the assets of the
> east;[24] or [3] of the lord of the Lot of Fortune (or [the lord] of the Lot
> of money) of the seventh with the corresponding Lots of the east or
> [with] the lord of the second; or [4] even of the lord of the east with
> the aforesaid Lots of the seventh—and the testimonies of discovering
> [money] stated above, were in agreement—the attainment or
> conveying of the matter will invariably follow.

> [al-Rijāl I.25]:[25] And if the lord of the house of assets applied to the
> Ascendant or with the lord of the Ascendant, or the lord of the
> Ascendant with the lord of the second, or the Lot of Fortune [were] in
> the seventh house, or the Lot of assets of the seventh [were] with the
> lord of the Ascendant or with the lord of the second, or the lord of the
> Ascendant and the lord of the Lot of assets of the seventh [were] with
> the Lot of Fortune, and the fortunes [were] testifying, he will have the
> assets just as we stated in the chapter before.

§468. But their different causes and their mutual status and manner (just
as has often been said), render a different opinion.

---

would project the usual Sun-Moon distance from the Descendant instead of from the
Ascendant.
23 That is, the lord of the Ascendant with the lord of the eighth.
24 That is, the lord of the eighth with the lord of the second.
25 Reading this paragraph with the 1485 edition of al- Rijāl, as it contains a phrase missing
in 1551.

# CHAPTER 14: ON ACQUIRING REAL ESTATE & LANDED PROPERTY[1]

### Chapter 14.1: Election: Acquiring real estate for agriculture[2]

§469. The distribution of lands is in two parts: for one is given to buildings and the habitation of men, the other to agriculture. The Ascendant and its lord, moreover the lunar lord and the Moon herself, even the pivots and their lords, [and] in the same way fortunate ones placed in the pivots and having some dignity in them (particularly in the Ascendant and the fourth), preserve that [part] which farmers are allotted. Moreover, let the infortunes be established as remote from the pivots. Likewise, let the Sun and the Moon be regarding the fourth in a friendly way, and be themselves strong. But of those which rule the pivots, none [should be] retrograde, nor should any retrograde star hold onto the pivots.

§470. For the prosperity of the fourth watches over the health of the land and the increase of [its] fruits. But the Midheaven signifies [trees and][3] cliffs and rocks, and—if they are in them—mountains. The Ascendant looks at the possessor of the land and his buildings. Also, the seventh claims the farmers and inhabitants and partners dwelling [there].[4]

§471. Let the Lot of Fortune even, and the lord of the twelfth from the Moon,[5] moreover the lord of the second, be supported by an aspect of fortunate ones, [and] let their lords be strong and appear in the pivots. Likewise, let the Lot of Fortune rejoice in the friendly view of the Sun and Moon and lucky ones.

§472. Wherefore it seems one must beware with the utmost effort lest some infortune appear in the ninth or eleventh or fifth: for it introduces harm and loss from the farmers.

---

[1] Parts of this chapter appear in al-Rijāl's material on elections; this is a case in which elections and questions blend together.

[2] For this subchapter, see al-Rijāl VII.22.

[3] Adding with Robert.

[4] But al-Rijāl's account allots these differently: the Ascendant for the buyer and the success of the venture (since it is an election), the Midheaven for things above the earth (such as trees), the fourth for the lands and inhabitants and servants (he also mentions that some assign it to the vegetation), and the seventh for its fertility and sowing.

[5] This probably means the twelfth-part of the Moon (*ITA* IV.6). But it may also indicate the lord of the Moon's sign itself.

§473. Moreover, we warn you to avoid there being a fiery sign in the fourth, or some fiery [planet] in it, and one estranged from the fortunes. For it corrupts the fruits with fire or heat and thirst if Mars would regard it, but more expressly if the regard would proceed from a pivot. Moreover, Saturn regarding the fourth and it being a watery [sign], does not free it from heavy rains and the damage of waters. The hostile regard of each, I say (namely of Saturn and Mars), and they being raised up above the ether,[6] increases the same.

§474. On the other hand, one must beware lest they corrupt the Midheaven, with it being an earthy sign. The perversity of Mars in it scorches the fruits, [and] afflicts with heat and dryness. But Saturn spoils with thirst and a lack of water. Moreover, should Mars corrupt it (it being a watery sign) [while] also descending,[7] it consumes the harvests with rot. The descent of Saturn in the ether, and corrupting [the Midheaven if it is a] watery sign, weakens the fruits, being deprived of maturity.

## Chapter 14.2: Election: Building on land[8]

§475. Furthermore, whenever a question about land destined for buildings were made known, let a firm sign be arranged in the fourth place (likewise the rest of the pivots), with the fortunate ones bearing themselves as was stated above; moreover, the lords of the pivots eastern and adding in course and being raised up in the north:[9] they portend the steadiness and firmness of the buildings, and the respectability and appropriateness of those affairs which pertain to that; finally, that all things are suitable and wholesome.

§476. One will even have to beware of the aforesaid status of the infortunes. For Mars bearing himself as was now said above, and corrupting, does not remove thieves and scorching. He being in a human sign admits thieves, enemies, plunderers, often even the violence and hand of the king. In a sign of another form, he threatens fire. But if Saturn would take up the role of Mars in that same status, it testifies to the ruin of a collapse, and

---

[6] Robert reads, "ascending in the circle," apparently referring to ascending in the circle of their apogee (see *ITA* II.1).

[7] Probably descending in the circle of the apogee.

[8] This might rather be for acquiring land for building, since Ch. 15 is on laying the foundations for buildings.

[9] In northern ecliptical latitude.

hastened dissolution.[10] Which if Mercury will be associated with Saturn, being invested with the virtue of Saturn himself,[11] and being estranged from the fortunes, and corrupting the fourth, it indicates the family's diseases, death, and scarcity.

---

[10] This "dissolution" refers to decay.
[11] This probably means that because Mercury is a very flexible planet, he takes on the nature of Saturn by mixing with him.

# CHAPTER 15: ON LAYING THE FOUNDATIONS OF CITIES & HOUSES

§477. The solution of this question engages the lunar counsel. For, the Moon made fortunate by lucky and eastern [planets], and set up in a place of her own authority, moreover her reception and that of the fortunate ones, approves [the construction]; or if the Moon would be set up in a pivot and ascending into the north, quick in course, in a fixed and straight sign,[1] even regarded even by her own lord; moreover the Lot of Fortune in some pivot and made fortunate (as was already said); also, let the pivots be set up as being firm and immovable, nor drawn down.[2] Moreover, the lords of the fourth and of the Ascendant [should be] in a place of their own power, and eastern, and all that we said before [should be] cleansed of the infortunes, even the pivots free of the infortunes.

§478. But [let] the lord of death[3] be estranged from [and] absent from the lord of the Ascendant and the Moon and the pivots. Also, the Tail in the twelfth, moreover let the lord of the sixth be entrusted to be estranged from the Ascendant and the Moon. Let the lord of the degree of the assembly or opposition be in a place of its own proper quality,[4] free of the infortunes, appearing in a pivot or after the pivots. Which if it were possible, Venus or Jupiter should be arranged in the pivot of the fourth or the tenth.

§479. In fact, such a disposition of these [planets] introduces no [merely] moderate money: [that is], the highest joy; but a special heap of gladness is amassed [with] Venus dwelling in the fourth, especially while she would favor the lord of the second and the Lot of Fortune and the Lot of money.

§480. Again, one must beware with the utmost effort lest Saturn or Mars hold onto the pivots: for Saturn devastates, expels the inhabitants, portends the unsteadiness of fragility, slows profit, blocks joys, and tries to put off better outcomes. Moreover Mars declares plunder, burning, the constant

---

[1] That is, a sign of straight or direct ascensions.
[2] Reading *nec* ("nor") for *vel* ("or"), since "drawn down" is normally used by Hugo to mean "cadent," which is not at all what one wants for a firm and upright building. So, I take this instruction to mean that the degree of the Midheaven should not be in the ninth sign (which is a cadent sign). See Bonatti's discussion of this idea (and al-Rijāl) in *BOA* Tr. 7 Ch. 11 (pp. 673-74).
[3] The lord of the eighth.
[4] Robert: "dignity."

attacks of enemies, (and as though eager to devour), the harming of the citizens, and wars breaking out.

§481. Moreover, in building cities it is good that Mars (as was stated above) be held back in [his] corruption from those who assist the lord of the Ascendant and the fourth and the Moon, [but] to favor [an aspect of] peace and health, [and] for them to be complected to part of them by some kind of reception.[5] Moreover, Venus being established in a trigon or tetragon introduces no moderate triumph from plowing.

---

[5] I take this to mean that these other significators will have receptions amongst themselves. But Robert plausibly reads, "but if [Mars] would be applied to them in any way, let him receive [them]."

# CHAPTER 16: ON DIGGING CANALS, CULTIVATING THE LAND, & CONSTRUCTING WELLS & DAMS[1]

## Chapter 16.1: Digging canals

§482. In digging out canals, let the Moon be in the first tetragon of the Sun, made fortunate, and received in a pivot; let even the pivots be disposed firm and straight,[2] also the lord of the Ascendant should be eastern and in some place of its own dignity, in a pivot or after a pivot; let even the ascending sign be watery and favored by a thriving fortune. Let the pivot of the fourth be strong, not deprived of the blessing of the lucky ones.

§483. But let the lunar lord be in a place of its own authority, received, blessed. Moreover let the Lot of Fortune be supported by the regard of the Sun and Moon. Let the degree of the assembly[3] be favored by the regard of fortunate ones. But let the application of the Moon (after her first withdrawal from the assembly or opposition of the Sun) come to be with a strong fortune in a pivot or after a pivot. Moreover, the lord of the assembly or opposition should bear itself in the same way. But let the infortunes be cadent from the pivots and from the Sun and Moon and Lot of Fortune, [and] the lunar lord.

§484. Which if it would be possible [for this] to happen as we have determined, it repels [any] hindrance from the digging out of the canal, it multiplies the waters and makes it support not-moderate profit [from them],[4] and keeps them harmless, and guards those sailing and the ships unharmed, and renders them unfailing.

---

[1] For this chapter, I have been helped by Burnett 1993.
[2] Again, signs of straight or direct ascension.
[3] *Alestima*, a transliteration of the Ar. *al-ijtimā*ᶜ, "assembly." That is, the lunation prior to the election (I would include the opposition, since the next sentence includes that).
[4] Reading with guidance from the Arabic.

## Chapter 16.2: Digging wells[5]

§485. Moreover, in [constructing] certain irrigation instruments for wells (which tend to be used among some peoples for drawing forth the depths of waters, which are even called by the common name of "storks" on account of the likeness of their form),[6] let the Ascendant and pivots be established as firm and immovable, nor drawn down,[7] even straight [in ascensions]; also, the Ascendant [should be] an earthy sign. The pivot of the earth and the rest [of the pivots should be treated] in this manner.

§486. Let the pivots be cleansed of the infortunes and defended, being made fortunate by the lucky ones. Venus in the Ascendant or in the fourth, namely in an earthy sign, produces a more powerful effect; also, the Moon in an earthy sign and dominant in the north or the south,[8] and in a place of her own authority, received by an eastern fortune, [indicates] the same.

## Chapter 16.3: Constructing dams

§487. Likewise the construction of dams follows the art of the aforesaid wells. For wells are dams.[9]

---

[5] Hugo seems to think at the beginning that this section is about constructing the irrigation mechanism above the well (see the next footnote), but the Arabic al-Kindī is describing the construction of the well itself. Probably the same mechanism used for drawing out the water, was also used to draw out the dirt while the well was being dug.

[6] According to Burnett (1993 p. 113), Hugo is describing a *shādūf* (Ar.), a long pole resting on a fulcrum, with a bucket dangling down into the water of a well. By pulling down on the free end, the pole lifts up the bucket full of water.

[7] This seems to mean that al-Kindī does not want the axis of the MC-IC to fall into a cadent sign. See §477 above.

[8] Reading with Burnett's translation from the Arabic (1993, p. 113). It probably means, "ruling the fourth or tenth."

[9] Reading with Burnett again. Again, Hugo seems to have latched onto the irrigation mechanism rather than the earthworks and digging itself: thus in his own version he thinks al-Kindī means the construction of waterwheels, saying "waters are extracted with the benefit of each instrument in the irrigation of fields."

## Chapter 16.4: Cultivating lands[10]

§488. But the Moon being received by fortunate ones consults for the cultivation of lands, [and] let the one by whom she is received be pivotal or after the pivots (but more powerful is [if] it or at least the Moon [is] in a pivot). Moreover, let the status of the lord of the Ascendant be corresponding to the status of the lord of the Moon.[11] Moreover, let the pivots be strengthened, cleansed of the infortunes [and] defended by the lucky ones, particularly while one of the fortunate ones would be set up as the lord of the house of money or of the Lot of Fortune or of the Lot of money. Moreover, let the [degree of the] assembly or the opposition fall into a pivot.[12]

§489. Then, the Moon's application by assembly or opposition of the Sun[13] should be directed towards some fortune in a pivot or after a pivot. But let the lord of the assembly be lucky, moreover the lunar lord and [the lord] of the fourth acquire the benefit of happiness.

---

[10] Reading with Burnett on this topic for Hugo's "inhabiting lands." As Burnett (1993, p. 117) points out, Hugo and Robert thought this section was about clearing land for the first time rather than simply cultivating it. But one can see why they might have thought so: cultivating land can be done every year, and has to be done on a schedule—unlike the special act of clearing it for the first time, which is more suitable for an election.

[11] Al-Rijāl (VII.23) clarifies that their condition should be *good*.

[12] Al-Rijāl's list of conditions differs somewhat, such as having a benefic *in* the second house rather than simply being its ruler.

[13] That is, the degree of the conjunction or prevention of the luminaries which most recently preceded the horary question or election. But I am not sure what is being timed here.

# CHAPTER 17: ON CONSTRUCTING SHIPS

§490. For organizing the construction of ships, let comfort of this kind be conveyed. Therefore, in the first place the Ascendant should be made firm, and the rest of the pivots established as immovable, nor drawn down[1]—but we should ascribe these to the fixed and straight signs. Also, let the Moon and the lord of the Ascendant be set up in a pivot and received by the lucky ones. Moreover, let a strong fortunate one,[2] in [its] easternness and in a place of its own authority and in quick step, strengthen and defend the Midheaven. Also, let the Moon be borne by her greater and faster course, and raised up in the ether.[3] Also, let her and the lord of the Ascendant be cleansed of the infortunes.

§491-492a. And so, Mars in a pivot, corrupting the Moon and lord of the Ascendant (or at least one [of them]), burns the ship up—especially from a fiery sign. In an earthy sign, it shakes and breaks the ship by a small bump or collision with a mountain or rocks.[4] In an airy sign, it sinks it through the loss of the oars and the blowing of winds. Moreover, with him appearing in a watery sign, it is sunk through the carelessness of those navigating, or the amount of the cargo. Which if Saturn would perform the role of Mars, it is believed to be harmful through a corresponding misfortune. However, he being in a fiery sign brings the wrecked ship down to the depths, but on account of those things which we established above with respect to the signs. Mars being in a human sign [means] the calamity of sinking, an assault of robbers, and an assault by enemies seem to follow.

§492b-493. In addition, the prosperity of the ship comes to be discerned in this ranking. For, Jupiter in the Midheaven preserves the full and general health of the cargo and of those sailing, and multiplies the profit and reward. If however Venus would favor and comfort the ship from the Midheaven, it greatly increases the common safety of the ship and cargo (though it happens more powerfully from Jupiter), [and] multiplies the joys of the captain or [the one who acts] on behalf of [its] owner.

---

[1] I believe this means that the degree of the Midheaven should not fall on the ninth sign.
[2] Reading the singular with Robert; Hugo begins with the singular but uses verbs in the plural.
[3] Ascending in the circle of her apogee.
[4] *Montis et saxorum.* Or perhaps this should simply be read as "a mass of rocks."

§494-95a. Further, the lord of the assembly or opposition should be noted [and] established in the way it was stated before in the above chapter.[5] Moreover, let the application of the Moon (after she leaves the assembly or opposition of the Sun), come to be or happen with a fortunate one.

§495b. Likewise, let the lord of the second make the lord of the Ascendant fortunate, and also establish the lord of the Midheaven in its own sovereignty, if it is permissible, and [make it] everywhere strong; also let the infortunes fall down from[6] the Sun and Moon, but let the Lot of Fortune be situated in a more powerful[7] aspect of the Moon.[8]

---

[5] Perhaps referring to §483 above.
[6] That is, be "in aversion to."
[7] Robert: "friendly."
[8] Robert: "And let the Lot of Fortune and the lights regard the east at the same time, in a friendly way; and let the infortunes be cadent from the pivots."

# CHAPTER 18: QUESTIONS ABOUT SHIPS: WHAT GOOD OR BAD WILL HAPPEN TO THEM[1]

## Chapter 18.1: Significators & overview

§496.[2] If someone often gapes at the false calm or amassing of winds, and wants to count his passage-money [and keep it safe], then let him await the beginning of this chapter, so that the ship does not totter in its motion due to a bad decision in this art.

§497. With the Ascendant being noted first, let the rest of the pivots be established with a precise method of computation. For the Ascendant designates the front part of the ship (namely the prow), but the seventh the stern, also the Midheaven the mast;[3] the underside is left to the pivot of the earth. In addition, four parts are reckoned as being on the right side, and that many on the left.

§498.[4] For example, with two parts on the right bordering on the water, [we give] the second to the forward one, the fifth to the rear one. To the two upper ones near the mast [we give] the third to the forward one, the sixth to the rear one. Of the two next to the water on the left side, [we give] the eleventh to the forward one, the eighth to the following one. Of the two lofty [parts], [we give] the twelfth to the leading one, the ninth to the rear one.

---

[1] For this chapter, cf. al-Rijāl III.14.
[2] This paragraph is only in Robert. I have substantially rewritten its tortured, self-indulgent style (which suggests that it is not a translation from Arabic).
[3] Reading with Robert for Hugo's "each edge."
[4] Using Robert's more succinct paragraph for Hugo's.

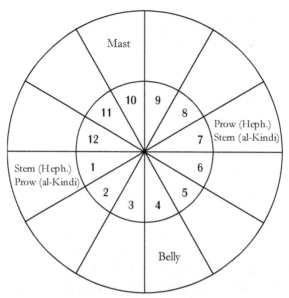

**Figure 54: Angles of the chart & ship:**
**Dorotheus-Hephaistio *vs.* al-Kindī**

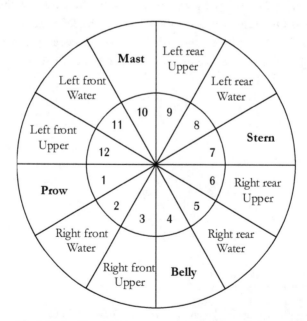

**Figure 55: Al-Kindī's ship-house associations (Robert & Hugo)**

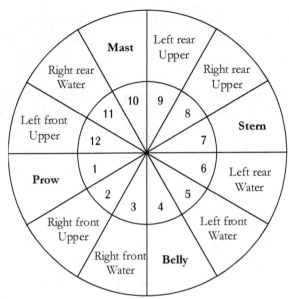

**Figure 56: Al-Kindī's ship-house associations (Latin al-Rijāl III.14)**

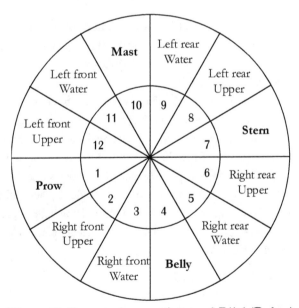

**Figure 57: Proposed correction to al-Rijāl (Dykes)**

*Comment by Dykes.* The attributions of houses to the parts of a ship are somewhat troubled in the literature.[5] Two types of differences are shown here: [1] in the assignment of the angles, and [2] the assignment of the rest of the houses.[6]

[1] The version according to Dorotheus (in Hephaistio III.14) gives the prow to the seventh and the stern to the Ascendant, as though the ship is sailing toward the 7th and the west. But the version according to al-Kindī reverses these, as though the ship is pointed towards the Ascendant and the east. What accounts for this difference? On the one hand, the seventh is usually envisioned as the destination of a journey:[7] in that case, Dorotheus imagines the ship *sailing away* from home (the Ascendant) *into* other waters (seventh), while al-Kindī imagines the ship *returning to* home (the Ascendant) *from* other waters (seventh). In that case, the attributions would really depend on the kind of question: "Will the ship reach its destination" (Dorotheus), and "Will the ship return home" (al-Kindī)—and indeed, §§499 and 506 suggest just this. But it seems to me that the disagreement is probably not intentional, and that the extent of the differences in the various versions are due to an error by al-Kindī or his sources—which brings us to the second difference:

[2] Robert and Hugo give a different attribution to the other parts of the ship than even the Latin al-Rijāl does, though both Robert-Hugo and al-Rijāl have their own kind of logic (and provided that one accepts my proposed correction to al-Rijāl in Figure 57).

[2a] For Robert and Hugo (Figure 55), everything above the horizon is the left side, and everything below it is the right side (which does *not* make sense if the ship is pointed eastwards, as they claim); likewise, everything in the eastern hemisphere is the front half of the ship, and everything in the western hemisphere is the rear part (which *does* make sense if the ship is indeed pointed eastwards). From there, the succeedent places all pertain to the lower sides of the ship touching the water, and the cadent places to the upper sides of the ship. I do not see why succeedent and cadent places should be divided in this way.

---

[5] The zodiacal signs are also attributed to parts of a ship: see al-Rijāl III.14 and 'Umar (*Judges* §9.44), both of whom credit "Ptolemy." Lilly also uses this zodiacal scheme (*CA* pp. 157-58).
[6] As Jiménez (2007, p. 29) points out, another and apparently jumbled and unclear version is attributed to Rhetorius in *CCAG* VIII.1, p. 265).
[7] See for example Ch. 29 below, §§604*ff.*

[2b] The Latin al-Rijāl (III.14) has a much more logical scheme for the non-angular parts of the chart. One may refer above to the scheme as actually written in the Latin version (Figure 56), which seems to mix up several of the attributions in ways that do not make sense. But I believe my own correction (Figure 57) is probably what al-Rijāl intended: like Robert and Hugo, my corrected al-Rijāl gives the upper and lower, eastern and western parts of the chart of the left, right, front and rear parts of the ship, respectively. However, from there, the attributions of the parts near the water or upper sides follow more logically: the places on each side of the Ascendant-seventh axis are higher up, near the upper points of the prow (Ascendant, second, twelfth) or the stern (seventh, sixth, eighth). The places flanking the Midheaven-IC axis are closer to the water. In this way we can follow a semicircular path around the ship on each side: from the point of the prow (Ascendant) we can trace from the upper part (second) to the lower part near the water (third) to the belly below (fourth), then up again to the water's surface again (fifth) and then to the upper side (sixth) toward the top of the stern (seventh)—and likewise down and around on the other side (provided that the fourth indicates the belly itself, no matter what side we are on).

[2c] However, my correction to the Latin al-Rijāl not answer the puzzling problem of the sides and direction of the ship itself. For in my corrected version, if one stands and faces the prow, toward the east, then the southern side of the chart (to one's right) indicates the left side of the ship, and vice versa—which does not make sense. But, the sides of the chart and ship *would* be consistent and logical if we adopted the Dorothean attribution of the angles and switched the stern and prow around. And so, I propose the following attributions, using the following: Dorothean angles, corrected al-Rijāl sides and upper/water distinctions, and switching the front/rear attributions to match Dorotheus:

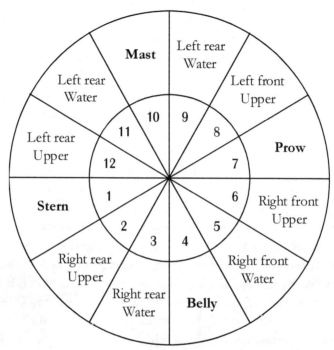

**Figure 58: Proposed correct attributions (Dykes)**

## Chapter 18.2: The safety & harm of the ship

§499. Therefore, with a question proposed about the course of a ship, if the pivots would gleam with the fortunate ones' own proper light,[8] but with the infortunes being estranged and cadent and scorched, they promise a safe and longed-for [return to] port without impediment, for both the ship and the cargo. But the infortunes in a pivot or after the pivots introduce danger into that part of the ship designated by the sign which the infortune is holding onto.

§500. Saturn [as that infortune] sinks it, wrecked. Moreover, Mars being in some place of his own dignity or in its regard,[9] and in an earthy sign, indicates the same as Saturn, but warns that one should fear an excessive collision of waves and overturning by rough seas.

§501. Also, with the infortunes bearing themselves thusly, if the regard of fortunes would be brought to bear, even the pivotal lords being safe and clean [of the infortunes], [and] particularly the Ascendant [and] the lunar lord, [then] after the aforesaid threats of rough seas and seething waves, they look after the integrity of the ship, and for the most part the cargo. But if Mars himself would corrupt the lords of the pivots and the lord of the Moon, it brings in the trouble of excessive storms and various attacks of enemies.

§502. If however unluckiness would accompany this corruption of the signs, it generates war, afflicts with wounds, pilfers goods through theft, particularly while the infortunes appear in signs defending the upper parts of ships (namely those adjacent to the edges [of the ship]). Also, the perversity of Saturn and Mars [together] inserts death and captivity. However, Saturn as the sole author of this corruption expels death [itself], but binds captives together and squanders the money.

§503. Which if Mars would hold onto the Midheaven, it being corrupted ([for the Midheaven] takes the signification over the upper parts of the ship, with the rest), it brings flashing [and] lightning down from above, and[10] what the fiery adversity of clouds tends to bring. He being in the pivot of the earth

---

[8] That is, if the fortunes were bodily in the pivots (al-Rijāl).

[9] Reading with al-Rijāl and Robert: that is, if Mars is in one of his own dignities or aspects a place of his own dignity (presumably this would only include his domiciles). A problem with this interpretation is that there is no sign in the zodiac in which Mars will not aspect at least one of his domiciles.

[10] Omitting *si*, which may have been *etsi* but still does not help.

scorches the lower parts of the ship. Moreover, in a human sign it burns the ship by an enemy hand, and it attacks[11] the part possessed by that corrupted sign, with iron. But if Saturn would enjoy the role of Mars in the Midheaven, it tears down the mast (namely the "tree" of the ship), shaken by the force of the winds, it shatters the sail, and induces danger according to the nature of the infortune and the estrangement of the fortunate ones, or even [according to] their testimony.

§504-05a. Also, an infortune (namely Saturn) being in the seventh, shocks the rear of the ship [and] breaks the ornamental stern. Which if Mars would be taking up that position, it incites enemies and renews the fires and lightning strikes just as was said before. Moreover, an infortune in the Ascendant contaminates the forward part of the ship with loss, just as I think has already been said enough with respect to the nature of the danger with the effectiveness of the infortune [in the seventh].[12]

§505b-506. But the retrogradation of the lord of the Ascendant impedes the journey and leads the ship back with it being incomplete. Likewise, with the lord of the Ascendant in a convertible sign, and it[13] retrograding, it brings it back to the place whence the ship had set out, with the journey being cut short. Which if retrogradation of [the lord of the Ascendant] would happen, and it is fortunate, it promises a useful return; being unlucky, it makes a return with loss.

§507. Then, the lord of the eighth (particularly with it being in the seventh) corrupting the lord of the Ascendant, threatens harm to the ship according to the manner and nature of the one harassing [it]. Moreover, the lord of the eighth (it being in the eighth) corrupting the Moon and the lunar lord and [the lord] of the Ascendant, exposes the master of the ship (and very often all of those whom he takes [on board]) to harm. The Lot of Fortune corrupted, and the Lot of money (and their lords)[14] corrupted, testify to the loss of the cargo according to the nature of the one making it unfortunate. If however fortunate ones would take up this role of the infortunes, they convey profit.

---

[11] Reading *afficit* for *appetit*.
[12] Again, all of this assumes that the Ascendant really does signify the prow and the seventh the stern (unlike with Dorotheus-Hephaistio).
[13] Reading with Robert for *eiusdem signi domino*. But al-Rijāl reads, "the lord of the fourth sign."
[14] Reading with al-Rijāl; Robert and Hugo include only the lord of the Lot of money.

## Chapter 18.3: Speed

§508. Also, the slowness of the lord of the Ascendant and of the lunar [lord], particularly with their lords bearing themselves that way, suggests a delay in completing the journey. The quickness of their course leads it more quickly to the destined place.

## Chapter 18.4: Death

§509. Which if the unfriendliness of contrariety would be found between the lord of the Ascendant and the lunar [lord], namely so that one would be situated in the seventh of the other without mutual reception (but rather if one would taint the other), it inserts mutual dissension [between] those sailing and the one whom the infortune afflicts with its own nuisance of adversity, will meet death, conquered.

## Chapter 18.5: Supplies & food

§510. Moreover: [1] the lord of the second being estranged from the second, likewise [2] the lord of the second from the Moon standing back from[15] the lunar second, moreover [3] the lord of the Lot of Fortune being estranged and absent from the Lot of Fortune, afflicts the cohort of those sailing, with a lack of food and supplies and those things which pertain to the sustaining of life.

§511. But if this should happen in watery signs, they are restricted by a lack of water. In airy or fiery ones, they are vexed with anxiety over starvation. Also, in fiery signs they are pressured by starving for those things which generally have the essence of sustaining [people] through the benefit of fire.[16] And so, remember to consider it for the rest in this manner.

---

15 Again, "in aversion to."
16 In other words, cooked foods.

# CHAPTER 19: ON ACQUIRING SLAVES[1]

§512. When someone is eager to buy slaves or admit certain slaves into his own employ, let the Ascendant and the Moon be situated in fixed[2] signs, and straight ones, and ones having the form of gentle [animals]. Moreover, let the lords of the house of slaves (namely the sixth) and of the Lot of slaves[3] be applying with the lord of the Ascendant, and let them be received by it in a friendly way. No less, moreover, should they apply with the Moon and the lunar lord, and be received, while they make the Ascendant and the Moon fortunate.

§513. Which if a requisition[4] of slaves should come to be because of some official duty or work, the application of the lord of the Midheaven with the lord of the house of slaves and the lord of the Lot of slaves should be noted, and [let them] be received.

But the infortunes should be put down from[5] the sixth, and let them be established in the friendly regard of the Ascendant and the Moon, with the fortunate ones in the pivots or after the pivots.

§514. Moreover, I think one should beware, with the utmost effort, lest the Moon or the Ascendant or the lord of [the house] of slaves be in Leo. Which if it happened to be so, they show a bold slave, brazen and in rebellion [against] his own master, often even making use of the laws of liberty unjustly for his own [benefit].

§515. But in Cancer they will indicate an inert and weak man, and one of no counsel or uprightness. Likewise in Pisces. But with them appearing in Scorpio, the slave is confirmed as being cautious, cunning, a liar, bad, morally corrupt. Which if they dwelled in Libra, it reveals a fugitive. But in Capricorn,[6] they do not deny flight and sexual immorality, and one about to

---

[1] For this chapter, cf. *Carmen* V.11, Sahl's *On Elections* §§71-73, and al-Rijāl VII.50 (which is more abbreviated than Hugo/Robert).

[2] Reading with al-Rijāl for Hugo's "watery."

[3] There are two Lots of slaves: that attributed to Hermes is taken from Mercury to the Moon (but authorities disagree as to whether it should be reversed at night); that attributed to al-Andarzaghar (which is the same as the Hermetic Lot of Necessity) is taken in the day from Mercury to the Lot of Fortune, and conversely at night. Both are projected from the Ascendant. See *ITA* VI.2.20.

[4] *Coemptio*, a forced purchase.

[5] That is, "in aversion to."

[6] Or perhaps, only in its first half, since the second half is mentioned separately below.

convey much disgrace to his master. But in Aquarius they indicate a man of long-lasting deliberation, silent, sparing in speech, cautious, persistent in [his] duty, but they demonstrate he is lazy in working.

§516. At the beginning of Sagittarius, he is confirmed to be arrogant and prideful; but at its end, his vigor and strength is highly praised. Moreover, at the end of Capricorn one unsound in his work is denoted. But if those which we have stated before happened to be in Taurus, they will exhibit vigor, a tolerance for labor, a lover of the one ruling over him. Also, in Aries they portend quarrels, dissensions, flight, rebellion; and [in Gemini],[7] a manner of elation.[8]

§517. And so, whatever good or prosperity from the slaves any one of the signs signifies, the lord of that sign and a regard of the fortunate ones increases it. Moreover, a regard of fortunate ones mitigates whatever malice of the slaves is denoted by any of the signs. But whatever prosperity is meant, is restrained by a regard of the unfortunate ones.

§518. Moreover, the Tail being situated in the Ascendant, or at least being with the Moon at the hour of the purchase, incurs loss from the slave because of low-class and abject matters. Again, it being in the sixth or with the Lot of slaves, affirms the slave's lack of skill, groveling, negligence of his own person and whole sense of honor, whence he incurs the crime, blame, and disgrace of his own master.

---

[7] Adding with Robert.
[8] *Consuetudinem elationis*. That is, the slave tends to be satisfied.

# CHAPTER 20: ON MARRIAGE

## Chapter 20.1: Whether he will marry

§519.[1] In establishing a marriage,[2] the lord of the Ascendant and of the seventh should be consulted. For, an application of the lord of the Ascendant with the lord of the seventh, and they being regarded by their own lords, and in the pivots or after the pivots, consecrate the nuptials.[3]

§520.[4] Moreover, a lunar application with Venus, and she being received by Venus, moreover an application of the Moon with the lord of the seventh, are asked to be noted. For all of these convey that the husband's vow and devotion to marry is present. But if the lord of the seventh or Venus herself would apply with the lord of the Ascendant or with the Moon, or if the lord of the seventh [would do so] with the Moon, the nuptial union agrees with the fiancée's wishes.

§521. No less does the application of the Sun with Venus bring about nuptials, particularly while the Sun would obtain some dignity in the Ascendant. Moreover, the Sun being received (namely regarded by his own lord) indicates the same thing. Moreover, the cadency of the one applying and the one to which the application happens, dissolves marriages, especially with the estrangement of their own lords from them, once the hope of nuptials they had is virtually complete.

§522. The Sun and the Moon and Venus, even the lord of the seventh and of the Ascendant, being in the pivots, [even if they do not regard each other but they are][5] regarded by their lords, and strong, [indicate that] the effecting of the marriage will follow a wholly extinguished hope of nuptials—then, I say, [it will be] when the direction[6] of the significator [which shows that the

---

[1] From here through §522, cf. al-Rijāl II.29.

[2] This has to do with love and relationship questions, not electing a time for the marriage. For the election, see Ch. 20.6 below. As usual, most of this chapter assumes a male querent, and should be adjusted accordingly. But see also §§523a and 533 below.

[3] Al-Rijāl only has them applying, and omits reception or angularity.

[4] For this section, see also §534 below.

[5] Adding with al-Rijāl.

[6] *Atazir*, omitting Hugo's explanatory *computatio videlicet aut transmutatio*.

marriage would happen][7] reached a pivot, by appointing days or months or years.[8]

## Chapter 20.2: Whether she is a virgin

§523a. Furthermore,[9] if someone suggests a question about the purity (or rather, sexual immorality) of the wife, the sign of the Ascendant should be noted—if, I say, it is asked specifically about the self-control of her whom he has arranged [a marriage contract with],[10] [that is, whether she] will be led astray. Which if someone [only] burning with the delight of [possible] conjugal fetters should seek [to know] whether or not he is going to marry a pure woman, let the lord of the seventh be consulted in place [of the lord] of the Ascendant. Venus and the Moon are supportive for both [kinds of questions].[11]

§523b-24a. [The significators] being in firm signs and in the regard of the lucky ones, promise she is pure, with her virginity unimpaired. In fact, the infortunes possessing the role of the fortunate ones, do not take away [her] virginity, but they do exhibit sexual immorality.[12]

§524b. But if these significators are holding onto double-bodied signs and are regarded by the fortunate ones, they do convey that she has been violated, but they preserve [her] purity.[13] Moreover, if the infortunes are

---

[7] Adding with al-Rijāl.

[8] I imagine this procedure could also be followed in nativities.

[9] From here through §525, cf. al-Rijāl II.30a. But al-Rijāl's account is very abbreviated compared with either Robert or Hugo.

[10] Adding based on Robert.

[11] Like Hugo, the Latin al-Rijāl simply groups the Moon and Venus along with the other lords; nor does al-Rijāl mention the seventh at all. Robert distinguishes the Moon and Venus, saying: "First one must discern whether the question comes to be after the contract has been made firm, or before. Therefore, after the contract we embrace the lord of the east and the Moon; but before, the lord of the seventh and Venus." (See also §533 and the differences between Robert and al-Rijāl there.) Robert's (or al-Kindī's) rationale seems to be this: the Moon is consulted once the engagement is settled, because she represents a female spouse (or fiancée); but Venus is consulted before it is settled, because she signifies *desire*. But this does not really answer the question as to why the Ascendant is chosen in one case, but the seventh in the other.

[12] The benefic or malefic quality of the planets shows conventional moral purity or impurity respectively, while the quadruplicity indicates the extent of actual sexual activity—such that fixed signs show self-control, but the movable signs something more like promiscuity.

[13] In other words, she has some sexual experience but has not lost her virginity.

allotted the role of the fortunate ones, they claim a corrupted and sexually impure woman. (This is affirmed particularly by the regard of Mars.) Moreover, the mutual regard of the Sun and Moon designate public sexual immorality, if they would even be looking at Mars.[14] Which if the Sun and the Moon were deprived of mutual regard, and estranged from Mars, they conceal the crime of longing.

§525. Moreover, should the Ascendant and the pivots be set up in convertible signs, and the infortunes in the same place, they indicate inextinguishable longing. Which if the regard of Mars is present, she will crave the sexual intercourse of each sex against moral [law], to boot. But if the fortunate ones would take over in place of the infortunes, they testify that she is of immoderate [sexual] longing, but [has] a sense of shame[15] and conceals her own crimes, [but] at last everything becomes public.

## Chapter 20.3: On her looks

§526-27a. Also,[16] [if someone is] worried about [her] form, let a view of the Ascendant be put forth, and the head and face ascribed to it. But to the second the neck, the third the hands and arms; but the chest obtains the fourth; also, the fifth the belly up to the groin; the sixth, the hips and sides; but the seventh, from the lower groin and the kidneys. Also the eighth, the places of longing; the ninth place, the buttocks and upper portion of the legs; but the tenth, the lower [part] and knees; the eleventh, the shins; the twelfth takes the feet. Therefore, it seems that the individual limbs must be noted individually according to the figure of the animal which is designated by them, and the form of its limbs.

§527b. And no little consideration is needed for this: [namely] in what place of the circle the Moon is made fortunate: for that limb ([designated] by that sign which the Moon is holding onto) being lucky, must be noted as being proper, and an appropriate marking is asserted as being there.

§528. But in a sign where a corrupted Moon dwells, it afflicts the limb belonging to its authority with some deformity or ugly sign. Moreover, the

---

[14] Mars can mean prostitution (which is what Robert and al-Rijāl identify), but perhaps it simply means there is scandal and gossip involved.

[15] Omitting the puzzling *et ad horam*, which is not reflected in Robert or al-Rijāl.

[16] From here through §532, cf. al-Rijāl II.30b.

augmentation or increase of the Moon[17] designates some augmenting [in that limb] beyond proper measure; decreasing, it suggests something is missing from the body. Moreover, [in] the middle between increase and decrease, it disfigures the skin and surface of the limbs [attributed] to that sign.

§529. But the color of the sign which the Moon is holding onto, and of the star by which the Moon is corrupted, designates of what color the blemish (or rather, mark) consists.

§530. But from what nature this foulness came forth, an earthy sign of the Moon, and her corrupting star being earthy, testify that it is cold and dry. But they being watery, cold and moist. Airy, hot and moist. But fiery, they establish that it is of a hot and dry nature.

§531. Which if the sign which the Moon is holding onto, and that of her corrupting star, consisted of different [natures], it is believed that the nature of each must be united in the discernment of this matter.

§532. However, [if] a fortunate one traverses the sign of any limb, it commends its looks; and an infortune exposes its ugliness. And so, in all things about whose status it is asked, let us remember to respond in a similar way, being instructed in an appraisal of this opinion.


### Chapter 20.4: Her background & status

§533. Discern[18] thusly whether she is rich or from a poor household. For, if such a question preceded [the engagement] (since the lord of the seventh claims the signification of that),[19] the lord of the eighth applying with the lord of the seventh, and made fortunate, likewise the Moon regarding the eighth and its lord, [but] the infortunes being estranged from the eighth, increase the woman's riches. Which if they bear themselves otherwise, they testify to scarcity. But their middling [quality] brings forth a mediocrity of assets and possessions. If however the significator of the question [were] the Ascendant [because the agreement has already been made],[20] let it be decided

---

[17] Al-Rijāl says that this is an increase in her motion, not in her size or phase.
[18] Cf. al-Rijāl II.31. This question is really directed towards learning the size of the prospective bride's dowry. This is still a very important issue in traditional marriages such as in India.
[19] Namely, of prospective partners *before* the engagement. See §523a above.
[20] Adding based on Robert. But the Latin al-Rijāl distinguishes the approaches this way: if a man asks about the woman, look at the seventh and eighth; but if the woman asks about the man, give her the Ascendant and the second. Now, on the one hand, the Latin al-Rijāl

from the Ascendant and the second, in just the way that advice is sought
from the seventh and eighth for the other [question].

### Chapter 20.5: Whether they will like each other

§534.[21] Once certainty about the marriage has been gotten, let such a
consideration be had as to whether one [spouse] would be conquered by the
obliged love of the other: for if the lord of the Ascendant and of the seventh
would enjoy a common aspect, [and] in the same way should the lord of the
Ascendant, and Venus, even the Moon [and] the lord of the seventh be held
[together] by a friendly regard, and be received, they signify the common
esteem of each. But if the regard of just one of them would be noted, the
affection is proven to belong only to the one whose receiving comes to be.[22]
And so it will be permitted to judge in this way with the rest of [matters]
about which a question of this kind proceeded.[23]

---

might simply mean that the querent gets the Ascendant and second in any case, and that
the betrothed always gets the seventh and eighth. But on the other hand, if Robert is
correct about the text, and the distinction is between agreements that are only potential
(seventh and eighth) and those already made (Ascendant and second), the rationale might
be this: when asking about a potential dowry, the question is essentially about a business
deal: one family is negotiating and contracting with the other. In that case, the seventh
and eighth represent the other family as business partners, so as to investigate their
wealth. But if the betrothal is already official, then the couple are legally united, and so a
question about their enrichment in the marriage is really a question about *their* finances:
hence the Ascendant and the second.

[21] Cf. al-Rijāl II.31.

[22] Robert puts this a bit more intriguingly: "if one of the significators conveys, [but] the
other refuses." This sounds like a case of "returning" (*ITA* III.19), but also see "not-
reception" in my comments to §94 and §101 above, Sahl's *Introduct.* §5.9, and al-Rijāl I.10.
In his own version of this passage, al-Rijāl says, "and if one of their significators received
the other, but the other did not receive it, say that the receiving one esteems the other,
and that the received does not esteem the receiving one."

[23] Reading *processerit* for *praecesserit*, following the verb in *Judges*.

## Chapter 20.6: Election: Choosing a time to affirm the marriage

§535.[24] In affirming a marriage, always let the signs ascribed to the significators (namely the Ascendant and the seventh, moreover the sign of the Moon and Venus) be established as straight and firm ones; furthermore, let the lord of the Ascendant and of the seventh be supported in common friendship and reception, with that same benignness existing between the Moon and the lord of the seventh. [But] let fortunate ones be in the pivots, [and] the infortunes thrust far from them. Moreover, let the lord of the house of children and Mercury be put as applying to fortunate significators, and cleansed of the infortunes.[25]

§536. Moreover, let the fifth and the lord of the fifth, even Mercury, possess signs of a manifold number and manifold form. Furthermore, let the fourth, the Sun even and the Moon, likewise the Lot of Fortune and the Lot of money, be made fortunate;[26] likewise let the application of the Moon after the assembly or opposition (which preceded the beginning of the marriage-[ceremony]) be to fortunate ones, and let her lord be lucky.

---

[24] From here through §536, cf. al-Rijāl II.32. This is for electing the time for commencing with the marriage ceremony itself.

[25] So as to produce many children.

[26] For wealth and a stable home.

# CHAPTER 21: ON PREGNANCY & CHILDBEARING[1]

## Chapter 21.1: Whether pregnant, & the number of children

§537. For a question as to whether or not a woman is pregnant, the lord of the Ascendant and of the fifth, and the Moon, should be consulted. If therefore some type of application would be noted between the lord of the fifth and that of the Ascendant (or the Moon), particularly if the Ascendant and the Moon would possess double-bodied signs, [and] in the same way the significators [would be] in the pivots or after the pivots, while a lucky star would be in the Ascendant or the second, they affirm she is pregnant. But if not, should they bear themselves [in] neither an application nor the pivots as we have said above, they deny[2] she is pregnant.

§538. Which if some star[3] would be arranged with the Moon and be received by her, or at least be with the lord of the Ascendant,[4] it claims she is fertile.[5] Moreover, some star with the Sun (namely in his degree[6] or under his rays), particularly a fortunate one, especially exhibits the signification of her being pregnant.

§539. If however the infortunes would fill the role of the fortunate ones in every signification of theirs, [she is not pregnant or][7] they promise a miscarriage.[8] Which if wicked Mars would appear in that same place, she is corrupted with a flowing of blood. But if Saturn, [the fetus] is dissolved through an excess of waters and winds.

---

[1] For this chapter, cf. al-Rijāl I.48.
[2] *Inficiantur.*
[3] I imagine al-Kindī means a fortunate star.
[4] Al-Rijāl I.48 says: "If perhaps there were a direct planet with the Moon, applying to the lord of the Ascendant." But probably the Latin of al-Rijāl is wrong, and mistakenly reads *directus* for the more accurate *receptus* ("received").
[5] That is, she has been fertilized and is pregnant.
[6] Reading with al-Rijāl and Robert for Hugo's *affinitate.*
[7] Adding with al-Rijāl.
[8] Or, "abortion" (*abortivum*).

## Chapter 21.2: The time left in the pregnancy

§540. With him asking you about the hour of conception, you will note how many ninth-parts of the Ascendant have passed by to completion: for, by taking months for individual ninth-parts, it asserts that that much [time] has passed by from the hour of the conception up to the time of the question. But how much of the Ascendant is left, designates the remaining time [until] the birth, as a month is granted to each ninth-part.

§541. But sometimes, the degrees by which the applying star and the one with which the application is, are distant [from one another], determine the hour of giving birth, by representing months in this judgment—if, I say, the degrees appeared to be fewer than the time [left in] the pregnancy. But[9] if not (namely if the degrees would indicate more months than is possible), the number of degrees explain the same thing in terms of days.

## Chapter 21.3: Sex of children

§542. Moreover, male significators (or at least being in male signs) will indicate the male sex; but bearing themselves otherwise, they testify to a female.

## Chapter 21.4: Twins or more

§543. Likewise, the plurality of the significators [occupying] signs of much offspring and number, reveals that she bears many in her womb.

---

[9] Translating somewhat freely from Hugo's very cramped style, along with al-Rijāl.

## Chapter 21.5: How the pregnancy will be

§544. Moreover, you will diagnose how she would be doing while she was pregnant, from the second and its status.[10] Likewise, the twelfth place makes clear how she is going to be after the birth. For the presence of the fortunes in it portends good, [but] the infortunes the contrary, just as their nature demands.

§545. Which if Mars does not corrupt the significators of birth[11] but [would be receiving them][12] and would be supported by a friendly aspect[13] (particularly from a hot sign), it beings about a birth without labor. But Saturn (Mars's role being taken [by him]) indicates an anxious and difficult one.

But the most recent application of the Moon upon exiting [her] sign,[14] and the manner and nature of her application, and the place which it is allotted (in the arrangement of the square of signs), will declare the mother's status after the birth.

---

[10] The idea is that she is represented by the Ascendant, her time so far in the pregnancy by the second, and the events after pregnancy by the twelfth.

[11] Reading *partus* with Robert for *aut eorum partem*.

[12] Adding with al-Rijāl.

[13] Al-Rijāl says, "and that a fortune would aspect Mars."

[14] That is, the last aspect she will make before leaving (al-Rijāl).

# CHAPTER 22: ON SEEKING FRIENDSHIPS
## & PARTNERSHIPS[1]

### Chapter 22.1: Friendships & partnerships

§546. If someone would arrange to enter into an agreement of friendship
or a partnership, the Moon being received by Venus from a trigon ([and]
more powerfully a reception from house or sovereignty) seems to approve it.
But[2] with this being impossible, [make] the Moon be received by Jupiter
[while] in the trigon of Venus, or [received] by the lord of her own sign from
a trigon or hexagon or assembly by body. Which if this would [only] happen
with difficulty, arrange the Moon in some place of Venusian authority,
received by Jupiter,[3] cleansed of the infortunes.

§547. If however someone would enter into an agreement because of
some partnership or common living situation, let the Ascendant be situated
in a place of Venusian authority.

### Chapter 22.2: Partnerships for wealth & success

§548. Which if he is eager to do the same thing because of acquisition and
profit, remember to place the Lot of Fortune in the trigon of the Ascendant,
or in the Ascendant itself, or in the Midheaven or in the seventh or the
fourth.

§549. But if he would strive to enter into this with the king, establish [the
Lot] in the Midheaven; but if with a merchant, in the seventh; but if he
desired to achieve success because of the cultivation of lands, let it be placed
in the fourth. Which if he would be disposed to wrench out the profit of his
family and the fruits of his own domestic household, you will place it in the
Ascendant. But if he would be led by the benefit and love of gifts, in the
fifth. Which if it is by those things which pertain to the law, in the ninth.

---

[1] For §§546-48, see al-Rijāl VII.96.
[2] Reading this sentence with Robert. Hugo's sentence is worded oddly, contains an
improper negative, and replaces the reception by hexagon/sextile with one by
tetragon/square.
[3] Robert has: "made fortunate by Jupiter," which is probably more accurate.

Moreover, should he be touched by the success of some favorable opinion or hope, [let it be] in the eleventh.

§550.[4] But in all of these things, the Lot of Fortune and her lord should be in a strong place or blessed by the fortunes with reception. Furthermore, to the extent that opportunity permits it, let the star (through whose signification the decision is sought),[5] regard, assist, and receive the lord of the east and the Moon and the Lots of Fortune and of money.

§551. If therefore someone about to accept [such] benefits would strive to be attached to a prince of wars for the same reason, let Mars assist the lord of the Ascendant and be received[6] by the Moon, and console [them] by a friendly aspect. But if he desired the profits of borrowed money, the reception of Saturn should be sought in the place of Mars. But again, if he should insist on it because of computation, writing, and books, let a Mercurial reception be arranged. But [if he sought it] from the king, let the Solar reception be preferred. But from a judge and the underofficials of the king, and prominent people, Jupiter's.

### Chapter 22.3: General advice about significators in all elections

§552. Therefore, whenever a question came out into the open about those things which pertain to the signification of some house, let the reception of its lord be sought, namely [let the lord receive][7] the Moon and the lord of the Ascendant and the Lot of Fortune and the Lot of money; also, you will place the lunar lord (no less even the lords of the Ascendant and of the fourth) cleansed of the infortunes, and strong. For the leadership and signification of these lays bare the end of the question.

---

[4] Reading this paragraph with Robert. Hugo only has the first sentence: "Moreover, greatly desire the Lot of Fortune or its lord to be made fortunate, received from a strong place."

[5] This seems to mean the natural significator of the partner, as described in the next paragraph.

[6] Reading *receptus* for *receptos*. But Robert's version of §550 has the general significator receiving *them* (which is probably correct). The same ambiguity appears below in §552, where both Robert and Hugo add *in* to the formulation of reception, which does not make sense to me.

[7] See the footnote above.

# CHAPTER 23: ON PRISONERS

## Chapter 23.1: His condition

§553. A question having been proposed about the liberation of some captive, an understanding of the hour at which he was led into captivity releases no little part of the doubt, through its own signification. It being unknown, let the question proceed in general terms: the lord of the Ascendant and the Moon, or the one who is asserted to be stronger in the Ascendant and question,[1] receding from an infortune [who is] the lord of the twelfth or seventh or eighth, and applying to fortunate ones, means freedom and safety. The significators being led down from the pivots[2] even bring about this same thing.

## Chapter 23.2: The hour of his liberation

§554. Moreover, the degrees of application of that star which recedes from infortunes and applies to the fortunate ones determine the hour of obtaining freedom—namely, by substituting for hours, days or months, or years for [the degrees] by which it seems to be thus far distant from a fortunate one. For an application in a convertible sign, and its lord in a convertible sign, [and] in the same way the significators (or the majority of them) in convertible signs, suggests hours. Which if the application [would be] in a convertible sign and its lord in a fixed one, it decrees days. In a double-bodied one, months. But in a fixed one, years.

§555. Moreover, the quick course of that receding significator, seems to confirm the same thing. In fact, its quickness sometimes transforms years into months, months into days, days into hours. Likewise, its slowness very often changes hours into days, days into months, months into years.

§556a. Furthermore, the stationing[3] of the significator whose recession and application is chosen, [indicates] what is written above.[4]

---

[1] Robert: "the lord of the question or the victor."
[2] I.e., "cadent."
[3] *Status.*
[4] I take this to mean it will slow things down, as in §555.

## Chapter 23.3: Whether he would die in prison

§556b. Likewise, the same [planet] being foreign and weak in a sign, testifies to the harshness of prison and the difficulty of faring badly. [But] strong and received, the contrary. Moreover, an application of it with the fortunate ones from retrogradation, means an unexpected departure, particularly [if] received by those fortunate ones.

§557. Which if it would be corrupted by the lord of the eighth while [the lord of the eighth] is Saturn, and if it would apply itself to the aforesaid lord of prison, it promises death in prison. Mars taking up the role of Saturn, destroys him. The lord of the eighth being corrupted by the aforesaid infortune, and [that infortune] in the Midheaven, also the other infortune in the pivot of the earth, threatens hanging. But if it would be corrupted by Mars but not the lord of the eighth, it adds blows and blood. Moreover, corrupted by Saturn, it heaps on the labor of torture.

## Chapter 23.4: Whether he would be tortured in prison

§558. If therefore the corruptor and giver of anxiety appeared as the lord of the Ascendant, he earns his affliction in prison [because of] his own crime. Which if [it were] the lord of the second, he incurs this punishment because of money and his clients,[5] [or] even those whose help he hopes for.[6] But if it would be established as the lord of the third, he is punished because of friends and those types, and travel. The lord of the fourth afflicts with blows because of parents and something of antiquity or land. The lord of the fifth, he is punished unjustly because of children.

§559. But if it appeared as the lord of the sixth, it is caused because of a lower order of slaves, and by the impediment of beasts and disease. Which if it would be established as the lord of the seventh, it reprimands him through an attack of adversaries, women, merchants. Placed in the rulership of the eighth, the supporters of the adversaries, women, or business [partners]

---

[5] Or, lesser associates and dependents (*clientum*).
[6] Reading with Robert for *quorum spes magni habetur.*

testify that this wrong is done [to him] because of inheritances or his own captivity or some death.[7]

§560. The lord of the ninth, he is made crooked because of law or travel. In the rulership of the tenth, it brings the king or the duty of his own profession, or his mother, against him. It even being the lord of the eleventh, it afflicts him because of the royal family and money, friends, and hope. Which if it appeared as the lord of the twelfth, he is punished with this suffering because of enemies and prison. And so, in this manner you will remember to indicate it with respect to the fortunate ones and their causes.


## Chapter 23.5: How long he would be held

§561. Furthermore, the firmness of the signs which the significators and their lords are holding onto, suggests openly enough the long-lastingness of the captivity: for they designate the period of the captivity. The significators being in convertible signs and drawn down from the pivots, promise a quick exit. The signs being in the pivots or after the pivots, [indicate] a slower exit.

§562. Furthermore, the departure of the lord of the Ascendant from scorching at the hour of the question, [and] in the same way the liberation of the Moon or of the lunar lord or of a star in some authority of theirs (namely of one appearing in her house or sovereignty) from under the rays, permits freedom from prison.

§563. Furthermore, the lord of the assembly or opposition which preceded the captivity (or at least, the question) withdrawing from being scorched or being drawn down from a pivot, being fortunate and cleansed of the infortunes, indicates [his] exit can in no way be impeded.

---

[7] This seems to be a more natural reading of the rulership issue. As written, the text says that the supporters of the adversaries (and so on) testify that *he has committed* his offense because of inheritances (and so on).

## Chapter 23.6: What would happen after his release

§564. Moreover, with that freedom already being indicated through the benefit of the stars, the lunar lord and [the lord] of the Ascendant [indicate] the status of the captive and what should happen to him after the captivity. Being made fortunate and lucky, they testify to respectable events and an appropriate end. Which if the lord of the Midheaven would be the one favorable to them, it promotes him to [a position of] authority and to a dignity. But if [it were] the lord of the second, they introduce prosperity. And so, in this manner of consideration it will be permitted to judge with respect to individual houses and their lords.

§565. But this is the analogy which we state:[8] insofar as the Sun himself would be the lord of the Midheaven, it raises him into royal service. But if Jupiter, he is made a judge. Saturn too, arranges him into the rank of senior people, but more often it establishes him as a guard of revenues and personal property, and an inhabitant of agricultural areas, and a minister of buildings. Mercury makes him a writer or merchant. Venus claims he is a teacher of (or devoted to) cheerfulness, jokes, and women. Also, the Moon commends him as a minister of legations and servitude and leadership. Finally, Mars calls forth a minister of wars [or] a soldier.

§566. And I say that the aforesaid distribution or association of the stars' [signification] should be made through the individual houses by this analogy. [With this exception, that the significator returning by retrogradation into the sign which it had held onto at the hour of flight, or being in combustion, signals [his] return.][9]

---

[8] That is: when looking at the planet which is making the aforesaid planets fortunate, the house it rules will show the area of life providing the benefit (§564), but the planetary nature modifies that area (§565). See §566.

[9] Adding with Robert.

# CHAPTER 24: ON AN ABSENT PERSON

## Chapter 24.1: On his status

§567. If someone would propose a question about the status of an absent person, namely as to what would happen to him on his journey, and whether he would be able to complete what he proposed: the lord of the Ascendant, and the Moon, likewise the Sun and the Lot of Fortune, even the degree of the assembly or opposition, necessarily seem to reinforce [the matter].[1] Therefore, you will note the victor (namely the stronger star) in all of these: which if it would be situated [and be] fortunate between the Ascendant and the Midheaven, it testifies he is staying in the first half of his journey.

§568. But if it would be receding from the fortunate ones, between the Midheaven and the west, or at least should [its] receding come to be from none of the infortunes, you will report that he is unharmed [and] in the second half of the proposed journey, but not yet in the region [he has] considered [as his destination].

§569. But receding from the infortunes in the aforesaid places, but applying to fortunate ones, it declares he is unharmed [and] in the corresponding places of the journey, but he has had fear or grown ill according to the nature of that unfortunate one from which it recedes, and of the sign [the infortune] is holding onto, and of that house in the circle in which it is situated. Which if it would be receding from one of the fortunate ones, you should not doubt that he has achieved good according to its nature and its house and place in the circle, just as was said above about an infortune.

§570. But if you would discover that it was applying with the lord of the seventh, between the seventh and the Ascendant itself, and was received by it, in any event he has completed what was proposed in the journey. Finally, dwelling in the seventh, he is in possession of the proposed thing he wished, in the land to which he was going.

---

[1] These are virtually the five releasing places described in Chs. 3.2-3 for finding a weighted victor for the querent, and the releaser for the whole chart. But since al-Kindī (or his sources) wants to analyze this victor as a planet, he uses the *lord of* the Ascendant and of the degree of the assembly/opposition, instead of simply those degrees themselves.

§571. Moreover, it seems that the proper quality of the star to which it applies must be combined, just as its nature and its dignity in the circle seems to demand.

## Chapter 24.2: On his return

§572. Also, with a question made about [his] return (once you were certain about his life),[2] if [the victor or significator] would be established in the seventh, it detains him thus far in the region [whence he had gone]. Also, being drawn down from the seventh, it does not permit him to have departed for very long.[3] Retrograde, it leads him back without question. Drawn down from the four pivots, likewise. Which if it would appear fortunate (or [else] unlucky), you will remember to affirm it in the same way, and in the corresponding places of the path,[4] just as was said about his departure.

§573.[5] In discerning the hour of [his] arrival, you will note how many degrees [it is] from where it began to go retrograde, up to the one in which its step will go forward. For, the individual degrees insert hours or days or months or years, just as was said in a heading above.[6] Or, more strongly, [giving] days for individual degrees from the degree of the significator up to the Ascendant. Sometimes the degrees of its application with the Ascendant suggest the same. In all of these, the Moon and the lord of the Ascendant present no little evidence.

## Chapter 24.3: Whether he is living or dead

§574. Furthermore, [if] being asked about [his] death or life, a strong and fortunate significator, and strengthened by the seventh,[7] and free of the troubles produced by the lord of the eighth, preserves him as living. If it is

---

[2] That is, if you knew he was still alive. See below.
[3] *Nondum longius abscessisse permittit.*
[4] That is, in the diurnal path down from the seventh, through the fourth and back up to the Ascendant.
[5] For this section, see also §607 below.
[6] See Ch. 2.6.
[7] Robert reads, "and should it give aid to the seventh." This probably means being in a favorable aspect to the seventh sign and particularly the Descendant.

corrupted by the lord of the eighth, it designates he is dead. Receding from [the lord of the eighth], he is dead, [and] it will be permitted to describe the death according to the nature of each (namely the corrupter and the significator) and [its] place in the circle.

§575. Moreover, the significator itself being placed between the two infortunes,[8] and in a fixed sign (particularly being arranged in the eighth or twelfth),[9] claims he is a captive. [Besieged] by the lord of the eighth, but corrupted in its own place, threatens the death of prison.[10] But being scorched in that same place, it claims he has met death at the very hand of the king. Which if the lord of the Midheaven would be corrupting it, he is killed [when] found by the king.

§576. Moreover, being corrupted by the lord of the house of death, or scorched, and in the seventh, it confirms he has undergone death in the region to which he has gone. Also, being free of these infortunes and what is like them, brings him back to his own family.

§577. Moreover, being tainted by the lord of the house of death, namely [while the significator is] between the Ascendant and the fourth (particularly being scorched with another infortune), prepares death during [his] return, unless [the significator] would be freed, sustained by no [merely] moderate prosperity of some one of the fortunate ones[11]—provided (I say) that the lord of the Ascendant appeared stronger than the corrupter, and the decreasing light of that infortune would be reduced.[12] For in such a way, he would be able to avoid death, [but only] after bringing no [merely] moderate care and intention to bear.

---

[8] See Ch. 1.1.3 above, and *ITA* IV.4.2.

[9] Robert adds, "or the sixth."

[10] This sentence could also be read as, "Being corrupted by the lord of the eighth, but in its own place…". But if it were in a sign which it ruled, it would not be in so difficult a position.

[11] That is, having the siege broken. See *ITA* IV.4.2 and my comment to that section.

[12] That is, that it would be decreasing in light. Perhaps this means that the infortune is about to go under the rays of the Sun?

# CHAPTER 25: ON BUYING AND SELLING ANIMALS & SLAVES[1]

§578. The buying of animals looks out for the Moon appearing in a sign of the same kind of animal, particularly [if] made fortunate by the lord of that same sign. Also, let the lord of the Ascendant be set up in a corresponding way: each one even being received by the fortunate ones, particularly by the lord of that same sign. Which if [the receiver] were not lucky, it still should not refuse to regard them from a trigon. But let the infortunes be turned awry[2] and their virtue cut off, removed from the sign of the question and from the Moon.

§579. If therefore you are arranging to buy a slave for use as labor, select some fortunate celestial shape (namely the one which obtains the command and likeness of that job), and establish it in the Ascendant or in the place of the Moon, and let each be made fortunate.[3] If however you are taking it for use in a matter at home and for one's own [household] slavery, ascribe the form which we said before to a human sign, such as Taurus[4] and the end of Sagittarius and the sign of Gemini, if [the form] were made fortunate. Let them be arranged in Aquarius in the same way, but in Aquarius it means art and science[5] and long deliberation.

§580. But a stronger place for the significators would be one be set up as male. But if a woman would be procured, the stronger place for the significators would be one arranged as female—particularly Virgo, if he is arranging to introduce her for the sake of sexual intercourse and offspring. Also, let the infortunes fall away from it[6] and let it become bright with the light of fortunate [planets].

---

[1] For this chapter, see al-Rijāl VII.50 and 52, which distinguish between slaves (VII.50) and animals (VII.52).Cf. also *Carmen* V.11-12, which have bear some resemblance. I do find it odd that al-Kindī does not use the 6th house at all in this chapter.

[2] *Perversa*. Robert reads "weak" (*debiles*). This probably means being cadent.

[3] Reading with Robert for Hugo's *utriusque fortunatis*.

[4] Taurus is not a human sign, but perhaps al-Kindī is thinking of Taurus as a domesticated animal that does hard labor.

[5] Any organized body of knowledge.

[6] I.e., be in aversion to it.

§581. Which if you wanted to decorate[7] some limb of this [slave], let the Moon be put in a sign of that limb, made fortunate, in the illumination of the aforesaid sign (namely, Virgo).

§582. In the sale of sheep, let Aries be arranged.[8] In selling goats, Capricorn. But if a cow or ox is being sold, remember to arrange Taurus. Which if [it is] for use in riding, as are courier horses and that type, Sagittarius (but more powerfully, let its last parts be arranged). But if camels, [use] the shape which incurs the name of "armchair."[9] Also, the sale of birds and that type of thing, demands the arrangement of Libra.

§583. And so, [the animal's] soundness and intactness is preserved by the figure of the individual things, the presence of the fortunate ones, [and] it being blessed by the estrangement of the unfortunate ones.

---

[7] That is, to brand an animal or human.
[8] That is, in the Ascendant or the sign of the Moon.
[9] Hugo: *cathedrae*; Robert: *decalcurci/decalcurti*. This might be Cassiopeia, whose name in Arabic means "Woman in the chair," but Cassiopeia is a bit high in the sky to be relevant.

# CHAPTER 26: ON HUNTING & FISHING

§584. The skill of hunting seems to demand that the lord of Ascendant be strong, fortunate, in some one of the pivots, but the lord of the eighth[1] cadent from Mars, [while being] corrupted from a strong place.[2] Which if someone would be pursuing a hunt in the mountains or forests, an earthy sign will have to be applied to the seventh.

§585. But if he is pursuing four-footed animals, [then] if it is permissible, arrange the lord of their sign as being corrupted in an earthy sign. Which if [he pursues] flying things, it is good to arrange an airy seventh sign, and its lord in an airy sign. But if he is going after fishing by some art, let it be a watery sign, and its lord be affected by the aforesaid corruption, in a watery sign. [By how much more corruption was in them,[3] the catch will be that much easier and productive.][4]

§586. Moreover, let the star from which the Moon's receding comes to be, be a lucky one, received; but the one to which she applies herself should be noted as cadent, weak, unfortunate. And likewise the lords of the east and of the fourth.[5]

---

[1] Robert reads, "the seventh."

[2] The sense is that the lord of the eighth (or of the seventh, according to Robert) should be corrupted from a strong place. But I think the instructions are supposed to read as follows: (1) make the lord of the *eighth* be *in aversion to* Mars, but (2) make the lord of the *seventh* be *corrupted by* Mars. Thus the significator of the hunter's death (the lord of the eighth) is kept unaffected, but the significator of the game or animal (lord of the seventh) is harmed. The following paragraph seems to verify this, as the instructions say to make lord of the seventh be corrupted.

[3] That is, the lord of the seventh, and probably the planet to which the Moon applies (see the next sentence).

[4] Adding with Robert.

[5] Reading with Robert for Hugo's awkward and unclear "No less will the lord of the Ascendant and of the fourth be profitable, especially [if] it is making fortunate, and [they are] strong."

# CHAPTER 27: ON BANQUETS[1]

§587.[2] [If] arranging to go to banquets, [whether] of one's own accord or invited,[3] establish the Ascendant for yourself, but the seventh designates him who has invited you. The second place from the Ascendant will indicate him who sits down on the left, but the twelfth the one on the right. And so, in this way, it declares those sitting down: the sixth on the right of the one inviting, the eighth from on the left. The Midheaven portends that man because of whom the rest are called and enter the banquet; also the eleventh on his left, but the ninth will indicate those reclining on the right. The fourth signifies those serving, the fifth the bartenders,[4] the third the attendants for the drinks.

| | Robert/Hugo | Al-Rijāl |
|---|---|---|
| 1st | Inceptor | Inceptor; beginning, food, games |
| 2nd | On inceptor's left | On inceptor's left; the presider's servers |
| 3rd | Serving staff | Serving staff; siblings of hosts |
| 4th | Attendants | The venue/home; paternal relatives of presider |
| 5th | Entertainment/bartender | Wine, gifts; friends of inviter |
| 6th | On inviter's right | On inviter's right; other servants |
| 7th | Inviter | Inviter; inviter's wife |
| 8th | On inviter's left | On inviter's left;[5] attendants of inviter's wife; wine barrels and glasses |
| 9th | On presider's right | The door; where servants enter and exit |
| 10th | Presider | Important people; lighting |
| 11th | On presider's left | Middling people; people hanging out; friends of the hosts |
| 12th | On inceptor's right | Wife of inviter;[6] low-class people |

**Figure 59: Houses at a banquet[7]**

---

[1] For this chapter, cf. also al-Rijāl I.51.

[2] This paragraph is according to Hugo; al-Rijāl's treatment differs quite a bit. See the figure below.

[3] Al-Rijāl explicitly mentions wedding receptions, so many types of parties are meant.

[4] Or generally, drink servers and preparers (*pincernas*).

[5] The Latin al-Rijāl puts them on his right, which seems to be a mistake.

[6] This does not seem right, as the wife was mentioned above for the seventh.

§588. Finally, the Moon designates the whole home, the lunar lord the last parts of the stay [at the banquet], the second from the Moon the dinner guests, but the first triplicity lord of her second [the food],[8] and the second one the drinks.

§589. Moreover, a fortunate significator for both, or the first triplicity lord of the second from the Moon being more praiseworthy than the second one, claims the foods are more powerfully embellished than the drinks. The second triplicity lord of the second from the Moon being stronger and lucky, testifies that the drinks are to be preferred to the dishes. The luckiness of either one summons prosperous things, but [their] adversity [brings] adverse things according to the signification of the one corrupting. It will be permitted to speak in a corresponding way with respect to the aforesaid things.

§590. Moreover, the first lord of the lunar triplicity looks over the beginnings of the assembly, but the second one the last parts.

§591. The Midheaven from the Moon claims the actors and dancers. The seventh from the Moon will exhibit the status of those partying after[9] they leave. But the fourth lays bare the seating of all, in the same way the fifth from the Moon [indicates] the singing, the sixth the instruments, the third whatever is discussed, from beginning to end. The eleventh from the Moon determines the friends of the one inviting [the guests], namely by whose counsel and favor these acts are asserted to be. Also, the twelfth disposes the misfortune of his home and whatever corruption (or rather loss) would happen in it. The ninth from the Moon [indicates] him who takes the partygoers away after [their] departure. But the eighth possesses the drains[10] and baths and places of washing, and that type of thing.

---

[7] For the most part, al-Rijāl agrees with the Hugo-Robert list, but mainly adds other significations based on natural and derived house meanings: for example, the second is the sixth from the tenth, so it indicates the servants (sixth) of the presider or the one who is responsible for the event (tenth).

[8] Adding based on Robert.

[9] Reading with Robert and al-Rijāl for Hugo's "before."

[10] Or, "sewers" (*cloacas*).

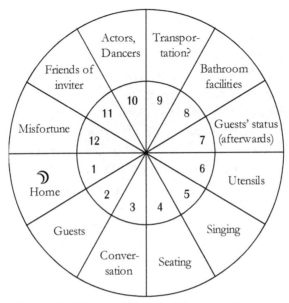

**Figure 60: Houses from the Moon at a banquet**

§592. Therefore, whenever fortune and prosperity would come into the knowledge of any of these places, it will be all right to report the goodness, glory and fame of the place or job designated by it, according to the nature of that star making [it] fortunate, and [according to] the virtue of its lord. Once their misfortune is understood, let it not annoy [you] to explain the misfortune and harm of corruption according to the status of the one corrupting, and of its lord, and what dignity it retains in the circle. For the respectability of their status suggests charm, but its ugliness [suggests] foulness. Venus principally testifies to and adorns the form and look of all of these. Also, Jupiter distinguishes the more eminent [people], the more elegant, and their success.

§593. But the enormity of the whole corruption, and the harm of unluckiness, proceed from Saturn. Mars heaps on fears and the rest of the bad emotions of the soul, and those which pass by quickly. But the luckiness of Mercury commends the advantageous appearance and glory of business matters and any talent [performing at the party]. Finally, the Solar virtue establishes the public praising of matters, and eminence. The Moon [does] the same, but in a more relaxed way.

§594. Furthermore, a significator being retrograde [but] established in a dignity of its own, raises up the excellence and advancement of [its] matters.

But the fallenness[11] of the significator furnishes their abjection (namely, death and depression).[12] The significator dwelling in the opposite of its own house will generate whatever adversity occurs. Moreover, Venus in a pivot of the Moon (particularly in [her] Midheaven), makes the home resonate with the sweetness of the partygoers' singing. Jupiter (having taken over her role), [signifies] gifts and glory. But the luckiness of Mercury designates the resounding of voices; but being adverse, the contrary.

§595. Moreover, the lord of the Ascendant being corrupted by Mars (and with him being the lord of the house of death) wounds the invited person at the hour of the invitation, [and] often even afflicts him with death. Likewise, Mercury commingled with the nature of Mars attacks with the reproaches of the partygoers. Saturn, too, introduces loss and contempt.

§596. Which if Saturn[13] would attain the rulership of the sixth, even [if] assisted by others, it contaminates with disease according to the nature of his place and of his own house which he claims in the circle.[14]

§597. But Jupiter, taking on the role of Saturn,[15] [indicates] the success of convenience,[16] according to the status and place and house of Jupiter in the circle. In the same way, Venus having taken the role of Jupiter multiplies joys [and] decorations, just as the status and place and house in the circle ([which is] had by her) seems to demand. Finally, the Sun, increasing the role of Venus,[17] makes it glorious and venerable, faithfulness in speech, [and] applies an observance of proper rules of conduct.[18]

§598. Finally, a corrupted Moon interferes with the prosperity of the partygoers, disturbs [them], and introduces harm and calamity according to the nature of the one making [her] unfortunate. Her luckiness furnishes those reclining and the place [itself] with the praise of all exultation and the hope of respectability, according to the weight of the prosperity she takes on, and the manner and status and strength of the one by whom she is blessed. Moreover, the prosperity of the second place from the Moon commends the

---

[11] *Hubut*, a transliteration of *hubūṭah*, being in fall or descension.

[12] Reading in the accusative for Hugo's nominative.

[13] Robert simply says that the lord of the sixth in general will introduce illness.

[14] Or more probably, that domicile of his which he aspects (or aspects more strongly), as al-Kindī states elsewhere.

[15] I do not believe this means "if Jupiter were the lord of the sixth," but rather if he were combining with the lord of the Ascendant.

[16] Or perhaps, "comfort" (*commoditatis*).

[17] Or rather, with him *taking* her role for himself.

[18] *Praeceptis*.

glory of the dishes according to the weight of the luckiness it takes on. But unlucky, it shows blameworthy things.

# Chapter 28: On the Truth & Falsity of News[1]

## Chapter 28.1: True and false *vs.* good and bad rumors

§599. The firmness of the pivots,[2] even the significators being in the pivots or after the pivots, decree [the truth of] whatever propitious or malicious rumors someone would announce. Moreover, a messenger [with bad news] is established by an infortune, but [bad news] is refused by the lucky ones: fortunate ones increase good [rumors], the infortunes pervert it.[3]

§600. The firmness of the pivots, and the Moon being received in a firm sign, likewise the luckiness of the Ascendant and of the Moon, attest to the truth of the rumors. If [the rumors] announce good things but the pivots are turning,[4] [and] if even the Moon and the lord of the Ascendant would hold onto turning [signs], and they are made wicked,[5] they falsify rumors of the aforesaid kind. Moreover, if [the news were bad but] the pivots were firm, and should the Moon be dwelling in a firm [sign] and likewise the lord of the Ascendant, received, and if a significator or some assistant would be unfortunate, they do not recede from what is true. But if the pivots bore themselves thusly, and if infortunes would be regarding the Moon and the lord of the Ascendant, the truth of the rumors is [also] affirmed.

## Chapter 28.2: The cause of the rumors

§601. Furthermore, in discerning the cause of rumors, you will note what sign the lord of the Ascendant and the Moon would be holding onto: for the judgment proceeds from these same places. Also, the lords of their signs, and their nature, make the causes clear.

---

[1] For this chapter, cf. al-Rijāl I.30.2. Lilly (*CA* pp. 193-94) reports these passages without commenting on them, and instead proposes his own approach—but then immediately uses many of these rules anyway in evaluating a chart about rumors (pp. 200-01).

[2] That is, if they are in fixed signs.

[3] To put it more simply: fixed signs tend to show truth, but movable signs falsity; malefics show bad news, benefics show good news.

[4] That is, in the movable or convertible signs.

[5] That is, "unfortunate" (Robert).

## Chapter 28.3: The outcome of the rumors

§602. If therefore certainty is had over the truth of the rumors, the lunar lord and the lord of the Ascendant suggest the end. For the indication of the end depends on their nature and their places which they claim in the circle, likewise from [the places of] their lords and the dignity[6] they hold onto in the circle. For fortunate ones portend good according to the nature of the one making [them] fortunate, [but] unfortunate ones the contrary, according to the manner of the one corrupting.

## Chapter 28.4: How public the rumors are

§603. Moreover, the lord of the Ascendant being scorched or under the rays, hides it from the majority of the whole public. Being eastern or in the aspect of the Sun (especially while [the Sun is][7] regarded by the Moon, or should each consider[8] the Ascendant), they announce it in public (whether it is true or false).

---

6 Al-Rijāl reads, "power" (*potentia*).
7 Adding with al-Rijāl.
8 That is, "aspect."

# CHAPTER 29: ON MESSENGERS & MAIL[1]

## Chapter 29.1: The status of a messenger sent somewhere

§604. The lord of the Ascendant and the Moon give counsel as to whether a messenger would reach the desired place.[2] For, each (or either) of them in the seventh, or an application of them with the lord of the seventh already being made, suggests he is already persisting in the desired region. But a withdrawal from fortunate ones conveys health and opportunity on the journey; withdrawing from infortunes, the contrary. Therefore, it seems one must report [this matter] according to the nature of the fortunate or unfortunate ones, and their dignity in the circle, [and] strength and weakness. Moreover, an application of [a significator] made with fortunate ones, renders everything prosperous in that place; with the infortunes, the contrary. The nature and place and dignity of the fortunate and unlucky ones in the circle ([and] even their weakness and virtue) will show what must be said about the matter.

## Chapter 29.2: Whether he would find whom he was seeking

§605. If therefore certainty would be had about reaching the place, for a question as to whether he has come to the person he was heading for, an application of either (or each) of the aforesaid significators with the lord of the seventh, or at least one [of them] applying with the lord of its own place, testifies he has found him. Otherwise they mean a contrary judgment. But [if the applying one were] received by the one with which it applies itself, it makes him be taken in diligently and in a friendly way. But with it made from the opposition, [it means] the opposite; from the tetragon [it means] the same, but makes it less slyly.

---

[1] For this chapter, cf. al-Rijāl I.50.2

[2] As al-Rijāl explains in his version, the Ascendant and the Moon represent the one who has sent the messenger, while the seventh and its lord signify the person to whom he is sent.

## Chapter 29.3: On the messenger's return[3]

§606. A question coming out into the open about the return of the messenger: each significator (or either one) drawn down from the seventh or from the pivots,[4] and receding from the lord of the seventh, means his return. Which if it would apply with its own lord while it is being drawn down from the pivots, the same.[5] Also, an admixture of the infortunes seems to speak against [his return]: which will seem to consist of the nature and status and place of the infortune, and what dignity it would claim in the circle. But the fortunate ones also [speak in favor of his return] in this manner.

§607. For if it would be asked about the hour of his return, an application of them with the lord of the Ascendant or with its own [lord], the degrees, I say, of the application sometimes put hours or days or months or years in between,[6] according to the nature of the convertible or fixed or double-bodied [signs], or even according to the quickness or slowness of the significator, also especially if[7] the [number of the] degrees of the aforesaid application would be equal to that of the Moon [in her application] with the degree of the Ascendant [by body] or with her own [lord], or [her application with] that of the lord of the Ascendant. Also, the exit of a star from scorching, or the application[8] [of a star into][9] the degree of a dignity which it possesses in the heavens, explains the same thing. No less, moreover, does the retrogradation of the significator indicate [his return], at the point where it goes direct: for, how many degrees are left until going direct, we bid you to compute that many hours or days or months or years.

---

[3] For this subchapter, see also Ch. 24.2 above.
[4] That is, being cadent.
[5] Robert (but not al-Rijāl) adds: "and likewise [if] retrograde."
[6] That is, between the time of the question and the messenger's return.
[7] For the rest of this sentence, adding material in brackets from al-Rijāl.
[8] Reading with Robert (*inire*) and al-Rijāl (*applicatio*), for Hugo's *status*.
[9] Adding with al-Rijāl.

# CHAPTER 30: ON REQUESTING SOMETHING FROM SOMEONE[1]

§608. Let the lord of the east and the Moon (or the one of them [more] powerful in the question), be received by the lord of the sought matter, and let them occupy the place of the matter itself. For example, if anything is sought from old men or farmers or builders, let Saturn rule over the place of that matter. However, Jupiter if we are striving to advance among judges, proposers of law, generous people, the wealthy, truth-tellers and those of this kind. Mars, if among leaders of armies, soldiers, craftsmen or anyone doing mechanical work through the power of fire. The Sun, among lofty kings or the more elevated people of the kingdom.

§609. Venus, if among women or females, mimes, and those doing Venusian crafts, such as painters, polishers, and those who put together any ornamented things and [produce good-smelling] odors. Mercury, if among scribes, teachers, clever calculators, precise machinists[2] and geometers. Finally, let the Moon rule over the place of the thing if anything is demanded of legates, runners, wanderers, royal attendants, nocturnal robbers, ambushers of roads or those who lease carts.[3]

In all things of this kind, let the lord of the east and the Moon be made fortunate and received, just as we said before.

§610. Also, in the seeking of money, let the Lot of Fortune and her lord be both received and looked at by the lord of the east and the Moon, moreover let the lords of the fourth and of the east and of the Moon be set up as blessed and received: for this makes the end fine. Conversely, the opposite.

§611. But one must beware with the greatest effort lest any infortune obstruct[4] the Moon or her lord and the ruler of the matter, or that it should corrupt the lord of one of them or [the lord] of the east, especially if it in no way appeared as the one presiding over that place. But let every reception prefigured by each kind of star[5] be from a trigon or hexagon—but only by the lucky ones [if] for an assembly by body. One must observe (if possible)

---

[1] This chapter is only in Robert.
[2] *Machinatores*. But this word also connotes inventiveness generally.
[3] *Equiturae*. This suggests shippers of goods.
[4] Reading *intercedat* for *intercidat*.
[5] Namely, either the benefics or malefics.

lest the lights or the lords of the east and of the matter dwell in remote signs.[6] But if not, let the victor over the five releasers mix itself together with the victor of the matter, with each one of them being both fortunate and received.

---

[6] Omitting the odd *praedictis segnius*, which seems to be out of place.

# CHAPTER 31: ON SICK PEOPLE & THEIR CONDITION

### Chapter 31.1: Significators & overview

§612a. The Moon and the Sun and the lord of the Ascendant, being cleansed of the infortunes (especially from the lord of the house of death), promise the health of the one who has grown ill. But if two bore themselves thusly, no matter if the third one would apply with the lord of the house of death, they convey health. Also, with the third one bearing itself thusly but the remaining two being cleansed of an application with the lord of the house of death or with an adverse infortune (particularly one who appears as a partner of the fourth or of the second in something), as long as they were cleansed, they liberate.

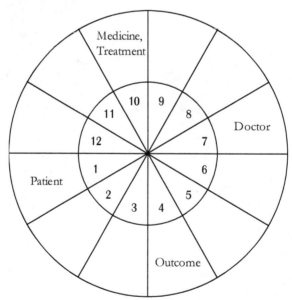

**Figure 61: Al-Kindī's angular scheme for medical treatment**

§612b. The proper quality of the [planet] by which the significator is corrupted will demonstrate the nature of the disease. Also, the place of the corruptor (in the arrangement of the signs), suggests the causes of the infirmity.

§613. The[1] degrees of the application by which the stronger significator approached the fortunate ones, judge the days between the question and the hour of health, especially if it were the lord of the Ascendant or the Moon, and if the Moon claimed the shift (no less too does the Sun [do so] as the lord of the shift). The application of the stronger significator especially with the lord of the house of death does not expel death, but rather introduces death according to the degrees of application.

Therefore, the application of any significator to the infortunes increases the diseases, up to where it recedes from it. Also, [its application] with the fortunate ones soothes and mitigates [the illness] until [its] withdrawal. And so, it will be right to diagnose the days of the whole infirmity in this manner. Which if the infortune would be likened to the nature of the illness, it enlarges it; but a dissimilar infortune mitigates it.[2]

## Chapter 31.2: In what limb he will suffer

§614. In whatever house the corrupted significator appeared, the limb indicated by that same house will suffer manifestly. The proper quality of the corruptor suggests the kind of illness, [and] moreover the house of the corrupting star (namely the one it strengthens by a benign aspect) ascribes the causes of the suffering.

§615.[3] Also, once the avoidance [of disease, or rather] future health has been understood and made certain, the lucky one liberating [indicates] the nature of it, and the domicile of it which is looked at more luckily by it, [indicates the] occasion.

§616. You will even explain in what part of the body (namely the upper part or middle or lower), or finally in what limb he suffers, in this order, [according to the place of the corrupted significator.][4] For, the Ascendant designates the head; by the second is denoted the neck; the hands and shoulders are designated by the third; but the fourth indicates the[5] chest and

---

[1] Reading this sentence with *Judges* §6.21.
[2] Which must mean that if the disease is cold and dry, then the involvement of Mars should mitigate it due to Mars signifying heat and dryness.
[3] This paragraph only in Robert.
[4] Adding with Robert.
[5] Omitting *tenus* with *Judges*.

lungs; the fifth portends the stomach and liver and what are the receptacles of foods.

§617. But the sixth [indicates] the sides and rear parts.[6] The seventh, the kidneys and vital organs. The eighth portrays the virile parts, the bladder, testicles, *rignones*.[7] The ninth declares the buttocks and colon (which in Latin we call the anus). The[8] tenth, the haunches and knees; the eleventh, the shins; but the twelfth, the feet.

§618. Moreover, such a judgment is given for what part of the body he is vexed in. For, the significator corrupted above the earth [indicates] the right [side]; but under the earth, it afflicts the left with pain. If the infortune would be set up in a sign of many ascensions,[9] it indicates the disease will be in a [more] enlarged [part] of the body;[10] but in others, the contrary.

§619. If therefore the truth of the question would promise health, [then] if one is asked about a doctor, one will have to relate this according to the nature of the fortune which liberates [him]. Even the house of the fortune itself (namely the one which it looks at with a more loving aspect) lays it out clearly.

### Chapter 31.3: The value of the doctor

§620. But the lord of the seventh will indicate whether it is possible to be healed by the doctor who is brought in. For if it would make the lord of the Ascendant fortunate, or if it would aid it in something, it testifies that the doctor will be useful for the sick person. But if not, [then] not at all. Which if it would corrupt [the lord of the Ascendant], it promises he is harmful. But if it would be the lord of the house of death or of the second (along with this corruption), it signifies he will be killed by him.[11]

§621. Again, the lord of the seventh receiving the lord of the Ascendant, means a merciful, pious doctor, and one dealing diligently with health. Moreover, the lord of the Ascendant receiving the lord of the seventh, makes

---

[6] *Terga.* That is, the back parts above the waist or hips.
[7] Unknown at this time. Robert omits this.
[8] Adding this sentence with *Judges.*
[9] That is, those of straight ascension: see Ch. 1.1.11.
[10] Literally, in the "enlargement" of the body. I am not quite sure what this means: perhaps in the thicker part of whatever limb is indicated.
[11] Reading *perimi ducetur* with *Judges* for Burnett's *primi dicetur.*

the diligence of the one who has grown sick, be suitable to the healer.[12] But the mutual reception of these indicates mutual courtesy.

§622. Moreover, the lord of the seventh being eastern, in its own light, received, and fortunate, confirms the prudence of the healer and the effect of [his] remedies. Moreover, the same thing amplifies the wisdom and grace and courtesy of the healer.

§623. Furthermore, the shape of the seventh, and its lord, will indicate the form of the healer.

§624. Moreover, you will note whether the one about to take the remedies, would approach [it] willingly. The lord of the Ascendant being received by the lord of the Midheaven, will indicate the effectiveness and appropriateness of the remedies that are taken. Which if they would bear themselves otherwise, they pervert the judgment. No less do the lord of the seventh and the Moon and the lord of the Midheaven come to be considered in this matter.

§625. Also, the final conclusion [of this] for the sick person depends on the lord of the Ascendant and the lunar [lord] and [the lord] of the fourth, according to their luckiness or corruption. But the lord of the significator in particular decrees the same thing.

---

[12] That is, the patient will do what the doctor instructs.

# CHAPTER 32: ON BLOODLETTING & CUPPING[1]

§626. The letting of blood maintains this in common with cupping, that blood is drawn off in both cases; but in what characteristic they differ, will be stated separately in its own place. For, the cutting of veins which they call "phlebotomy" always seems to differ from cupping in this, that the use of cupping glasses comes to be more suitable after the opposition of the Sun and Moon (namely in the latter half of the [lunar] month). Also, phlebotomy claims the prior half of the [lunar] month as being more useful, while the fortunes bear themselves as was stated above.

§627. But as for what [these practices] are partners in, it is good to establish the lord of the Ascendant and the Moon in an airy or fiery sign, made fortunate in a pivot or after the pivots, in its own light,[2] but no less [should you make] their lords fortunate.

§628. If someone desired to purge the defects of the sanguine [humor], let the Moon or the lord of the Ascendant be arranged more suitably in earthy[3] signs. But [to purge] choler, it seems that watery [signs] are more powerful than fiery or airy ones. Which if [it is] black bile, they will hold onto airy ones better so than fiery ones. But a purgation of phlegm seems more appropriately to demand fiery ones.[4]

§629. In all of these, we warn you to beware lest that limb which belongs to the sign the Moon or the lord of the Ascendant is holding onto, should ever by hurt by iron.[5] To make this matter evident, we entrust the limbs of the body to the individual signs by such a distribution:[6] and so, Aries looks to the head, Taurus the neck, Gemini the shoulders and hands, Cancer the chest and what belongs to the chest, but Leo the stomach and vital organs and what is next to these, Virgo takes the loins and back and sides.

---

[1] Al-Kindī's title read "scarification," because cupping was sometimes practiced by scratching (Lat. *scarifo*) or cutting the skin before applying the cup (which must have left a scar). Cupping could be used on many surfaces of the body, whereas bloodletting (phlebotomy) draws blood directly from a vein. See the interesting discussion of cupping in Ibn Sīnā's *Canon*, pp. 521-24. For this chapter, see also al-Rijāl VII.7, which has much additional information.

[2] This generally means that it is out of the Sun's rays.

[3] Reading with al-Rijāl for Hugo's "airy."

[4] Thus the sign indicates the opposite of the type of humor being purged.

[5] That is, for such a surgical intervention.

[6] See a similar list above, in Ch. 1.1.2.

§630. Moreover, Libra claims the *findas*[7] and what is adjacent to these, Scorpio the cock, bladder, buttocks,[8] Sagittarius the testicles, colon and *hiran*,[9] Capricorn the thighs and knees, Aquarius the shins. To Pisces are granted the feet. Therefore, someone instructed in this distribution will never presume to cut (with iron) the limb belonging to the sign which the Moon or the lord of the Ascendant possesses.

§631. Moreover, let the lord of the eighth be deprived of the companionship of the Moon and the lord of the Ascendant, [and] in the same way be estranged from their lords and from a pivot; also, [it is] best if the lord of the Midheaven [is] lucky, regards the Moon and the lord of the Ascendant, [and] moreover that the Moon or the lord of the Ascendant in no way should possess the fourth.

---

[7] Unknown, but Libra generally has the area around the hips. *Judges* reads "calves" (*suras*), which does not make sense.

[8] Reading Hugo's euphemism *renes* for the unknown *rinones* and *rignones* (*Judges*).

[9] Unknown. *Judges* reads *yram*.

# CHAPTER 33: ON SURGERY

§632. The use of surgery demands the same care as the cutting of veins, namely that the limb designated by the sign which the Moon or the lord of the Ascendant is holding onto, should not incur any wound by iron, nor should someone presume to risk it.

§633. Moreover, one must take care with a vigilant soul, lest the lord of the Ascendant or the Moon be falling down from the pivots, nor should they be set up as scorched or retrograde: their preferable position is in a pivot. Furthermore, the lord of the Ascendant should be put in the Ascendant or the Midheaven, [and] likewise the Moon in the Midheaven or the seventh. Also, let the infortunes lack the regard of the Ascendant and its lord (moreover that of the Moon and of the lunar lord), but remember to place them in the falling of the pivots.[1]

§634. The establishment of all of these will finally be perfect if the strength of the lord of the Ascendant and of the Moon would be present, and the lord of the sixth would be set up as being unsound (more often however, it profits no moderate amount to support [the lord of the sixth], wherever it happened [to be]). The end of the matter should be observed in the way it was stated above with respect to phlebotomy. Moreover, the light of the fortunate ones will increase the advantageousness of the pivots.

---

[1] That is, the infortunes should be cadent.

# CHAPTER 34: ON PURGATIVE MEDICINES[1]

§635. The Moon in the last half of Libra or in the first [half] of Scorpio[2] supports the taking of potions. Let her lord[3] be fortunate, strong, eastern and in a pivot, but the one by whom it is blessed should be pivotal and eastern (also, let the lord of the Ascendant be likewise). Likewise let the infortunes be cadent from the Moon and from the pivots, with the Moon received by fortunate ones. Which if the lord of the Moon were unlucky, let him still regard her from a trigon [or hexagon].[4]

Therefore, whoever will have to apply a cure to a limb, let one of the fortunate ones be set up strongly in the sign to which [the limb] is reckoned [to belong], [and] moreover let the lord of the Ascendant[5] and of the fourth be situated in the same way the lunar [lord] is.

§636. One should even avoid placing some significator in a sign which presents the form of [animals] chewing the cud, nor the Ascendant being one of this type: for then, he will vomit forth the remedies he has taken, [and they will be] ineffective.[6] Which if the purging is arranged to take place in the upper parts [of the body], let them be in these [signs] which were [just] prohibited [for laxatives], with the above-written prosperity of the signs and significators.

§637. Whenever it was good to chill or heat the body, to moisten or dry it out,[7] let the Moon and the lord of the Ascendant (or either of them) hold onto signs of a corresponding nature; apart from that, [follow] what was written above about [their] prosperity.

§638. However, the cadency[8] and unluckiness of the significators should be avoided, with the virtue of the infortunes being removed[9]—for these convey no little harm. Let the lord of the house of death be dwelling in none of the pivots, nor should it enjoy partnership or any companionship with the

---

[1] For this chapter, cf. al-Rijāl VII.47.

[2] The so-called "burnt path" or *via combusta*.

[3] If we followed the previous instruction, this would have to be Venus or Mars.

[4] Adding with al-Rijāl.

[5] Al-Rijāl uses only the lord of the fourth, not the lord of the Ascendant. Hugo may have repeated this because it appears above.

[6] This is for laxatives.

[7] That is, if the potion is supposed to provided these medicinal effects.

[8] Reading with al-Rijāl and Robert for Hugo's "fall."

[9] Al-Rijāl has this as "nor should an infortune be firm," suggesting that it is in a fixed sign.

significators. Therefore, a diligent observation of all of these things furnishes the rest as you wish.

# CHAPTER 35: ON FINDING TREASURES & HIDDEN THINGS[1]

## Chapter 35.1: Finding a hidden thing

§639. With a question being proposed about treasure and any hidden thing, namely as to whether or not a place (which has already been considered) contains it, before all else the Ascendant and the pivots should be established. Therefore, any lucky star in the Ascendant [or any of the pivots],[2] affirms it is in the allotted place. Wherefore, one will be able to decide the status of the concealed thing, and the proper quality of [its] nature, and the price, according to the manner and nature, strength and weakness of the fortunate and lucky [star].

§640. In fact, that lucky [star] being corrupted by a powerful infortune, spoils the hidden things, as it portends that the whole (or the majority of) it has [already] been carried off.[3] Which if it is blessed by the luckiness of other [planets], it preserves what he was seeking in that same place.

§641. But the lord of the Ascendant and the Moon respond to the question as to whether it could be found. For their common application with the significator of the concealed thing, [with reception],[4] affirms its discovery. But if it happened differently, let the opinion of the judgment be changed.

§642. Therefore, once one has faith about its discovery, let such a description of the place where it is shut up lead right to it. And so, let a division of its place (which [one's] masterful assessment has indicated) be drawn from its center to every outermost limit, in twelve directions, bounded in right angles.[5] Moreover, let the line of the sign which the star is holding

---

[1] For this topic, see also *Search* (Ch. II.2 generally, but especially Ch. II.2.3); also *Judges* §§4.18-20 and §2.8-9. William Lilly drew on Robert's translation in his own *CA*, p. 218.

[2] Adding with Burnett 1997, based on the Arabic.

[3] See a similar but different view of 'Umar's in *Judges* §4.18.

[4] Adding with Burnett 1997, based on the Arabic.

[5] Probably because al-Kindī supposes the house or property is roughly square-shaped; but he also seems to mean that the lines should be evenly spaced and form right angles just as the lines dividing the signs of a quadruplicity do. See diagram.

onto (dividing a triangular place according to the quantity of its course),[6] be drawn out from the center of that same door:[7] so that if [the planet] is crossing one-third or one-fourth of the sign, the line will either cut off or enclose one-third or one-fourth of the triangle.

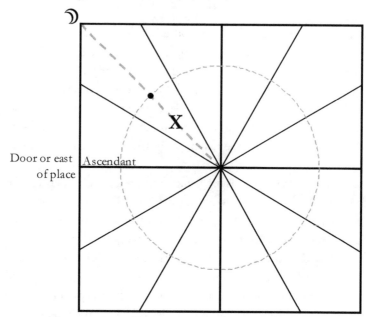

**Figure 62: Al-Kindī's example of finding treasure[8]**

---

[6] What Hugo means is that one should divide the significator's sign into three (or four, see immediately below) parts so as to estimate where in that direction the treasure is, proportionate to the significator's position in the sign.

[7] Or rather, that portion of the house.

[8] In this example from al-Kindī's *Letter* (Burnett 1997, pp. 70-71), the treasure is in a house, and the Ascendant represents the door. The square house is divided into twelve equal parts representing the signs (§642). The Moon happens to be the significator of the treasure, and is 45° to the south of the Ascendant, with 2° northern latitude. *The Forty Chapters* has us estimate which third of the sign the planet is in (§643), but al-Kindī's *Letter* recommends using the exact degree. We draw a dotted gray line from the center of the house towards the southeast, at an angle of 45° from the Ascendant (§642-43). Then, divide this line in half with a mark (§644), and use a compass to draw a circle representing the ecliptic (the circle is actually unnecessary, what matters is dividing the line). Then, determine what the maximum latitude of the planet is, and what its latitude actually is at the time (§644-45): in this case, the Moon's maximum latitude is 5°, but she is actually at 2° N. Northern latitudes will be between the mark and the center of the house, southern latitudes between it and the circumference of the figure (§645). Since she is 2/5 of the way towards her northernmost latitude, the treasure will be at a distance 2/5 of the way from the mark to the center of the house, marked by the X. Her distance towards or away from

§643. The[9] line produced from the center separates the whole space [within] the outermost [limits] of the sign, [according to] how[ever] many degrees of the sign the significator of the hidden thing has passed through. So that if it is now leaving one-third [of the sign], the line will cut off, by [its] angle, one-third of the sign which the significator is holding onto. To make this matter obvious, the point of the Ascendant designates the degree of the east in that same place or home. Therefore, by how great the distance the significator[10] was from the Ascendant, you will note that much distance of the concealed thing from the east.

§644. Again, if you wanted to determine whether it is closer to the center or to the end-point of the line in which it is discovered to be, cut that same line in half. The mark of its division [in half] also represents the circle of signs[11] which we call the zodiac. Then the latitude of the star from the ecliptic (namely its departure towards the south or towards the north) should be noted. For a northern [latitude] invites us towards the north [and the center][12] from the point fixed before, but a southern [latitude] towards the south [and the circumference].[13]

§645. Moreover, it will be good to divide the distance [between] the mark[14] and the center [of the room] according to the degrees of its latitude. For example, if the [maximum] latitude of the star from the ecliptic were proven to be 5°, the aforesaid distance [between] the point and the center shares in [those] five equal degrees. If therefore the star departed somewhat from the ecliptic, what is sought is asserted to be distant from the mark [in the center of the line] by that same amount. Like if it completed one-fifth of [its] latitude from the ecliptical point, it means one-fifth of the line extended from the center to he mark. But if one-third, [then one-third of the line], in this manner. So, if it departs towards the south, the matter warns [us] to measure that portion in such a manner [toward the circumference]; likewise toward the north [and the center of the home].

---

her apogee (or perhaps, her elevation in the sky) will determine how high up or low the treasure is (§647).

[9] Reading this and the next sentence with the Arabic as a guide, since Hugo seems to have misunderstood what was being divided or determined.

[10] Reading with the Ar. and the logic of the paragraph, for Hugo's "of the lord of the significator."

[11] Omitting the transliteration *deirataburoig* (Ar. *dāʿirah al-burūj*, "circle of signs").

[12] Adding with Burnett 1997, based on the Arabic.

[13] Adding with Burnett 1997, based on the Arabic.

[14] That is, the mark indicating the center of the line.

§646. Which if the [planet][15] came to be discovered in the middle of the signs,[16] with the southern and northern part being left behind, search for what you intended in that sign, [in the place] where the line is divided.

§647. Moreover, the depression of the star, or [its] loftiness above the ethers,[17] should be noted. For, a consideration of this matter shows how far below the earth it is being held. Its middle loftiness means [it is] between the surface of the earth and the impenetrable bedrock or water.[18] But its uppermost status suggests a place of height, in the way it was said about the status of a home, above.[19]

## Chapter 35.2: Election: When to dig it up

§648. Moreover, in choosing the hour for digging it up, an application of the Moon with the fortunate significator should be noted, [and] in the same way an application of the lord of the Ascendant at that hour to [that same significator]—indeed an assembly[20] of each with it is more powerful. In the hour of extracting it, you will no less take care to make the infortunes be absent from the pivots.

---

[15] Reading *planetam* for *notam*.

[16] That is, right on the ecliptic.

[17] This appears to mean whether the planet is ascending or decending in its apogee (*ITA* II.1). Burnett believes it is the star's altitude above or below the horizon (1997, p. 60), but that does not seem right to me. The translator of the version in *On Hidden Things* §7 (in *WSM*) explicitly names the apogee.

[18] Reading with Burnett's Arabic (1997, p. 75) for Hugo's "intact earth which the Arabs call *gibel almuntaneah*."

[19] This appears to be a reference to finding the home of a thief: see above in Chs. 6-9, but I do not find a similar statement there.

[20] Reading with Burnett's Ar. for "with reception." An assembly is a conjunction within the same sign: see Ch. 2.1.1 above, and *ITA* III.5.

# CHAPTER 36: ON HORSE RACING[1]

## Chapter 36.1: Significators & overview

§649. The arrangement of the Ascendant and the pivots manages the racing of horses and the status of those running [in it]; whence, the Ascendant and its lord designates the master of the whole cohort.[2] Moreover, seek vigilantly for any star which claimed the rulership of the hour for itself: for it signifies the horse [who wins], but the lord of the second [hour] the following one, that of the third [hour] will indicate the third, and the lords of the rest of the hours take the rest, in whatever order they were.

## Chapter 36.2: Identifying the winner by color & markings

§650.[3] Therefore, if the nature and manner of whatever ruler of the hour [it was] would be diligently looked for, they indicate his horse as a whole. For example, [if the color is that] of Saturn as the significator, a dark horse is expected. Jupiter, blonde or whitish; Mars, red; the Sun, white, more consistent with bright white; Venus, intensely black and glittering;[4] Mercury, less black; the Moon, white verging more into blackness.

§651. But once the significators distinguish these colors, if there were a commixture of the stars with them, the commixture of their colors with those of the applying ones, will follow—but the color of the significator will always prevail in it. For example, if Jupiter applied to the significator Saturn, the majority of the hair will appear dark, [but] a lesser blonde [amount] will be mixed in with it. With Mars being mixed with [Saturn], it exhibits a color of dark and red, verging more to blackness. With the Sun joined to [Saturn], middling white; Venus, middling black; and likewise Mercury, but going more towards the dark. Finally, the Moon joined to [Saturn] will be dark, [but] consistent with brightness.

---

[1] This chapter should be compared to Sahl's *On Questions* §12.1-3 and al-Rijāl III.33.
[2] *Cohortis.* This seems to mean the person who is hosting the race: see §661.
[3] From here through the rest of the chapter, the paragraphs are all from Robert, as Hugo is missing most paragraphs.
[4] Reading *renidens* for *renitens.*

§652. With Jupiter as the significator, his color will overcome the rest of those mixing [with him].[5] With Saturn as the applier [to Jupiter], an even blonde [color] with a little bit of dark hair, or [the body itself] partly verging on the dark; with Mars [as the applier to Jupiter], reddish; the Sun, either the shiniest white or a gleaming blonde; Venus, handsome and varied markings; Mercury, either of silver or iron color; the Moon, either shiny white or yielding more to this color.[6]

§653. But with Saturn applying to Mars as the significator, red verging on blackness. Jupiter, reddish, the forehead and tail of which are bright white. The Sun, reddish, and its hair[7] and tail red. Venus, varied in red and black, or whose redness yields more to blackness. But Mercury, less so. Finally, with the Moon applying, a mixture of color from silver and red.

§654. Saturn joined to the Sun as the significator, of a rusty color. Jupiter, bright white, with the legs and eye sockets[8] and forehead black. Mars, leaning red, similar to royal horses. Venus, white with innate black markings in the Lunar manner, and that kind of thing. Mercury, likewise white but taking on redness. Finally, with the Moon applying to him, middling white.

§655. With Venus as the significator [and] applying to Saturn, the horse will be blackish. She being mixed with Jupiter, bright black, tending a little bit to blonde, or of a silver or varied color. Mars, reddish. The Sun, of a gleaming and handsome variety. Mercury, muddy.[9] The Moon, approximately whitish-black.[10]

§656. Saturn mixed with Mercury as the significator, black approximately similar to dusky. Jupiter, black verging on blondeness. Mars, a rosy color close to red. The Sun, reddish or tending to blackness. Venus, a nearly blue-black[11] or varied. The Moon, ash-colored.

§657. Then, with Saturn mixed with the Moon as the significator, a dark color in no way bright, but commendable. Jupiter, very bright white. Mars, blackish white. The Sun, white verging on redness. Venus, likewise but with white markings. Virtually such is Mercury, too.

---

[5] Bringing this sentence down from the previous paragraph. It had been placed above by Burnett so as to match Hugo's paragraphing.

[6] I take this to mean, "the color indicated by Jupiter."

[7] On its head and mane.

[8] *Oculorum orbibus.*

[9] Or, clay-colored (*luteus*). But with a long initial *u* (*lūteus*), golden-yellow. I prefer clay or mud here, since Mercury is elsewhere darker.

[10] *Subalbus fere niger.*

[11] Or perhaps, "a black [that is] nearly blue" (*niger fere blavus*).

§658. Moreover, no little notice should be taken of those ruling the four faces (namely of the place and pivots of the significator of the horse),[12] just as we will soon teach. For, Jupiter or the Sun or Venus or the Moon ruling the face which the significator of the horse is holding onto, makes a distinguishing mark on the forehead. But otherwise, none. However, one of these ruling the face of its fourth, makes the belly white or distinguished with marks; of the face of its Midheaven, the back and sides; of the face of its seventh, the tail.

### Chapter 36.3: Other characteristics of the horses[13]

§659. Moreover, the significator being eastern renders his horse young; western, aged (for a measuring of this type of status); direct: one moving in a straight line and readily so; retrograde: crooked, running back, difficulty, bad; stationary: stupid, standing still; hastening in [its] course: quick; slow: the contrary; treading in a pivot, in some dignity of its own, going out from under the rays: good, strong, well-mannered; conversely: the contrary; made fortunate: beautifully put together and fortunate; made unfortunate: the contrary.

§660. A lucky one ruling over its bound: [the owner is][14] noted and famous; and if Venus would rule it, [he is] Arab and what is like these; if Jupiter, a Latin or that type. But an unlucky one ruling over the one asked about,[15] [he is] ignoble and without any name, except for his own good behavior.

§661. Thus, the lord of the hour determines whose horse achieves the victory. Ruling over the east, it announces the winning horse will belong to the master of the race and the gathering.[16] [Ruling] over the second, the

---

[12] That is, the planetary decan of the lord of the hour itself, and of the cusps of the derived angles from it. See the following instructions.

[13] This material is a bit difficult for me to understand, since the lord of the hour is supposed to indicate the winning horse: how can it do this if it is running slowly or crookedly, etc.? This is another reason for all of the horse-racing material to be examined together.

[14] I take this to indicate the owner, but perhaps al-Kindī is mentioning the background and pedigree of the horse.

[15] *Quaesiti*, which in Robert appears at the end of the sentence.

[16] *Curiae*, which could also mean the quarter or ward of the city (such as when different parts of the city compete against each other). Normally this refers to a law-court or where the royal court gathers itself.

horse of some follower or ally of the master of the race. Over the third, that of his brother or one having the role of a brother. Over the fourth, that of his father or one just like a father, or that of the republic, [or] one given to fights and the defense of the fatherland.[17] Over the fifth, that of his child, or one equally loved. Over the sixth, that of a slave or one bearing the responsibility of one. Over the seventh, that of a partner or equal or spouse. Over the eighth, that of the ally of partners, or that type. Over the ninth, a proposer of laws or one equal to brothers. Over the tenth, that of the king or a craftsman.[18] Over the eleventh, that of a friend. Finally, ruling over the twelfth, it designates the winner is the horse of an enemy or of a blood-relative of his.[19]

---

[17] *Seu rei publicae, pugnis patriaeque defensioni datum.*
[18] *Artificis.*
[19] That is, a blood-relative of the enemy.

# CHAPTER 37: ON PRICES & COMMODITIES[1]

§662. If someone worried would inquire into the price of things for sale, let him note studiously the victor of the degree[2] of the assembly or opposition which preceded the Sun's ingress into the first point of Aries), and let it take possession as the significator. If therefore the significator itself would be adding, or there would come to be an application of it with a star [that is] adding,[3] it seems to signify that the price of things will be more burdensome, and according to the nature of the sign which it is holding onto. No less should the understanding of the lord of the Ascendant of the year and of the Ascendant of the conjunction [or opposition] be judged as necessary.

§663. Moreover, the pivots being blessed with the light of the lucky ones makes the price of things for sale more burdensome; but that of the unlucky ones, the contrary. Moreover, the Sun and the Moon in a pivot declare coin to be costly. And so the Sun designates gold, the Moon silver.

§664. Venus [and] Mercury even testify in this manner: for Venus resembles the Moon in signification, Mercury the Sun. Which if these significators would be cadent from the pivots, they mean the cheapness of gold and silver, but they commend what is bought with these at a greater price.

---

[1] Although the mechanics of the method are clear, I am somewhat uncertain about the effects of the planetary positions on prices. First there is the fact that our writers were living in the days of the gold standard. Second, some of their language is a bit tricky because of the conflict of interest between buyers and sellers: normally, buyers want prices low and goods plentiful, but sellers want prices high and goods scarce. Well, these texts (see also *Judges* and *ITA* VI.5) seem to be written with the value of the commodities themselves in mind: benefics, pivots, and good conditions make prices rise and the goods scarce; but malefics, cadents, and bad conditions make the prices cheap and the goods abundant. But see §667, in which Hugo seems to mean that cadents indicate low prices, but uses the word that typically means high prices.

[2] Reading with Robert. Hugo reads, "the victor, namely the lord of the degree...". But the victor assumes a decision procedure: it is not merely the lord of a place of a degree. Note however that Ch. 3, which lists several victors, does not explain the victor of a particular degree. Perhaps al-Kindī is thinking along the lines of §§699-700 below, which suggests the most important ruler of the degree which also regards it.

[3] This probably refers to increasing in speed, but I would not rule out increasing in the circle of the apogee (see *ITA* II.0-4).

§665. Therefore, one should note with an ever-watchful mind, what kind of assent the fortunes show.[4] But the fortunes make things more expensive, the infortunes the contrary.

§666. This same thing must be considered in the individual quarters [of the year] for the price of things at that time, and in the individual conjunctions and oppositions (just as done here at the beginning of the year), and a moderating judgment [made] from all of these.[5]

§667.[6] If therefore the significators of things for sale were cadent, they convey low[7] [prices] or a manifold abundance of them. Then the ingress of [the lord] of the Ascendant [of the year][8] or of the opposition or the assembly, into the Ascendant itself or into one of the pivots, determines the hour at which these things should happen. The lords of the annual quarters do not even deny what the lords of the Ascendant [of the year] and of the assembly [or opposition] testify to.

[Robert]: The ingress of the aforesaid significators into the places designated above will bring about the time of the foreseen alleviation or burdensomeness [of the cost]: namely, [1] the [ingress of the] victor of the degree of the conjunction or opposition into [that place itself], or [2] the entrance of the ruler of the east of the year, or the lord of the conjunction or opposition, into the east itself.

§668. Moreover, the ascent of the stars into the north,[9] increases the price of things; but into the south, the contrary.

---

[4] This probably means that we must keep watching the transits throughout the year, and not only at the ingresses.
[5] Using Robert's more succinct version of this paragraph.
[6] I add Robert's version below, because he gives a slightly different version of the ingresses. Hugo has the lord of the Ascendant or of the assembly/opposition entering the Ascendant of the year or any of the pivots. Robert allows these significators to enter the Ascendant, but also lets the lord of the assembly/opposition enter the place of the assembly/opposition.
[7] *Graves.* I am a bit unsure about this, because in other places *gravis* and *gravescor* refer to higher and more burdensome prices. But one would expect the price and value of things to go down in the cadent places.
[8] Adding based on Robert.
[9] That is, by ecliptical latitude.

# CHAPTER 38: ON CHANGES IN WEATHER[1]

## Chapter 38.1: The year, quarters, & months

§669. For a complete recognition of those things in the atmosphere which are renewed[2] through individual years, it is good that the Ascendant of the assembly or opposition[3] which came before the Sun's ingress into the beginning of Aries, be established. Therefore, whatever sign Saturn claimed in that hour, the year seems to imitate its nature: for a hot one means heat; cold, cold; dry, aridness; moist, moistening.

§670. Moreover, when the Sun enters the individual quarters or seasons of the year,[4] Jupiter comes to be noted: one will have to judge about him in that same quarter of the year, in the way it was stated above [about Saturn]. But the consideration that is made of the signification of a quarter, and the signification of the year, will exhibit the truth in revealing the judgment.[5]

§671. Moreover you will note [1] with whom the application of the lord of the assembly or opposition[6] (preceding the beginning of the year or quarter) comes to be. For the sharing [of indications] that is made of that star (just as was stated above) lays bare what will be.

§672. Moreover, with no less attention should you care [2] with whom the application of the lord of the Ascendant of[7] the assembly, or [3] of the lord of the Ascendant of the year, comes to be. For once a discernment of all of them is had, they suggest what must be said. Moreover, [4] the lords of the assembly and opposition in every month should be noted. In this way, let there be a report about those future things which are imminent.

---

[1] For this chapter, I have consulted the Arabic version and English translation in Burnett and Bos, 2000. A fuller treatment with commentary will accompany the corresponding material in *Judges*, and in the weather volume of my *Astrology of the World* (forthcoming 2011-12).

[2] Hugo means the revolution or cycle of years: the Sun's return to Aries every spring.

[3] The Ar. has only the assembly/conjunction.

[4] That is, his ingresses into the other movable signs: Cancer, Libra, Capricorn.

[5] That is, by combining the indications. Burnett's translation of the Ar. makes it seem that we should also look at Saturn at every quarterly ingress, but to me the sense is that Saturn is for the year as a whole, and Jupiter for the quarters. Certainly Robert and Hugo read it that way.

[6] Again, the Ar. has only the assembly/conjunction.

[7] Adding with Robert and the Ar.

§673. In addition, if the significator and giver of hail (or heavy rains or dryness) is regarding the [Sun or Moon at the][8] assembly or opposition of the month or year—the Sun for planets of the year, but the Moon for the planets of the year and the months[9]—it signifies that those things which follow its nature are imminent—especially [if] placed in a bound or house of its complexion.[10]

## Chapter 38.2: Individual planets' indications

§674. And so it seems one must note that Venus principally signifies wetness, Mercury stirs up winds, Saturn multiplies clouds and the darkness of the air, and hail, Mars incites the southern winds [and heat] (but especially in Capricorn [or its pivots]);[11] moreover Jupiter in a house of some authority of his own (but especially in Cancer) sends in the northern winds. The Sun introduces heat and dryness.

## Chapter 38.3: The posts[12] of the Moon, the opening of the doors

§675. Moreover, let the [Ascendant of every assembly of the Sun and Moon][13] be principally established. But no less will you note, with the equal attention of your mind, [the following] twelve points, for they are these: the

---

[8] Adding with Robert and the Ar.

[9] Adding with Robert and the Ar. The sense seems to be that planets examined at the beginning of the year (Saturn, planets at the annual assembly just before the ingress) should aspect the Sun, but any of them may aspect the Moon when looking especially at monthly times. But this does not really make sense, since by definition any planet aspecting one luminary at the New or Full Moon will also be aspecting the other.

[10] Reading with Robert (Ar.: "according to its nature"). Hugo reads, "in agreement with the nature of the one to which it applies," but in this paragraph we are not considering applications.

[11] Adding bracketed material with the Ar.

[12] Ar. *marākiz*, which comes from a verb (*rakaza*) very similar to the Arabic (*watada*) and Greek (*kenteō*) verbs used to derive the words for the pivots or angles: "to ram into the ground, set up a pole, position or fix firmly." Burnett plausibly translates it as "centers," but I do not believe this really captures the sense of a firm position, or point of concentration, so I have used the English "posts," in the sense both of a pole and an organizational position or rank (these are also acceptable readings in the Arabic dictionary).

[13] Adding based on the Arabic.

assembly, opposition, the two squares (namely the tetragons), and the cross-quarters of the tetragons, the 12° before the completion of the assembly and opposition, [and] the same amount after their completion.

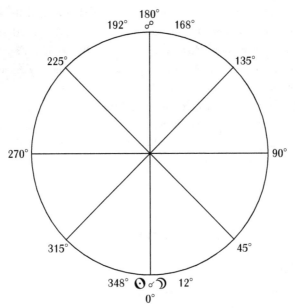

**Figure 63: Al-Kindī's twelve posts of the Moon**

§676. Therefore, when the Moon is found in any of these, if any of the inferiors would apply to a superior by an opposition,[14] it testifies that what is in agreement with its nature will happen, if a common regard of the Sun and Moon would be present, and if the Ascendant of the region or city does not lack their regard,[15] [and] even should they be supported by a regard of their own lords.

---

[14] The Ar. reads as though any inferior can apply to any superior, but al-Kindī is describing the "opening of the doors/portals," in which an inferior must apply to the superior planet which rules the domicile opposite its domicile: Mercury to Jupiter, Venus to Mars, and the luminaries to Saturn. Here, al-Kindī says the *aspect* must be an opposition.

[15] This may mean the Ascendant of the founding of a city or country. In modern times we have assumed Ascendants for the formal establishments of nations, but how could medievals have known this for virtually any city or nation besides Baghdad (whose founding was determined by an electional chart)? Perhaps it could include the annual Ascendant of the year at the Aries ingress, or some other epochal Ascendant.

§677. In addition, if the Moon would advance and apply from some inferior to the superior opposite it,[16] both as mediator and key-bearer, it indubitably forces the natural [qualities] of its superior to come about. Which if this administration is ascribed to Mercury, in addition to heavy rains he begets winds; and if to Venus, it multiplies rain clouds; and if to Saturn, it sends down hail, covers the atmosphere, and prolongs [destruction],[17] putting clouds over clouds. Moreover, the Moon brings about a multitude of rain clouds. Finally, in the same way the Sun taints the atmosphere alternately: now with fire, now with clouds.[18]

§678. The significators (or [especially][19] the Moon) being individually in the regard of Mars, stir up thunder and send down lightning strikes. Moreover, Saturn as the author of this administration, even [indicates cold and][20] overturns buildings. [The judgment must be made analogously for all qualities.][21]

### Chapter 38.4: Other indicators

§679. Furthermore, the moistening places of the circle seem to be worthy of consideration, because they multiply waters.[22] Moreover, the retrogradation of significators furnishes an overflowing of waters.

§680. And[23] this happens at the hour of the Moon's separation from an indicator of [rain], and likewise at the hour of the inferiors' departure from the superior significators. [By separating from an indicator, it means] the lunar departure from the four principal [posts],[24] which tends to alternate and vary any quality of the air [from one] to another. The Sun's [standing] there [does] likewise, but more powerfully so the Moon.

---

[16] The Ar. only says that the Moon is applying to an inferior planet.
[17] Adding with the Ar.
[18] Ar.: "air, and darkness."
[19] Adding with the Ar.
[20] Adding based on Robert and the Ar.
[21] Adding with Robert, mirroring the Ar.
[22] Apparently, if significators are in them. There are several versions of these places (see Burnett and Bos 2000, Table III). Al-Kindī's two *Letters* on this topic mainly agree on Cancer, Scorpio, Pisces, and add Leo, Aquarius, and Capricorn (or the end of Capricorn).
[23] This paragraph is a *pastiche* of Robert, Hugo, and the Arabic. The Arabic, however, does not speak of the inferior planets separating, but only that the Moon's departure from the four principal quarters indicates changes in weather.
[24] That is, at the lunar quarters.

§681.[25] Furthermore, the rest of the stars imitate the Sun in this, but not so manifestly nor with such effectiveness. For example, they operate their own effects in their own orbits [of the apogee and perigee] and the rest of their own places, just as the Sun does in corresponding places, even though they do it more secretly and known to fewer.

§682. Finally, a studious reader should not neglect to scrutinize this attentively: any [star] traversing in north [latitude] seems to enlarge the effects of its own peculiar signification and indication; also, in the south [it is] weaker. Moreover, ascending into the north is more powerful than if it is descending in the [north]. But declining in the south [is] more slack than if its ascent in [the south] would be happening.

---

[25] Reading this paragraph with Robert.

# CHAPTER 39: ON YEARS OF PLAGUE
## & GOOD HEALTH

§683. First of all, with the Ascendant of the year being placed, then too will follow an awareness of the Ascendant of the assembly or opposition which precedes the Sun's ingress into Aries. And so, let those Ascendants and the Moon be made clean of the infortunes, and no less should the lord of the assembly or opposition appear free [of them]. An application of [that lord] having been made with fortunate ones, or that same [lord] being in the regard of the Sun and Moon (or at least the one which obtains the shift), introduces a healthful year and one without disease.

§684. Moreover, the lords of the [two] Ascendants, and the Moon, and also the lord of the assembly or opposition (or the majority of them), being unfortunate and unlucky, convey the pestilence of disease, and this is agreed[1] to happen according to the manner and harshness of the corrupting [planet], and the nature of the infortune, and the place in which the corruption comes to be.

§685. Which if there would be an application of those which rule the Ascendants, and of the Moon (the aforesaid infortune having been observed), with the lord of their eighth,[2] a plague is designated which will kill many. But if it happened otherwise, [it will kill] very few. Which if a manifold disease[3] is present, still it will oppress few.

§686. Furthermore, these significators (or one of them), retreating from scorching, and applying with the lord of its own eighth, introduces a sudden kind of ruin but without disease. But if any lord of them would apply with it, once a signification of disease would already be had, the slowness of its natural course multiplies the disease and renders it long-lasting; but the quickness[4] of [its] course removes the steadiness of its long-lastingness.

§687. Which if this corruption would proceed from Mars, it generates acute diseases, particularly [assuming] the quickness of his course, [and] he even being strong and dwelling in a hot and dry sign. But Saturn arriving as

---

[1] Reading *constat* for *constans*.
[2] That is, of the lords with the eighth from that Ascendant, or of the Moon with the eighth from her own position. See a similar treatment in §692 below, and §403.
[3] Robert: "much and difficult." Al-Kindī could mean a serious illness that kills few, or perhaps many diseases that kill few.
[4] Reading *celeritas* for *caelestis*.

the corruptor, indicates the steadiness of the disease, particularly [with him being] slow, strong, and arranged in a cold and dry sign.

# CHAPTER 40: ON THE REVOLUTION OF THE YEARS OF THE WORLD[1]

§688. In revolutions of the years of the world, the east[2] of the conjunction or opposition (namely the one preceding the solar ingress into Aries) and the rest of the pivots must be established with the most subtle computation, and also the places of the stars. Then, one must note to what kind of star the Moon would apply after that conjunction or opposition (namely to a lucky or unlucky one, strong or weak). For, the nature of that [star] has an indication over the future things which will happen to the people.

§689-690. If therefore [1] the Moon, being in an advancing [place and] obtaining some dignity there, commingled herself with a lucky [planet], strong in an advancing [place] and in one of its own dignities, a fertile year and abundant sustenance will befall the people, and their happiness will follow happiness, and they will advance themselves to one good from another.

That conjunction being made with Jupiter, the people will pursue faithfulness, cleanliness, and good moods in that year, and will make many offspring and will rejoice in good health. With Venus, abundance and joy will come to pass, and the people will be devoted to[3] fornication and much ornamentation, [and] will even enter into marriage.

§691. But [2] the Moon being remote, nor applying in some dignity of hers, [but] applying to a lucky one in an advancing [place] in one of its own dignities, what was said before about good fortune will [indeed] happen, except that [the people] will incur the luckiness from a calamity, and it will be first weak, then strong.

But an inversion of this will happen if [3] the Moon is advancing and obtaining some dignity, [and] she applied to a lucky [but] remote star outside of [any] dignity.

But [4] each one[4] being remote and outside [any] dignity, [then] a change will happen: just as from a good status to a corresponding one before, so

---

[1] This chapter is only in Robert.
[2] That is, the Ascendant. See Ch. 39 above.
[3] *Militabit.*
[4] Namely, the Moon and the fortunate planet to which she applies.

here [it would be] from a bad one to a corresponding one—but with the health of the body as a companion.[5]

§692. If [5] the Moon, being weak and peregrine, commingled herself with an unlucky, strong [planet] holding onto an advancing [place], [then] evil, degradation, weakness, slight sustenance, and manifold disease will happen to the people.[6] And if that unlucky one would rule the eighth from the Moon, or it would even obtain a strong power in her eighth (even though it is not its lord), frequent death will follow; and likewise even if it is not unlucky [but] if, ruling the eighth of the Moon, it regards her. Indeed, with the unlucky one being Saturn, Saturnian diseases will happen (namely melancholic) which will be the occasion of the death. But it being Mars, acute and hot diseases will follow, and at the same time a pouring out of blood, and slaughter.

[With the infortune] holding a human sign—but especially if the year applied[7] either [a] to that place which Mars was allotted at the beginning of that people, or [b] to the place where [the Saturn-Jupiter conjunction] changed its trigon, or [c] to his[8] own place in the conjunction[9] which most recently preceded the revolution—that year will abound in battles and the pouring out of blood in the direction of the lands corresponding to the sign which Mars is allotted in that year and in the above-listed places, the end of

---

[5] In other words, people's health will be affected.

[6] The other relationships with malefics, corresponding to the benefics above, are mentioned briefly in §693 below.

[7] What follows seems to be a list of mundane profection places, probably from the Ascendant of the last triplicity change. On average, Saturn-Jupiter conjunctions take place every 20 years, and 12 times in a row in the same triplicity; after this average 240 years in the triplicity, they change to the next triplicity (and are at least sometimes supposed to identify a people and culture on the rise). The Persians frequently profected the Ascendant of this "change" (whether the calculated Ascendant for that moment, or the Ascendant of the Aries ingress for that year). So, al-Kindī seems to be listing the following profections of the Ascendant of the change to support the already-bad situation described above: (a) to the sign Mars was in at the change, (b) the sign in which the conjunction of the change happened, and (c) the sign Mars was in at the last minor Saturn-Jupiter conjunction (i.e., within the last 20 years). So for example, the Saturn-Jupiter conjunction of 571 AD, marking the change to water and Islam, took place in Scorpio, and the Ascendant of the change was often taken to be Gemini. So, let's suppose we were living in the 7th Century: if, at the Aries ingress, the Moon were in the difficult situation described in the first part of §692, and Mars were in a human sign, then the bad effects listed here would take place if the annual profection forward from Gemini in 571 came to (a) Mars's place at the change (Virgo at the actual date, but Gemini at the revolution in March), or (b) to Scorpio itself, or (c) to Mars's place at the most recent Saturn-Jupiter conjunction. For more, see *ITA* VIII.3, and my forthcoming *Astrology of the World*.

[8] Tentatively reading "his" (Mars) instead of the more neutral "its."

[9] *Alkiren*, a transliteration of Ar. *al-qirān*.

which will happen in that year when Mars will incur his own burning or fall, or Jupiter [would incur] burning.

§693. Then the place of Mars must be noted, namely whether he is eastern or western, right or left. For, his direction will attain victory,[10] by the command of God. And if Mercury were putting on[11] the nature of the corrupting Mars, mortality will fall upon the year. But with Mercury wearing the nature of Saturn in an earthy sign at the revolution of the year, an earthquake will shatter islands and seacoasts, cliffs and rocky places. Finally, every manner between the Moon and a lucky one indicated above (namely with respect to remoteness and advancing, strength and weakness, and the rest of that kind), should be considered here between the Moon and an unlucky one, and a change of this kind should be judged according to this: from evil into something similar, or into the contrary.

---

[10] That is, the people in or from that direction.
[11] This probably means that Mercury is closely aspecting Mars by degree.

# ADDITION 1: ON THE EFFECTS OF THE MOON[1]

§694. The Moon in turning signs alternates affairs quickly, whence [there is] hatred or unstable enmity, unsteady adversity. The Moon in firm ones [is good for] the planting of trees and the practice of grafting [plants]. But sowing seems to demand her being in turning signs. For planting demands the steadiness of stability, but [the sowing] of seed the contrary.

§695. The Moon in turning [signs] in no way agrees with laying the foundations of buildings, because instability threatens the ruin of collapse. The Moon in turning [signs] is wholly useful for selling and buying. If someone would grow ill and the Moon [were] in turning ones, it denies the long-lastingness of the disease. If someone detained would enter into flight, and the Moon [were] in turning [signs], it indicates a quick return. Disagreements and quarrels while the Moon is staying in turning ones, [will be] neither firm nor long-lasting. To make a journey with the Moon in turning ones is useful, [but] promises [made] in convertible ones are not delivered on, discussions and dreams in convertible ones are false and untrustworthy.[2]

§696. Furthermore, if things are bought with the Moon being in a movable or double-bodied sign, they do not remain, for they tend to be complicated with fraud and very often trickery, and violence. One who comes to you and the Moon [is] in a double-bodied sign—reckon him as a flatterer and fraudulent, whence it seems neither diligence nor faithfulness can be applied to him or his words, for [his] deeds differ from [his] words. The chains of marriages will be dissolved with the Moon in a double-bodied sign: sexual immorality and quarrels contaminate its end.

§697. Anyone disgraced by some crime, and the Moon in a double-bodied sign, will escape safe and free. If someone is led as a captive and the Moon [is] in a double-bodied sign, it hastens [his] freedom. One to whom exit from prison is given, and the Moon [is] in a double-bodied sign, is getting ready to be returned more quickly to chains. Anyone held, who enters into flight, and the Moon in a double-bodied [sign], is no less led back. Anyone approaching a judge, and the Moon in a double-bodied [sign], will bring back a doubtful and ill-advised, and even unexamined judgment.

---

[1] Much of this material can be traced back to Sahl's *On Elections*, §§12-17.
[2] Or perhaps, "conflicting, many-sided, fluctuating" (*varia*).

§698. He who grows ill, and the Moon [is] in a double-bodied one, will get well but will fall into disease all over again. Whatever good or adverse [things] someone would incur, and the Moon in a double-bodied [sign], it is necessary for him to undergo it doubly. If someone will die, and the Moon [is] in a double-bodied sign, it portends that another from the family of his house will perish before few days [more]. Victory and triumph are to be praised [if] the Moon is in a double-bodied sign.

# ADDITION 2: RECTIFICATION[1]

§699. Among the sages it is agreed that the generations and corruptions of things happen through the perpetual motion of the heavenly bodies, the effecting of which proceeds principally from the nature of the lights and the rest of the planets of heaven (together with [their] manner and rank), in the conjunction and opposition of the lights.

But the significator[2] of every generated thing is the more principal and more manifest one by nature: [namely, the single victor-star over the degree of the conjunction or opposition more closely preceding the nativity. First, calculate the approximate Ascendant and Midheaven of the birth. Then, let the number of degrees and a fraction which the victor-star is allotted in its own sign at the hour of the nativity, be the actual degree of the Ascendant or the Midheaven—whichever was nearer.]

§700. For example, at the hour of the concluded conjunction or opposition, the Moon held onto the tenth degree of Aries. Mars, regarding it from the tenth [degree] of Leo, appears as the victor. In whatever degree of whatever sign [Mars] was at the hour of the nativity which follows, the pivot near it at the hour of the nativity (whichever it was) will be established as being in that many degrees.[3]

But, it having been found thusly, [and] then with the rest of the pivots established, and together with the domiciles, the hour of the nativity should be established over the hour of the east.

---

[1] This material is only in Robert, and Burnett (1993, p. 80) believes it is probably not by al-Kindī himself. But it is based on Ptolemy's version of what the Persians called the *namūdār* or "indicator," from *Tet.* III.3. In the second paragraph below, I have supplied a brief explanation of it in brackets, replacing Robert's rather bizarre compressed version. For more rectification material, see the Study Guide to *Persian Nativities* in *ITA* Appendix F, or *PN1* and *PN2* themselves.

[2] Reading *dux* for *ducatus* ("signification").

[3] I take this to mean that the approximated pivot which is nearer *in ordinal or cardinal degrees* to the degree of Mars, is the one to be corrected—not the one nearer in absolute distance. For example, suppose that the approximate Ascendant were at 26° Gemini, and the approximate Midheaven at 5° Pisces. If Mars were the victor, and in 12° of some sign at the nativity, then we would correct the Midheaven and make it 12° (or close to it, subject to further rectification), since 5° is closer to 12° than 26° is. But I do not believe we would take the zodiacal longitude *between* Mars and the axes, to see which one is closer: for example, if Mars happened to be in Gemini he would be closer to the Ascendant in absolute degrees, but the number of his degree would still be closer to the number of the Midheaven's degree.

# APPENDIX A: THE *ESSENTIAL MEDIEVAL ASTROLOGY* CYCLE

The *Essential Medieval Astrology* cycle is a projected series of books which will redefine the contours of traditional astrology. Comprised mainly of translations of works by Persian and Arabic-speaking medieval astrologers, it will cover all major areas of astrology, including philosophical treatments and magic. The cycle will be accompanied by compilations of introductory works and readings on the one hand, and independent monographs and encyclopedic works on the other (including late medieval and Renaissance works of the Latin West).

## I. Introductions
- *Introductions to Astrology:* Abū Ma'shar's *Abbreviation of the Introduction,* al-Qabīsī's *The Introduction to Astrology* (2010)
- Abū Ma'shar, *Great Introduction to the Knowledge of the Judgments of the Stars* (2011-12)
- *Basic Readings in Traditional Astrology* (2012-13)

## II. Nativities
- *Persian Nativities I:* Māshā'allāh's *The Book of Aristotle,* Abū 'Ali al-Khayyāt's *On the Judgments of Nativities* (2009)
- *Persian Nativities II:* 'Umar al-Tabarī's *Three Books on Nativities,* Abū Bakr's *On Nativities* (2010)
- *Persian Nativities III:* Abū Ma'shar's *On the Revolutions of Nativities* (2010)

## III. Questions (Horary)
- Hermann of Carinthia, *The Search of the Heart* (2011)
- Various, *The Book of the Nine Judges* (2011)
- Al-Kindī, *The Forty Chapters* (2011)

## IV. Elections
- *Traditional Electional Astrology:* Abū Ma'shar's *On Elections* and *Flowers of Elections;* other minor works (2011-12)

## V. Mundane Astrology
- *Astrology of the World:* Abū Ma'shar's *On the Revolutions of the Years of the World, Book of Religions and Dynasties,* and *Flowers,* Sahl bin Bishr's *Prophetic Sayings;* lesser works on prices and weather (2011-12)

## VI. Other Works

- Bonatti, Guido, *The Book of Astronomy* (2007)
- *Works of Sahl & Māshā'allāh* (2008)
- *A Course in Traditional Astrology* (TBA)
- Al-Rijāl, *On the Judgments of the Stars* (TBA)
- *Astrological Magic* (TBA)
- *The Latin Hermes* (TBA)
- Firmicus Maternus, *Mathesis* (TBA)

# BIBLIOGRAPHY

Abū Ma'shar al-Balkhi, *Liber Introductorii Maioris ad Scientiam Iudiciorum Astrorum*, ed. Richard Lemay (Naples: Istituto Universitario Orientale, 1996)

Adamson, Peter and Richard C. Taylor eds., *The Cambridge Companion to Arabic Philosophy* (Cambridge: Cambridge University Press, 2005)

Al-Bīrūnī, Muhammad ibn Ahmad, *The Book of Instruction in the Elements of the Art of Astrology*, trans. R. Ramsay Wright (London: Luzac & Co., 1934)

Al-Bīrūnī, Muhammad ibn Ahmad, *The Chronology of Ancient Nations* (Lahore: Hijra International Publishers, 1983)

Al-Kindī, *The Forty Chapters (Iudicia Astrorum): The Two Latin Versions*, ed. Charles Burnett (London: The Warburg Institute, 1993)

Al-Kindī, *On the Stellar Rays*, trans. Robert Zoller and ed. Robert Hand (Berkeley Springs, WV: The Golden Hind Press, 1993)

Al-Kindī, *De Radiis Stellicis*, eds. M.-T. D'Alverny and F. Hudry, in *Archives d'histoire doctrinale du Moyen Age*, v. 41 (1974)

Al-Qabīsī, *The Introduction to Astrology*, eds. Charles Burnett, Keiji Yamamoto, Michio Yano (London and Turin: The Warburg Institute, 2004)

Al-Rijāl, 'Ali, *De Iudiciis Astrorum* (Venice: Erhard Ratdolt, 1485)

Al-Rijāl, 'Ali, *De Iudiciis Astrorum* (Basel: Henrichus Petrus, 1551)

Bonatti, Guido, Benjamin Dykes trans. and ed., *The Book of Astronomy* (Golden Valley: The Cazimi Press, 2007)

Burnett, Charles, "Al-Kindī on Judicial Astrology: 'The Forty Chapters,'" in *Arabic Sciences and Philosophy*, v. 3 (1993), pp. 77-117.

Burnett, Charles, "Al-Kindī on finding buried treasure," *Arabic Sciences and Philosophy* v.7, 1997, pp. 57-90.

Burnett, Charles and Keiji Yamamoto eds. and trans., *Abū Ma'shar on Historical Astrology: The Book of Religions and Dynasties (On the Great Conjunctions)* (Leiden: Brill, 2000)

Burnett, Charles, "A Hermetic Programme of Astrology and Divination in mid-Twelfth-Century Aragon: The Hidden Preface in the *Liber novem iudicum*," in Charles Burnett and W.F. Ryan, eds., *Magic and the Classical Tradition* (London: The Warburg Institute, 2006), pp. 99-105.

Burnett, Charles and Gerrit Bos, *Scientific Weather Forecasting in the Middle Ages: The Writings of al-Kindī* (London and New York: Kegan Paul International, 2000)

Dorotheus of Sidon, *Carmen Astrologicum*, trans. David Pingree (Abingdon, MD: The Astrology Center of America, 2005)

Dykes, Benjamin trans. and ed., *Works of Sahl & Māshā'allāh* (Golden Valley: The Cazimi Press, 2008)

Dykes, Benjamin trans. and ed., *Persian Nativities* vols. I-III (Minneapolis, MN: The Cazimi Press, 2009-10)

Dykes, Benjamin trans. and ed., *Introductions to Traditional Astrology: Abū Ma'shar & al-Qabīsī* (Minneapolis, MN: The Cazimi Press, 2010)

Dykes, Benjamin trans. and ed., *The Book of the Nine Judges* (Minneapolis, MN: The Cazimi Press, 2011)

Hermann of Carinthia, Benjamin Dykes trans. and ed., *The Search of the Heart* (Minneapolis, MN: The Cazimi Press, 2011)

Ibn Ezra, Abraham, *The Book of Nativities and Revolutions*, trans. Meira B. Epstein (ARHAT Publications, 2008)

Ibn Sīnā, *The Canon of Medicine* (Chicago: Kazi Publications, Inc., 1999)

Ivry, Alfred L., *Al-Kindī's Metaphysics* (Albany: SUNY Press, 1974)

Jiménez, Aurelio Pérez, "Περι Δειπνου. A Propósito de Heph., III.36," MHNH vol. 2 (2002), pp. 237-54.

Jiménez, Aurelio Pérez, "*Dodecátropos, Zodíaco y Partes de la Nave en la Astrología Antigua*," MHNH vol. 7 (2007), pp. 217-36.

Jolivet, Jean and Roshdi Rashed, "al-Kindī," in *Dictionary of Scientific Biography* v. 15 suppl. 1 (New York: Scribner, 1978), pp. 261-67.

Kennedy, Edward S., *Astronomy and Astrology in the Medieval Islamic World* (London: Ashgate Publishing Company, 1998)

Maternus, Julius Firmicus, *Matheseos Libri VIII* [*Mathesis*] (Stuttgard: B.G. Teubner, 1968)

Niermeyer, J.F., *Mediae Latinitatis Lexicon Minus* (Leiden: E.J. Brill, 1993)

Pingree, David, *From Astral Omens to Astrology: From Babylon to Bīkāner* (Rome: Istituto italiano per L'Africa e L'Oriente, 1997)

Ptolemy, Claudius, *Tetrabiblos* vols. 1, 2, 4, trans. Robert Schmidt, ed. Robert Hand (Berkeley Springs, WV: The Golden Hind Press, 1994-98)

Ptolemy, Claudius, *Ptolemy's Almagest*, trans. and ed. G.J. Toomer (Princeton, NJ: Princeton University Press, 1998)

Schmidt, Robert H., trans. and ed. *Definitions and Foundations* (Cumberland, MD: The Golden Hind Press, 2009)

Sezgin, Fuat, *Geschichte des Arabischen Schrifttums* vol. 7 (Leiden: E.J. Brill, 1979)

# INDEX

Please note: Where a whole chapter or long passage is devoted to a single topic, the reference is to the section or chapter heading only.

# Also available at www.bendykes.com:

Two classic introductions to astrology (by Abu Ma'shar and al-Qabisi), are translated with commentary in this volume. *Introductions to Traditional Astrology* is an essential reference work for traditional students.

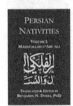

The three volumes of *Persian Nativities* represents works on natal interpretation and numerous predictive techniques by Masha'allah, Abu 'Ali al-Khayyat, 'Umar al-Tabari, Abu Bakr, and Abu Ma'shar. These works represent the natal portion of the *Essential Medieval Astrology* series.

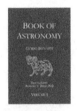

This classic medieval text by Guido Bonatti, the *Book of Astronomy* is now available in paperback reprints. This famous work is a complete guide to basic principles, horary, elections, mundane, and natal astrology.

This compilation of sixteen works by Sahl bin Bishr and Masha'allah covers all areas of traditional astrology, from basic concepts to horary, elections, natal interpretation, and mundane astrology. It is also available as two separate paperbacks.

Expand your knowledge of astrology and esoteric thought with the *Logos & Light* audio series: downloadable, college-level lectures and courses on CD at a fraction of the university cost! It is ideal for people with some knowledge of traditional thought but who want to enrich their understanding.

n can be obtained
.com

19
0001B/70/P

CPSIA information
at www.ICGtesting
Printed in the USA
BVHW0810561808
556127BV0